THE
DISAPPEARANCE

Remigiusz Mróz is the author of 46 novels across 9 series and various standalones and is recognised as the most popular author in Poland according to the National Survey and Book-scan. He has sold eleven million books in the country alone, with each book becoming a number one bestseller and remaining in the charts for several months post publication.

A recent novel, *Never Found*, won the Translated Literary Prize 2021 at the Festival of Giallo Garda, and film and television rights to six further series have been bought and are at various stages of development for the screen. Remigiusz's work has been sold in multiple territories including Germany, Italy, Japan, Czech Republic, Hungary, and more.

THE DISAPPEARANCE

REMIGIUSZ MRÓZ

ZAFFRE

Originally published in Poland by Czwarta Strona in 2015

First published in the UK in 2024 by
ZAFFRE
An imprint of Zaffre Publishing Group
A Bonnier Books UK Company
4th Floor, Victoria House, Bloomsbury Square, London, WC1B 4DA
Owned by Bonnier Books
Sveavägen 56, Stockholm, Sweden

Copyright © Remigiusz Mróz
Translation by Joanna Saunders

A CIP catalogue record for this book is
available from the British Library.

ISBN: 978-1-80418-762-3

Also available as an ebook and an audiobook

1 3 5 7 9 10 8 6 4 2

Typeset by IDSUK (Data Connection) Ltd
Printed and bound in Great Britain by Clays Ltd, Elcograf S.p.A.

Zaffre is an imprint of Zaffre Publishing Group
A Bonnier Books UK company
www.bonnierbooks.co.uk

To Ania and Maja
If you decide to be lawyers, you'll be even better than Chyłka.
(But don't forget – your uncle recommends a writing career!)

Qui accusare volunt, probationes habere debent
'Those who wish to accuse must have evidence'
Legal maxim

Part 1

1

Joanna Chyłka could hear the Iron Maiden guitar solo coming from somewhere. For a moment, she had no idea what was happening. Then she realised – it was her phone ringing. She forced her eyes open and looked around the room.

'Well, I'll be f . . .' she muttered, seeing the display screen flashing above the dresser. She got up, instantly regretting moving so fast, and staggered towards it. Leaning against the furniture, she looked at the screen.

`2.37 a.m. Unknown number.`

She sighed. This wasn't going to be good. It was Friday, it was scarcely an hour since she'd had her last drink, and everybody who could possibly want something from her knew better than to disturb her. She had no ongoing cases, and she wasn't on call. It was most likely one of Żelazny & McVay's clients.

She reviewed her options. She'd been a lawyer long enough to know she was still just about under the drink/drive limit – not officially drunk, but not exactly sober either. Just enough to have a good time, then fall into a blissful slumber. There would, no doubt, be echoes of tequila sunrise in her voice, but it was still better to answer the call than ignore it. The lesser of two evils.

She cleared her throat, then swiped her finger across the screen.

'Yes?' she said.

'Jo?' It was a woman's voice.

Chyłka froze. Everyone she knew, everyone close to her in any way, knew not to call her that. Even the postman had learned the hard way. She was relentless in informing everyone it wasn't her name.

'Who is this?' she asked, slurring slightly and frowning.

'I'm sorry to call at this hour,' said the caller, her voice cracking. It was as if she hadn't heard the question. Chyłka still had no idea who she was dealing with, but it definitely wasn't one of the firm's clients – she'd have known in a flash if it was one of the geese that laid the golden eggs.

'I was afraid you might have changed your number,' the woman continued.

'OK,' mumbled Joanna, searching for a pack of Marlboros then realising she wasn't going to find one. Swearing to herself, she reached for her e-cigarette.

'Don't you recognise my voice?' asked the caller.

'Not really.'

'We were at high school together. We played on the same team. Gracki coached us . . .'

As soon as the voice stopped speaking, Joanna realised who it was. She slumped down on the bed.

'Angelika?'

'Yes,' confirmed the woman, her relief palpable.

Chyłka took a drag of her imitation Marlboro. She could scarcely believe it. She'd never have expected the old skank to ring her after all these years, especially not in the middle of the night.

'It's good to hear your voice,' said Angelika.

'You too.'

'I hope I didn't wake you.'

'Don't be silly. It's not even three yet.'

'Good.'

Joanna rolled her eyes. Some things never changed.

'I'd never dream of bothering you, but . . .'

'You need help.'

'Is it that obvious?'

'You wouldn't have rung otherwise, would you?'

'True . . .' said the other woman. Then nothing.

Chyłka decided to take advantage of the awkward silence and bow out before her friend had a chance to get going.

'Listen,' she began, 'I'm up to my eyes in work at the moment, but I know a lot of good lawyers. Ring back in the morning and tell me everything. I'll put you in touch with—'

'I don't want anyone else.'

Joanna frowned. 'Why not?' she asked.

'Because I saw how you handled the Langer case. You and that young man. You gave them hell.'

Chyłka wouldn't have put it quite that way, but she wasn't about to start arguing. Maybe it had all looked different on television.

'Awit and I have a problem, and—'

'You and who?'

Angelika paused. 'Awit. My husband.'

'Is that even a real name?'

'My God, Chyłka, you haven't changed, have you?'

'I guess not.'

'And like the loser I am, I rang you in despair, trying to be polite and respectful.'

'Well, at least you tried.'

'What?'

'Nothing, it doesn't matter. Ring me in the morning.'

'If you fob me off, your bosses won't be happy.'

'They never are.'

Angelika fell silent again. Chyłka took the phone away from her ear and looked at the display. She should disconnect. There was no earthly reason why she should help her old schoolfriend. And yet she couldn't bring herself to end the call. She took a deep breath and straightened up.

'Right. I'm listening,' she said. 'Have you been accused of something?'

'No. At least, not yet. But the police are asking so many questions I feel as if I have.'

Chyłka got up and walked to the kitchen. If she was going to listen to what the old harridan had to say, she wasn't going to do it without a glass in her hand.

'OK, now talk,' she said, opening a bottle of tequila topped with a red sombrero instead of the traditional stopper. 'Tell me everything, beginning to end.'

'Before we start, I should tell you we won't be wasting your time, or money,' said Angelika. 'We've got more cash than we could ever spend.'

'OK,' said Chyłka. Although, to be honest, she didn't think Angelika and her husband would have enough to cover even the average bill charged by Żelazny & McVay's senior associates.

'Awit's company is one of the top players in the T&L sector. We can pay, don't worry.'

'T&L?'

'Transport and logistics,' said Angelika. 'They provide a range of services, from financing—'

'And what's the problem?' Joanna cut her off mid-sentence.

'Our . . . our daughter went missing the night before last.'

Chyłka, who had been adding grenadine to her tequila, froze.

'What?' she said.

'Our daughter—'

'Yes, I heard,' said Joanna. 'So you're telling me your child's missing, and you're going on about fucking transport and logistics?'

'I . . . I was only—'

'Tell me what happened.'

Chyłka could hear Angelika struggling to swallow. It didn't particularly surprise her – Angelika was probably still in shock, or maybe she simply couldn't believe what had happened. Or maybe the police had good reason to suspect her.

'We . . .' Angelika began, 'we put her to bed just before eight . . . Jo, she's only three years old. How could anyone want to . . .'

'You put her to bed,' Joanna prompted. 'Then what?'

'We closed her door, had a glass or two of wine and watched a film. We set the alarm before we went to bed. In the morning she was gone.'

Chyłka added orange juice to her glass and took a sip.

'No sign of forced entry?' she asked, although she already knew the answer.

'No. And we didn't hear anything either. We woke up in the morning, went to her room – and she wasn't there.' Angelika paused to steady her voice. 'Chyłka, they're going to charge us.'

The lawyer nodded.

'I don't doubt it,' she said. 'If I were them, I'd have done it on the spot.'

'So will you take it on? Our case, I mean?'

'I'd need more details.'

'But . . .'

'But I'd have hung up long ago if I wasn't going to help you,' she said.

They finished talking. Joanna put down her empty glass and went back to the bedroom, pulled out her overnight bag and stuffed in a pile of clothes and make-up. She was ready. Had she been sober, she'd have thought of plenty more things to pack. But equally, had she been sober, she probably wouldn't have taken this case on at all.

2

Kordian Oryński woke with a start, to the sound of his phone ringing. His studio flat on Emilia Plater Street was in the ideal location, a few steps from the law firm's offices in the Skylight building, but the acoustics were nightmarish, and the slightest sound echoed across the whole space. Picking up his phone, Kordian saw it was his supervisor calling. The timing was unusual, even for her.

'Did Żelazny finally kick us out?' he asked as a greeting.

'Are you sober?'

'What sort of question is that at three o'clock in the morning?'

'One to which I need an answer. Now.'

'I am.'

'Then get a cab and get over here.'

Kordian opened his mouth to speak, but no words came out.

'And bring a change of clothes,' Chyłka added.

'Are you suggesting what I think you're suggesting?'

'Get over yourself, Zordon. We're going on tour.'

'We're what?'

'Our fame has spread even to the godforsaken north of this country. We need to leave right now, and I need a driver. I've had one tequila too many. Or two.'

'But . . .'

'Maybe even three. I don't remember.'

'It's just that . . .'

'You get to drive my X5. Isn't that what you've always wanted? You have got a driving licence, haven't you?'

'You've known me for a year, and you don't even know if I've got a licence?'

'I don't know what size underwear you take either, and please God, I'll never find out. So, are you getting yourself together or what?'

'Yes, but . . .'

'Bring stuff to last you a week, then we can come back for more if we need to.'

Oryński took a deep breath, and instinctively looked around for a pack of cigarettes. But there were none to be seen, as a week ago, he and his supervisor had decided to try and beat their addiction once and for all. It was their second attempt – they had tried once before, after the Langer case, but had only lasted a few months. This time they were more optimistic, as they were using substitutes to give them that blissful nicotine hit.

Unfortunately, it wasn't going well so far. They were both as mad as hornets.

'Chyłka, I've got a case on at the moment,' he said. 'Falsification of documents. You must have heard about it.'

'A minor misdemeanour and a complete waste of your time.'

'Even if it is, I can't just—'

'I've already cleared it with McVay. He's assigned it to someone else.'

Kordian smiled and shook his head. He should have known. Whatever his supervisor wanted, she usually got, both in and outside the courtroom. Oryński knew he'd be hard-pushed to find a better teacher, particularly if he wanted to learn to be hard-nosed and ruthless.

'So, get your kit together and let's get going,' she said, and hung up.

Ringing back for more details would be pointless, so Kordian quickly packed a bag, and within fifteen minutes he was on his way. If there was one thing in their rather bizarre relationship he would never have expected, it was being invited to drive Chyłka's BMW X5. It was clearly a very urgent case.

Joanna was waiting for him by the car. He nodded to her, threw his bag into the huge boot and settled in behind the wheel. Rubbing his hands in anticipation of the drive, he felt the weight of Joanna's gaze.

'Listen, Zordon,' she said. 'We both know this is a dangerous situation, both for you and my X5. Be very, very careful.'

'OK.' He pushed the start button and the engine purred into life.

'Where to?' he asked.

Chyłka pointed to the sat-nav, which showed their unassuming destination – a dirt track in the village of Sajenko. Without any further questions, Kordian shifted into reverse and moved off, following instructions spoken by a deep, robotic male voice.

'Not exactly James Bond, is it?'

'What?'

'You know you can change the voice if you want,' he said. She looked at him mournfully, as if he'd upset her. Kordian was desperate to ask what she was dragging him into, but now didn't seem the time. He supposed she'd tell him when the time was right.

'This is Zygmunt,' she said at last, as if that cleared the matter up.

'It's who?'

'Don't you follow me on Facebook? That's where I write about the men in my life. Zygmunt and I have been together for two months or more.'

11

He probably should have known she had someone new, but the fact was that since the Langer case, they seemed to be working together less and less. Chyłka was still his supervisor and would be for another two years, but his bosses had assigned him to a different department: he was now working in Litigation. They even used the English word for it. Oryński had no reason to think he'd be moving back, so it was all the more surprising that Joanna had asked him to take on a case outside Warsaw with her.

'Don't you want to know where we're going?' she asked, settling herself into the passenger seat.

'I still have a forlorn hope you'll explain everything of your own free will.'

'Hope, and it shall be given unto you,' she said, adjusting her seatbelt. 'It's bloody uncomfortable on the passenger side. I feel like a priest in a minaret.'

'I don't expect a priest would be allowed in.'

'Just like I shouldn't be allowed to sit in this seat,' she muttered, and waved her hand. 'We're going to the Szlezyngiers' summer house.'

'Whose summer house?'

'Haven't you heard of Awit Szlezyngier? You read *Forbes*, don't you, and all those other business magazines?'

Kordian recognised the surname, although he was sure he'd never heard the first name. He spent a moment sifting through his memory, trying to link the name to a person. Finally, something clicked.

'You mean the logistics magnate?'

'Well done, Zordon, congratulations. I knew you knew your way round the business world.'

She was right, he did enjoy reading about business. He bought *Forbes* every month, and sometimes even picked up the

Polish *Law Daily* on his way to work to leaf through over coffee. On a couple of occasions the name Chyłka had mentioned had caught his eye. Szlezyngier was a big shot; if Oryński remembered rightly, in the previous year his company's turnover had exceeded one million zlotys.

'So where is this summer house of theirs?' he asked.

'That's the one question you have for me?'

'There'll be time for other questions later. At the moment I'd just like to know where we're going.'

'Wherever Zygmunt tells us.'

'Can't you be more specific?'

'Podlasie,' she answered, taking out her e-cigarette. Kordian did the same. 'Just north of Augustów.'

'Surely that's Masuria.'

'Officially, it's the Podlasie province. And when you're a lawyer, official is what matters.'

'True . . . I guess,' Kordian murmured, drawing so deeply on his e-cigarette that the LED light glowed red, informing him it had jammed.

'The Szlezyngiers' house is by a small lake called Sajenko.'

'That's an ominous start.'

'Not a great ending either,' said Chyłka, flapping her hand at him to suggest he overtake the car in front. 'Their child disappeared in the middle of the night.'

'Kidnapped?'

'Only if the suspect had teleportation superpowers.'

'Huh?'

'The house was locked up and the alarm was set.'

Oryński turned to her with a doleful stare.

'What are you gaping at?' she said. 'Keep your eyes on the road.'

13

'You're dragging me to the arse end of Poland to defend a guilty party?'

'Don't start with the guilty/innocent thing. What does it matter?'

He didn't answer – it really was a better idea to concentrate on his driving. Joanna was right, he was in a dangerous situation. One false move with the steering wheel and the ensuing lecture could go on for hours. The same would happen if he started discussing their clients' guilt or otherwise.

'Checking the alarm shouldn't be a problem,' he said.

'Exactly. We'll visit the Szlezyngiers' security firm first thing.'

'Do you know these people?'

'What difference does that make?' she snapped. 'Can't I just take a case on out of the kindness of my heart? Or for financial reasons?'

'You've got plenty of money, although I can't comment on the former.'

She forced a smile, and tugged so hard at her seatbelt that it locked.

'I know the wife,' she admitted after a pause. 'We were in secondary school together. Bit of a slapper, really.'

'A what?'

'A tart, Zordon. One day I'll buy you a dictionary.' He shook his head.

'Did she steal your boyfriend or something?'

'My boyfriend? Oh please!' snorted Chyłka, finally undoing her belt and sitting cross-legged on the seat. 'I stole hers, and let's say, she wasn't very dignified about it. This was school, remember. We had a few scuffles, but nothing worth talking about.'

'So why have you taken the case?'

14

'Her child is missing. What was I supposed to do?'

'Say no? It's going to be a heck of a mess.'

'But a heck of a mess can mean a heck of a lot of good publicity.'

Kordian smiled and shook his head. 'Now we're getting to the heart of the matter,' he said.

For a brief moment he'd thought his supervisor was stepping up to help for old times' sake, but he should have known better. The case had clearly not yet reached the media, but when it did, coverage would be nationwide. Everyone would be interested in the downfall of a famous businessman, and this one might well also be responsible for the disappearance of a child.

Oryński turned off Armia Krajowa Alley onto Highway 8 towards Marki, and put his foot down.

'Slow down,' bellowed his passenger. 'There's a speed camera ahead, and I'd be happy to give the traffic police the driver's details. It would be a clear-cut, quick and painful case – for you at least.'

'Like the Szlezyngier case.'

'We know nothing about it yet,' Joanna protested, putting her e-cigarette back in her jacket pocket.

'We know they got rid of their own child.'

'How?' she asked. 'Did they make her evaporate?' He looked at her, eyebrows raised. It was a good question. If they managed to find an answer, this journey wouldn't be a complete waste of time.

'There's a lake there, didn't you say?' asked Kordian.

'No doubt already thoroughly searched by divers.'

'And the Masurian forests?'

'It's in Podlasie.'

'Let's just agree it's the Suwałki region.'

'OK,' said Joanna, 'but in any case, they searched the area for two days. No stone unturned.'

'Did they find anything?'

'Zero, null, nada. Absolutely nothing. Whoever took this little girl – or her body – from the house knew exactly what they were doing.

3

Chyłka wasn't sure when she'd fallen asleep, but the X5's suspension ensured she slept like a baby for almost the entire four-hour journey. She didn't even wake as they drove along the bumpy roads on the outskirts of Augustów.

A few kilometres outside of town were several lakes – around five or six – along whose shores was a vast range of homes and farms offering guest accommodation. They weren't on top of each other; there was more than enough space for them all. Most of the countryside still consisted of unspoiled forests and lakes surrounded by peat bogs, and by the shore of one of those lakes was where the Szlezyngiers had bought a plot of land and built their summer house. Chyłka described it as off the beaten track, but that was a gross understatement; this whole area was off the beaten track.

She stepped out of the car, stretched, and looked at the building. It wasn't exactly grand – for a logistics magnate, Awit had scarcely excelled himself. It was a single-storey house, albeit with a usable loft room, painted white. A path led from the terrace to a wooden jetty over the lake.

It was gone seven o'clock, and the sun had risen an hour and a half ago. The owners were waiting on the steps, the personification of misery. Angelika raised her hand in greeting and gave a faint smile, while Awit simply nodded.

'Good to see you, Jo,' said the blonde with the surgically enhanced lips and patently artificial breasts, hugging her. Chyłka grimaced, but patted her old friend on the shoulder.

'You too.'

'How was your journey?' asked Awit, extending his hand to Oryński.

'Fine, although this isn't an easy place to get to,' he replied. Szlezyngier nodded. He didn't look anything like the ruthless businessman Kordian had read about in the papers. His eyes were dull, his hair wild, and his shirt was a crumpled mess.

'We wanted our own sanctuary, somewhere removed from everyday life,' Awit explained. 'We've got peace and quiet here, with no random passers-by.'

'So why the intruder alarm?' asked Chyłka, pointing to the security company's logo stuck to the window.

'For peace of mind. We never thought . . .' Awit fell silent and looked at his wife, who hurried to his side and allowed him to put his arm around her. To Joanna, the gesture looked staged, but on the other hand, it was clear neither of them had slept. Both had dark circles under their bloodshot eyes, and they were as white as their house.

'Let's go inside,' suggested Szlezyngier. Chyłka and Oryński picked up their bags and followed him through the door.

The outside of the building might not have looked imposing, but the interior left no doubt that these were very wealthy people. The flooring was light wood, the home cinema looked anything but homespun, and the kitchen was reminiscent of an aircraft cockpit, with all the equipment a gourmet chef could wish for.

'We prepared the attic room for you,' said Angelika. 'I'm really sorry, but that's all we've got. We never expected there to be anyone here other than the three of us. Nikola's room is still cordoned off.'

'No problem,' said Chyłka. 'Zordon can sleep on the stairs. He already looks like Quasimodo anyway.'

No one smiled. Kordian blinked at Joanna with disapproval, but she ignored him and hurried upstairs with her bag.

They stowed their luggage in a recess in the attic, and looked around their temporary field office. The room was extremely well-lit; with three large windows in the roof it would be bright enough to see even in the evening. Under normal circumstances, that would also mean it would be as hot as Hades during the day, but the Szlezyngiers' summer house was clearly air-conditioned.

'What do you reckon?' asked Oryński.

'I think they *look* pretty despondent, anyway.'

He turned to her. 'Meaning?'

'Nothing. Just that they'll look good for the cameras.'

'So you're really going to haul the media down here?'

She didn't answer; it would have been stating the obvious.

'Maybe you didn't see the same people I just saw?' Kordian persisted. 'Even the local rag would eat them for breakfast.'

'Szlezyngier is more than used to the media,' she said. 'And besides, journalists are quick to sniff out a scandal. If we go to them first, they may not bite the hand that feeds them.'

'I'm not so sure.'

'Trust me,' she said, and started down the stairs.

They went down to the living room, where Angelika was waiting for them with two mugs of coffee. Large, half-litre ones, Chyłka was glad to see. She helped herself to one, then sat down on the sofa and pulled out her e-cigarette. The others sat down too.

'Right,' began Joanna. 'To start with, I need to ask you something. Those windows in the roof.'

'What about them?' asked Oryński.

'They're not hooked up to the alarm system, are they?'

Szlezyngier looked carefully at the lawyer and shook his head. 'No, they're not. The only sensors are downstairs. We keep the external blinds closed upstairs anyway, so the house doesn't get too hot.'

That was normal. Not many people set up sensors in the attic: it would be no mean feat for a burglar to get a fifty-inch TV out through a rooflight. It would be equally hard to take a child that way, although not impossible.

'So in theory, could someone come in and go back out again without triggering the alarm?' asked Kordian.

'Yes. There are motion sensors outside which set off the lights, but no alarm or CCTV.'

'Do the police know?' asked Oryński. The couple nodded in unison.

'But they didn't find any traces around the house, of anything,' said Angelika. 'If Nikola had been taken, there would have been marks in the ground where the ladder had been. And footprints. Probably tyre tracks too.'

'So they only found your footprints?'

'That's right,' said Awit. 'And the security firm can confirm that no one switched off the alarm. The system was armed all night.'

For a moment, all was quiet, the only sound being the hiss of an e-cigarette.

'We know what this must look like,' Angelika began.

Chyłka shook her head. 'It doesn't matter what it looks like. What matters is what the court thinks.'

'Don't you care about . . . you know.'

'Whether you're responsible for your daughter's disappearance? No, I don't give a shit.'

Joanna looked from Angelika to Awit, then tucked the cigarette back into her pocket. She was sick of this electronic garbage, but a promise was a promise. It should have been easy enough to break, but there was a challenge involved: a week ago, she'd made a bet with Zordon about which of them could hold out longer. If she lost, she'd have to change her ringtone from the guitar solo from 'Afraid to Shoot Strangers' to some ridiculous Will Smith track.

The Szlezyngiers looked at her as if she was some sort of savage as they waited for her to continue. But Joanna had said her piece.

'I've no doubt you have all the social graces you need,' said Awit, 'but my wife warned me about this.'

'I bet she did.'

The businessman heaved himself off the sofa and studied her. 'But I'd rather slit my own throat than work with a lawyer who thinks we're guilty.'

Chyłka swore to herself. All clients, even the obviously guilty-as-sin ones, felt they had to convince their lawyers they were innocent. Completely ridiculous, of course, but it was the way of the world. Maybe hardened criminals were different, but people like Awit made these forceful statements in the hope that if their lawyers believed they were innocent, they'd be granted absolution.

For a moment their eyes met. Joanna got up slowly. 'That's not the way I work,' she said. 'I focus on defending my clients, not on what actually happened.' Awit looked at his wife, but she just shrugged. 'If you want drama, go to the press,' Joanna continued, 'and if you want a conviction, go to the prosecutor. But if you want a good defence come to me.'

'So who do I go to for the truth?'

'That I don't know.'

Szlezyngier ran his hand through his hair. 'In that case, I can't see us working together.'

'Awit . . .'

'Enough.' Awit glared at his wife. 'I won't be disrespected by our own lawyer.'

'You'd better get used to it,' said Chyłka, moving closer, 'because soon it won't just be your lawyer, it'll be everyone. People in the surrounding villages, journalists, your accusers – everyone. It's just a matter of time before your own families begin to treat you as *personae non gratae*. One by one they'll start to distance themselves, because the evidence points at nobody but you.'

'What evidence?' Szlezyngier protested. 'There's nothing to indicate a crime has even taken place. For God's sake, there aren't any forensics, and there's no trace of our daughter!'

'Exactly.'

'You can't start making accusations if you've got no proof,' Awit added. Chyłka turned to her trainee.

'Right, Zordon, time for a little test.'

'What?' he groaned.

'How would we say that in Latin?'

'Do we have to do this now?'

'Absolutely.'

'*Qui accusare volunt, probationes habere debent*,' he muttered.

'Excellent. Pity it has about as much truth in it as the idea that Kim Jong-Un is the Sun of his Nation. Now let's get out of here.'

Kordian glanced at his unfinished coffee. The Szlezyngiers still looked as if they didn't quite know what was happening.

Not to worry, thought Chyłka, they'll get used to it soon enough. 'Get a move on,' she said to Kordian, making her way towards the door.

'I was hoping we'd . . .'

'We'd what, get some rest? What are you, the Dalai Lama, needing time to meditate? Lawyers are there to get things done, and pretend lawyers are there to help them. So get up and help.'

Reluctantly, Oryński stood up. 'I thought we'd get at least a bit of sleep,' he said. 'I was driving half the night.'

'Sleep? What's that?'

'Chyłka . . .'

'You mean like when we blink?' she asked, waving him impatiently towards the exit.

As they left, she instructed their hosts not to talk to the police in her absence.

4

As they drove to Augustów, Kordian listened carefully to his supervisor speaking on the phone. It was amazing how she got others to do what she wanted, especially as her abrasive manner didn't exactly inspire cooperation.

Nonetheless, within half an hour Chyłka had managed to find out who was handling the case, and had persuaded a high-ranking officer from Central Headquarters to phone him and advise him to cooperate with the lawyers from Żelazny & McVay, who would be arriving any minute.

Oryński parked outside District Police Headquarters on Brzostowska Street and got out of the car.

'Is this going to come back and bite us?' he asked.

'No,' answered Joanna, shutting the door behind her. 'We're not formally representing a suspect yet, because no one's been charged. Żelazny simply called in a favour from someone in Warsaw.'

'Not exactly ethical.'

'What?'

'Nothing.'

'We're looking for a child, Zordon. At the moment, this is simply a missing persons case. There's nothing to stop them working with us. All we have to do is find Staff Sergeant Satanowski from the Search and Identification Team.'

'Now there's a name to arouse optimism.'

'Let's see, shall we, Oryjski?'

He glared at her, but she was already heading for the entrance. They went into the pale-coloured, two-storey building and confirmed where to find Satanowski. The sergeant had clearly been told to expect the two lawyers, as he opened the door and, without showing the slightest surprise, invited them into his office.

As far as it could be called an office, Oryński thought. It looked nothing like the offices on the twenty-first floor of the Skylight building in Warsaw: it was more like a cubicle, and the cast-iron radiator was a reminder of times gone by, when Donald Duck bubble gum, the ultimate symbol of life in the West, was all the rage.

'Come in, make yourselves at home.'

Kordian and Joanna looked at one another, then sat down on two rickety chairs by the desk. The paint was peeling off them, and they didn't look particularly stable. The desk at which the sergeant sat reminded Kordian of his desk at primary school. Satanowski grunted and folded his arms in front of his chest, sizing up the lawyers.

'I understand you're here about Nikola Szlezyngier.'

Chyłka just rolled her eyes, so Oryński thought it best to take the lead. 'Yes,' he said. 'We represent her parents.'

'So should we speak to Mr and Mrs Szlezyngier through their lawyers from now on?'

'No, it's just that—'

'We all want to find her, sergeant, or inspector, or whatever your rank is,' Joanna cut in. 'And the more resources we have on the case, the better. As human resources go, the two of us are pretty good. At least, fifty per cent of us are.' She looked indulgently at her protégé, then flashed the police officer a dazzling, if artificial, smile. 'And we'd be deeply grateful for a few bits of information. Starting with what you found at the scene.'

Satanowski leaned back in his chair.

'Our clients have said there were no traces of a ladder,' she went on, 'and that the child could only have been abducted through the rooflight.'

The sergeant nodded.

'Do you actually talk, or is keeping the roads clear all you're good for?' Joanna was beginning to lose her composure. Kordian raised his hand in a gesture of despair.

'Ms Chyłka, counsellor—' began the sergeant. But he wasn't allowed to finish.

'Let's stop with the faux formality.' Joanna was seething.

'Are we looking for this little girl or not?'

The officer gaped at her, but not as if she were mad – which was what Oryński had expected. No, Satanowski was looking at her as if she were his archenemy.

'Counsellor,' he tried again. 'I agreed to this meeting because I thought you had something to offer me.'

'What? A backhander?'

The sergeant opened his mouth, but nothing came out. He rose from his chair and pointed to the door. 'I thought you might have some new information, but I see I was mistaken.'

Joanna stood up too. 'Too right, and you have no idea just how mistaken you were. But I'm sure your superiors will explain it to you quickly enough.'

Satanowski seemed not in the least perturbed, but stood his ground, his arm still stretched out towards the corridor. Chyłka looked at Kordian, swore inwardly and stalked out of the room.

The minute they were outside the building, she pulled her e-cigarette from her jacket pocket. 'They're sticking two fingers up at Żelazny,' she hissed.

Oryński stood next to her and pulled out his own nicotine stick.

'What are you talking about?' he asked.

'The police, Zordon. They're getting their own back on us.'

'I can't imagine they'd—'

'They've had an axe to grind ever since that episode at the grey-haired man's place.'

Looking back on the incident, Kordian had to admit she could be right. They'd burned all their bridges and ruined any relationship they might have had with the police, and it had been naïve to expect any help from them now.

'Besides, they know the Szlezyngiers did it,' she added.

'But they've got no proof.'

'Don't they?' she asked, turning to him. 'Then maybe you can tell me how someone opened the rooflight from the outside, climbed in, took the child and then closed the window behind them? Without leaving traces.'

'We can't be sure there are no traces.'

'We know perfectly well there aren't any,' she said, trying to take a drag on her cigarette. She pulled it out of her mouth and looked furiously at the flashing red light. 'If there had been any evidence in the house, anything at all, the investigators wouldn't be targeting the Szlezyngiers.'

'The kidnapper could have worn gloves.'

'Bravo, Zordon,' she retorted. 'And a hat, mask and boiler-suit, to make sure they left no forensics, biological or otherwise? And as there are no tracks or footprints, do we assume they used a hoverboard?'

Oryński looked around and scratched his head. 'But we have to have something to take to court,' he said.

'You're right. But at the moment, I have no idea what that something could be. The way things are, any judge would sentence the Szlezyngiers the maximum penalty.'

'Without proof?'

'There'll be proof all right. In the form of a body.'

'Oozing optimism, as ever.'

'I'm simply telling it as it is. Dead bodies have a way of being found.'

They got back into Chyłka's X5, Kordian once again behind the wheel. It was, he thought, probably his last chance to drive this beast of a car. Surely Joanna would soon realise she had no reason not to drive it herself.

He sighed deeply, with a pang of regret that he'd let himself be dragged into this. Admittedly, it was good to be working with Chyłka again. But was it worth it? It seemed like they'd be defending the worst kind of lowlifes.

'The Szlezyngiers deserve credit for one thing,' he said, putting the car into reverse. 'They know how to fib.'

Joanna didn't reply, her eyes firmly on the rear-view camera. 'Careful,' she muttered.

'I'm being careful,' he retorted, noticing a passing cyclist in the nick of time and braking a little too sharply. Chyłka shook her head.

'You're right,' she said after a moment. 'They're industrial-grade liars. If common sense didn't dictate otherwise, I'd say they didn't do it.'

They glanced at one another, but dropped the subject. Chyłka pulled out her phone and dialled a friend at the NSI news desk. NSI were always happy to send a team out to wherever something was happening, twenty-four/seven, so chances were they'd get someone to their clients immediately.

Yet somehow Oryński hoped that this time, they wouldn't. Szlezyngier was used to being in the spotlight, but his wife definitely wasn't: one unguarded comment from her, one gesture, and their public standing could plummet.

Chyłka clearly thought otherwise. Her journalist friend quickly assured her she'd be there that evening.

'I wonder if you're in too much of a hurry,' Kordian remarked as his boss twirled her phone and put it away in her jacket pocket as if it were a gun. They turned onto Route 16 towards Przewięź, and Oryński took the opportunity to speed up a bit.

'We haven't got a lot of time,' Joanna said. 'Did you see his eyes? He's out for blood.'

'Who?'

'Satanowski. He won't be happy until he's found a victim and ripped them to shreds.'

'So you think they're ready to press charges?'

'I can't see any reason for them to wait.'

Kordian nodded. She was right. Why would they? The prosecution were probably already rubbing their hands in glee.

'Then aren't we shooting ourselves in the foot calling your journalist in?' he asked.

'Ourselves? You mean the legal bigwigs at Żelazny & McVay?'

'I'm being serious,' he said. 'If we cause a media frenzy like there was with little Madzia from Sosnowiec, and then the police find a body, every newspaper and news channel, TV and radio, will eat the Szlezyngiers alive.' The case he was referring to involved six-month-old baby Madzia, whose mother claimed she had been kidnapped. The child's body was not found until six months later, and the mother eventually admitted she'd killed her.

'We'll be OK. We need a good kick-start, and we won't get that without the cameras there.'

Oryński wasn't so sure, but he knew better than to argue. They drove the remaining ten kilometres without speaking, Iron Maiden blaring from the speakers. Kordian pulled up outside the house.

Chyłka set to work at once, instructing Angelika on what to say to the reporters and how to say it, and telling Awit to keep his mouth shut, as the story would sound better from a distraught mother. They had a dress rehearsal, made a few adjustments (and again, Chyłka blocked her e-cigarette by pulling too hard and too often), and finally, after one last run-through, she decided the Szlezyngiers were ready.

Oryński, meanwhile, looked on in horror. None of it looked good, and if it were up to him, he'd lock the couple inside their house and forbid any contact with the media. But it wasn't up to him: he wasn't the one with a track record of defendants walking free despite strong evidence against them.

Chyłka was rarely at a loss. She'd rarely had to grasp at straws, but everything about this case looked so hopeless for their clients that she'd grab onto even the most fragile one.

'Are you sure about this?' Kordian asked as soon as the last rehearsal was over.

'No.'

'Then maybe . . .'

'Zordon, we have to do something. Because if we don't, we'll fall before the first hurdle.'

Kordian hoped she wouldn't be proved wrong.

5

After the interview, Chyłka would have given anything to run to the nearest shop for a packet of real cigarettes. Anywhere would do – a supermarket, a petrol station, anything. Sadly, the one shop in the area sold only ice-cream and snacks, and that was just open in high season. Now it was firmly closed.

The interview was a disaster. Not only did Angelika come across as weak and indifferent when talking about her missing daughter, but Awit, who was supposed to keep stumm, couldn't help himself and joined in. Unfortunately, his many media appearances as a top businessman had left their mark, and his tone was arrogant and condescending.

As soon as the cameras had packed up, Chyłka and her journalist friend went outside.

'Thanks, Chyłka,' Olga Szrebska said happily. 'I've got enough material here for a super-tragic story.'

'Oh, come on.'

'Have you got anything that might get them out of this?'

'You'll have to wait till we're in court to find out.'

'I won't be there. I have to get back.'

'In that case, you'll just have to watch my fall from grace on-screen.'

Szrebska patted her on the back and winked, then she and her cameraman climbed into a car emblazoned with the NSI logo. Joanna waved them off, and stood for a while on the porch, trying not to think about anything. Especially not cigarettes.

Then she walked off towards the lake and sat down at the end of the jetty, dangling her feet in the water. Her pencil skirt would suffer for it, but at that moment, that was the last thing on her mind.

If Szrebska let the case go and handed the material to another reporter, there was a danger it would lose the multi-layered sensationalism that was her hallmark. The Szlezyngiers would be found guilty, and what's more, they'd be seen as the worst sort of scum. As soon as a body was found, they'd go to prison for years.

Joanna gazed at the glassy surface of the lake. The divers had already searched this part, and were now working further on. The killers could have dumped the body anywhere, using a small boat that had been left moored to the pier. The boat had been secured, but Chyłka doubted they'd find anything there, bar maybe traces left by the Szlezyngiers.

Sajenko Lake spanned almost thirty-six hectares, so the divers had plenty of work for the next day or two – unless, of course, they found the body sooner.

The girl could just as easily be in the woods. Augustów forest was pretty much impenetrable, and the Polish part of it stretched over a hundred hectares. They could be searching for months, especially if the killer had made efforts to cover their tracks.

Joanna sat in silence, gazing at a thicket of trees on a small promontory to her left, their overlapping crowns forming a dense wall of green. As she watched, a boat emerged from behind the headland. An elderly man sat in it, his back to her, calmly rowing away. Chyłka stood up.

'Hello!' she shouted. The man turned around and looked at her. 'You shouldn't be on the lake,' she shouted, cupping her hands around her mouth to make a megaphone.

The old man shrugged. A few straggly grey hairs surrounded the bald patch on his head, and Chyłka could see the wrinkles even from this distance.

'Come over here!' she shouted in a tone that brooked no objection.

The man hesitated, then did as she asked. He stopped at the jetty and extended an oar to Joanna to help pull him in.

'And who might you be?' she asked.

'I could ask the same thing.'

'I'm Joanna Chyłka, a lawyer, from Żelazny & McVay.'

It might impress your average Varsovian, but here she might as well have said she worked in McDonald's.

'And what do you want from me?'

'To know why you're on the water when it's clear there's a search going on.'

The man took a noisy breath. 'No one told me not to.'

Chyłka held his gaze for a moment, then reached out her hand. He climbed out of the boat, nodding his thanks, and sat down on the jetty. She was surprised he was so ready to sit with her, but she said nothing. Maybe he didn't get many opportunities to chat.

'The lake is closed,' she said, squatting down next to him.

'It's a pond.'

'Same difference. You still shouldn't be out on it.'

'I asked them and they said it was OK,' he said. 'They've already searched this bit.'

Joanna tried to ignore the fishy odour coming off the man's clothes. Zordon would have been in seventh heaven. He loved salmon and all those other floaty creatures.

'Even so, you're still interfering with the search,' she said.

'They won't find her here anyway.'

She turned to face him.

33

'Why not?' she asked.

The old man rubbed his few days' worth of grey stubble, reached into the pocket of his tartan shirt, pulled out a packet of Viceroy cigarettes and lit one. It stank to high heaven, but Chyłka still felt her heart leap.

'Because she's not in the water,' replied the old man.

'What makes you say that?'

'It's been an exceptionally hot summer. In fact, it still is.'

'And?'

'Put your hand in the water and feel how warm it is.'

Chyłka looked at him doubtfully, but did as he said. He was right. The water was warm. Very warm, even. And although the lake was small and the sunshine relentless, at this time of day she'd have expected it to be cooler.

'The water temperature in lakes and ponds isn't constant,' said the man.

'So?'

'So it can be cold on one shore and warm on another.'

She looked at him blankly. 'If you've got a point, please get to it.'

'Here, where we're sitting, the water is always cooler,' he continued, unperturbed. The old man clearly had a screw loose, but that didn't faze Joanna – most of her colleagues at Żelazny & McVay weren't exactly level-headed.

'Are you trying to tell me something?'

'Yes,' he said, taking a deep breath, and probably regretting it as he was seized by a bout of violent coughing. 'Do you know why dead bodies float to the surface?'

'Not really.'

'You're a lawyer. You should.' The old man eyed her as if she were mad, then started to cough again – quietly this time, although the wheezing in his lungs was clearly audible. For the first time, Chyłka thought that quitting smoking might have been a good decision. But she quickly pushed the thought away.

'The warmer it is, the sooner they surface. Ask the forensics guys.'

'And how would you know?'

'I read thrillers. It's the best way to learn that sort of thing. There's a drowning in Agatha Christie's *Halloween Party*. But I also read Chandler and Conan Doyle, and sometimes even Poe.'

'OK, I get it. Everything but J.K. Rowling.'

'What?'

'I can read Harry Potter over and over, but anything else by her is a chore.'

'What are you talking about?'

Chyłka ignored the question. 'So after reading your thrillers, you think the body would have surfaced by now?'

'I don't just think so, I know so,' he said, stubbing his cigarette out on the jetty. He'd smoked it down to the filter. 'If someone had dumped that child in the lake over there, the body would have surfaced by now. It's considerably warmer than it is here.' Without waiting for an answer, he held his hand out to Chyłka and moved off towards his boat. Joanna got up and helped him down from the jetty.

'Where do you live?'

'Not far from here,' he answered, and picked up the oar, passing her the other end. 'Can you give me a push?'

'Of course, if you tell me with whom I've had the pleasure?'

'Antoni Ekiel. I live over on Gwiezdna Street. Now make yourself useful.'

She pushed the boat away, giving him a perfunctory smile.

'We'll be round to see you!' she called. His only reply was to start rowing. He turned the boat around and headed towards the headland without once looking back. Joanna had no choice but to go and check if he was right.

She made her way to the opposite shore and asked the tech team what she needed to know. They were used to working in their own little police unit and had no experience of dealing with corporate lawyers, so she soon had them wrapped round her little finger.

It seemed Ekiel was right. One of the divers explained that under normal circumstances, a corpse would surface within about two weeks.

'When someone drowns,' he told her, as if revealing some hidden secret, 'the oxygen in the lungs is replaced by water. This makes the body sink. But after it's settled on the bottom, it begins to decompose, releasing gases. The rate of decomposition depends on how deep the water is, how much sunlight reaches the body and where the body's lying, as the temperature usually differs between the north side and the south.'

'You mean bacteria release gases?' asked Chyłka, uncertainly.

'Yes, and they feed on proteins in the body tissues – in fact, on decomposing organisms in general. The bacteria normally live in the large intestine, but they could also come from an infected wound. As they digest the flesh, they give off carbon dioxide and sulphur dioxide, which bloat the face, abdomen and, if the victim's male, the genitals. The body then rises and floats to the surface.'

He went on to tell her that women float face upwards, as do the excessively overweight. That, Joanna decided, was more than enough to be going on with. She set off to tell Zordon what she had learned.

Kordian looked at her with distaste, then frowned and returned to his coffee. They were sitting in the attic, and Chyłka hoped their conversation couldn't be overheard downstairs. The last thing she needed was the Szlezyngiers to start picturing little Nikola's decomposing body.

'Strange guy,' said Kordian.

'You're the strange guy. He's just an old, balding man.'

'Whatever. Do you think he might be involved in something?'

'Like what? Kidnapping a little girl through a rooflight? He could barely scrabble out of his boat.'

'So why do you think he rowed up to you?'

'No idea. Maybe he was looking for excitement,' said Joanna, but she didn't sound convinced. She'd instinctively felt there was something not quite right about the old man, but couldn't put her finger on what. And her intuition could be wrong: it wouldn't be the first time.

'We could get Kormak to check him out,' suggested Oryński, 'unless he's sitting in his McCarthy cave reading *The Road* for the hundred and fiftieth time.'

Kormak probably was. The skinny young man employed by Żelazny & McVay as their senior information specialist owed his nickname to the fact that he sat in his office – his 'cave' – from dawn to dusk, mostly reading Cormac McCarthy novels, but also spying on anyone the law firm needed to know about. He could work miracles with Facebook, Twitter, Snapchat and Endomondo – and it was all above board.

'He won't find anything on him,' Joanna answered. 'The old fossil probably hasn't even got access to the internet.'

'Still worth checking.'

She nodded reluctantly, then messaged Kormak. An hour later, she vowed never to doubt the young man's abilities again.

6

Kordian was standing right next to Chyłka when Kormak rang her with his findings, but despite his pointed gesturing, she refused to put her phone on loudspeaker. He had no choice but to wait until they'd finished, and that was a good fifteen minutes. At last Joanna put the phone down.

'Don't tell me – he's found something,' Kordian said, noting the familiar gleam in his supervisor's eye.

'Too right he has.'

'Well? Or do I have to guess?'

'Antoni Ekiel was once convicted under Article 207 of the Criminal Code.'

'Which means?'

'That, my dear trainee, is something you should know.'

'I don't have time to learn all this stuff by heart.'

'If I find many more gaps in your knowledge, that's exactly what you'll be doing.'

Kordian spread his hands helplessly. 'So what was the offence?' he asked.

'Abuse of a family member.'

'What, child abuse?'

'Got it in one,' she said with a smile. 'Ekiel was locked up for a year.'

Oryński sat down on the bed. 'Any more details?'

'Of course. Kormak went through everything there was.' Joanna sat down next to him. 'Our fisherman caught his four-year-old daughter in the act of cutting his trouser legs in half.

He started slapping her hands, and didn't stop until four of her fingers were broken.'

'And he got a whole year for that? What would the usual sentence be?'

'Three months to five years,' said Chyłka. 'He clearly didn't show any remorse.'

'When was this?'

'1999.'

'And where's the daughter now?'

'Kormak didn't manage to find that out. But we do know Antoni Ekiel lost all his parental rights. It all happened in the regional court in Białystok.'

'So he moved here to escape the stigma.'

'Bravo, Zordon.'

'And where do we go from here?'

Joanna nodded towards the door. She didn't need to add anything else. Oryński knew it was a flimsy lead, but at least it was a lead. If they'd been detectives, they'd have probably checked Ekiel out just to be certain, but as defence lawyers, they could use the old man and his story to their advantage. Under cross-examination, an exhausted Antoni Ekiel might let slip something that would at least cast doubt on their clients' guilt. And that would be enough to muddy the waters.

With Chyłka driving, they got to Gwiezdna Street in record time. They asked a woman working in her garden which house was Ekiel's, and she pointed them in the right direction. Moments later, the pair were standing on the doorstep, ringing the bell.

The old man with a bald patch opened the door and looked suspiciously at Kordian. It was only when he saw Joanna that he invited them in.

'Don't get too comfortable, I don't suppose you'll be staying long,' he said, going into the kitchen. 'I'm boiling water, but I'm only making tea for myself.'

He hunched over an old gas cooker. The two lawyers exchanged glances, then followed him.

'I thought the police would be the first to find me,' he said.

Kordian glanced at the ashtray on the countertop, where the cigarette butts stood up like candles on the birthday cake of a hundred-year-old.

'You know why we're here, then,' said Joanna.

'Of course. I know my name's in the Central Crime Register.'

'They changed the name in 2000. It's now the National Criminal Register,' said Chyłka. 'And the fact that you're on it doesn't mean that people like us can check it.'

'Really? I thought everyone had access.'

Oryński was afraid his supervisor would make him explain the ins and outs of crime registers from memory, but she barely even looked at him. He knew that since 2013, all evidence was also linked to the National Court Register, and that if you knew the right person, it was easy to check up on anyone listed on there. That was probably how Kormak had got his information, although if anyone had caught him doing it, he'd have been given a hefty fine. Which Chyłka would gladly have paid.

Antoni looked at them apprehensively. Had he said too much already?

'We tracked down the press releases,' Joanna lied.

'Did you?' His relief was palpable. 'What did they say about me?'

'Nothing good.'

He poured boiling water into his mug and sat down at the table. The chair creaked about as much as his joints did.

'I'm sure the police will turn up sooner or later,' said Chyłka. 'They can't just ignore the fact that a convicted child abuser lives a few hundred metres from the scene of the crime.'

'It was one child.'

Joanna moved closer, and looked down at him. 'What is it you want?' she said.

'What?' He swirled the teabag in his mug. 'You invite yourselves into my house, you remind me of things that happened in the distant past, and to top it all—'

'You spotted me from the headland,' Joanna interrupted. 'You rowed up to me and started talking about dead bodies floating.'

'Is that right?'

'Of course. You wanted my attention. And it worked, because here I am.'

She sat in the chair opposite him, while Oryński crouched beside them. He wasn't happy with the way this conversation was going.

'I wanted your attention, child, because you seem to doubt your clients' innocence.'

Chyłka froze for a second, then turned to Kordian and raised her eyebrows.

'This old curmudgeon's no good to us,' she said, standing up. 'He just wants something more exciting in his life than the daily crossword.'

Ekiel looked daggers at her, while Kordian rose from his squatting position. He knew she wouldn't leave this house without answers, although to be fair, he wasn't sure what the questions were. But that was nothing new. Chyłka had a habit of leaving it until the last moment to tell him even the most important things.

She made a move towards the door, but stopped in the hallway.

'Right. Last chance,' she said.

The old man took a loud slurp of tea. 'They didn't do it,' he announced.

'How do you know?' asked Kordian.

'Because I saw.'

'Saw what?' asked Joanna, turning to face him. She leaned against the doorframe and folded her arms. 'Come on. What did you see?'

Ekiel inhaled noisily and looked around for his cigarettes. To speed things up, Oryński grabbed the packet of Viceroys and handed them to him. He was tempted to take one himself, but didn't.

Antoni Ekiel lit up, and promptly started coughing as if his lungs would burst. 'Forgive me,' he said, 'I'm not as young as I used to be.'

'We're still waiting,' said Chyłka, 'but we won't wait forever.'

The old man nodded slowly.

'I don't sleep well,' he began. 'Sometimes I nap in the day, but then I can't get to sleep at night, so I go out in my boat. It calms me down. It's when I like to fish, too. I've got some good cork floats, and my neighbour ordered fishing lights for me online. Fifty sets for forty zlotys, that gives me a hundred lights, and each one lasts up to twelve hours.'

'Mr Ekiel . . .' Kordian tried to interrupt. The old man put his cigarette back in the ashtray.

'I was out fishing that night too. Although you can't really call it fishing, I was just sitting in the boat. The fish tend to be scared of the lit-up floats.'

'Did you see something?'

'I saw the child.'

'Nikola Szlezyngier?'

He nodded and lowered his gaze. 'I saw her walking along the shore with someone.'

'Who?' asked Joanna, unfolding her arms.

'I couldn't see,' he said heavily. 'All I could see were two figures, one tall, the other short.'

The lawyers looked at one another.

'I expect you're wondering why I didn't go to the police,' Ekiel continued. 'It's because I didn't want to draw attention to myself. Nobody here knows about my past. If it all leaked out . . . well, it's a small community here. I'd be finished.'

'So why are you telling us now?' Oryński wanted to know.

Ekiel gave a wheezing sigh. 'I watched the press conference,' he said, stifling a cough. 'I saw how you were all looking at those people, and I realised they were your prime suspects. But it's not true. Someone took their child.'

'A man? A woman?' Chyłka asked. 'You must have seen some sort of silhouette.'

'It was too dark.'

'Maybe an approximate height?' Kordian suggested.

'No,' insisted the old man, retrieving his cigarette.

'Is there anything that would help us narrow it down?'

Ekiel shrugged. His guests waited, but he clearly had nothing more to say. Even when Chyłka pressed him for more details, he remained silent.

'Are you going to call me as a witness?'

'We have to,' she replied.

'So it's all going to come out. My past, I mean.'

'No, that information remains confidential.'

He looked at them, unconvinced, and sipped his tea. They took his silence as an invitation to leave the house. They already had far more than they'd expected from him, so they thanked him and returned to the X5. Kordian sank into the passenger seat and sighed.

'The guy was convicted in 1999.'

'He was.'

'So after ten years, his conviction was cleared.'

'Yes.'

'So the old curmudgeon, as you call him, won't figure on any register.'

'Wrong,' said Chyłka, starting the engine. 'He has no criminal or court record, but he's still in the National Police Information System.'

'That's so unfair,' said Kordian. 'Clearing a conviction is supposed to be a means of social rehabilitation. There should be no traces of it anywhere. The whole point is to stop people being stigmatised for past crimes.'

'Zordon, Zordon, Zordon,' she said, giving him a black look to boot, as if her tone of voice hadn't been enough. 'The police have managed to get around that, and in 2005, the Constitutional Tribunal introduced a provision to make it OK for them to keep getting around it.'

Oryński nodded. He should have expected the authorities to have a way to look back on past convictions – especially as Kormak had found his way in.

'What Ekiel told us won't be much use anyway,' he said.

'It'll help us in court.'

'How? Surely the prosecutor will argue it was Awit walking with his daughter along the lake shore.'

'Let him argue what he wants. We can turn it to our advantage.'

Kordian wasn't convinced.

'Besides, maybe it wasn't Szlezyngier at all,' Chyłka added, setting off in the opposite direction to their clients' house. Oryński didn't need to ask where she was going. They were heading back to the lion's den, where the paint was peeling off the furniture and the old-fashioned chairs swayed alarmingly.

7

'And how did you come by this information?' Satanowski asked.

It was the million-dollar question. Chyłka plastered on her best, most friendly smile, which usually worked well on people like the sergeant, so she didn't foresee a problem. For a moment or two she gazed at him in silence. Satanowski's expression immediately softened, although he probably didn't realise it himself.

'The media, archives, the internet . . . you know how it is,' she said. 'It all gets put together by our expert at the Skylight. I don't have access to his office.'

'At the what?'

'The Skylight. It's our office. Parade Square.'

The officer looked helplessly at Kordian.

'In Warsaw. Right in the very centre, by the Palace of Culture. A big glass office building next door to the Golden Terraces shopping mall. Don't you ever watch TV?'

'I don't pay much attention to the topography of our capital city.'

'Whatever,' said Joanna. 'Just call this guy and let him tell you what he's found. Then get off my clients' backs.'

'But we haven't made any accusations—'

'Not yet, but you're going to,' she cut in. 'And now, get to work. Do something useful for once, before the prosecutor gets dragged into this.' She got up and made for the door, Oryński on her heels.

She'd been wondering how best to handle Antoni Ekiel's testimony, and decided it would be wisest to play for time. Every hour the police spent on their investigation would mean an extra hour of freedom for the Szlezyngiers.

She'd told Zordon earlier that maybe Awit was innocent, but that was increasingly hard to believe. If the girl had been kidnapped, surely they'd have had a ransom demand by now. The kidnapper could get a fortune from these people, and would be set up for life anywhere he chose – even the Bahamas.

But there had been no demand for money. Chyłka wasn't particularly surprised, as kidnappings were rare in Poland. She'd checked the statistics, and in 2013, of the seven and a half thousand children reported missing, ninety-five per cent had returned home within the first week, and the vast majority of the rest were back after two weeks. Children mostly went missing due to inadequate care; they were rarely abducted, unless it was by their parents. Looking at the Szlezyngiers, it was difficult to imagine they'd do such a thing. Neither of them had grounds to kidnap their own daughter: they weren't divorced or separating, or at any other relationship crisis point.

'What are you thinking about?' asked Kordian as they drove over a bridge across the River Netta.

'Our clients.'

Oryński loosened his seatbelt and turned to her. 'And your conclusions are?'

'I've got absolutely nothing.'

'So it's more of the same.'

She glared at him. 'This rarely happens to me, Zordon. You should know that.' The last time she'd been at such a complete loss was when they were working on the Langer case. She still remembered Piotr's 'nervous tic', and it still made her blood run cold. She pushed the thought away.

'The police will check out the evidence,' said Kordian. 'Maybe they'll find out something new.'

'Most probably that it was Awit walking along the shore with his daughter that night. Then all they'll have to do is persuade him to tell them where he buried the body.'

Oryński went back to his original position. 'Sounds to me like you still don't think they're guilty.'

'No, I have no doubt they are. At least I don't think I do.'

'Then what's the problem?'

'I'm wondering why they did it,' she answered, pulling out into a narrow road with no pavement either side. 'Why they resorted to doing something that would so obviously put them under suspicion.'

Kordian shrugged.

'I'd understand if they were in the same situation as that child-killer in Sosnowiec,' Joanna continued. 'She only had a few moments to kill her daughter and hide her body in some crumbling old building nearby. The Szlezyngiers could have been much better organised.'

'So there is some good in you after all,' Kordian said.

'Wait, what?'

'And you try to see the good in others too.'

'Don't insult me,' she said with a smile, and put her foot down. They sped along in silence, Kordian drumming his fingers on the door, watching the trees. After a while, ignoring the double white lines in the centre of the road, Joanna moved smoothly first to the left then back to the right lane, leaving in their wake a perfectly serviceable Ford.

'I don't know,' said Kordian at length.

'What don't you know this time?'

'Nothing about this case adds up,' he said. 'From the absence of forensics around the house and the Szlezyngiers' behaviour, to the reaction of the police and media.'

'The police are worried they may have a repeat of the Sosnowiec debacle. The media even more so. Do you remember how everyone was so invested in searching for the little girl? For two weeks it was all anyone in Poland talked about, and then it turned out that even before the murder, that cold-blooded harpy had trawled the internet looking for the cheapest coffins and checking the funeral allowance for infants. She made a fool out of everyone.'

'Even so.'

'No one wants to get taken in a second time.'

'OK, I get that,' he said. 'But what about the lack of forensics?'

'Don't try to play the detective.'

'I have to, if we're expected to defend these people. It would be an idea to have at least a tiny bit of evidence to prove their innocence.'

'Skill in putting their case will be enough,' she said. Then she spotted a TVN24 news van driving almost as fast as she was, and frowning, pointed it out to Oryński. 'They're going fast.'

'I can see that.'

Joanna changed gear and put her foot down. The BMW let out a deep growl, and sped down the left-hand lane. And that was when the pair noticed the string of news vans from other TV stations.

Chyłka hit the indicator and reached for her phone. She called Angelika, but there was no answer.

'Here, take this,' she said, passing her phone to Kordian, 'and keep trying her.'

She sped up even more, trying to overtake any vehicle with a news station logo on it. It was clear the procession was on its way to the Szlezyngiers' house.

'Still nothing?' she said.

Oryński shook his head. 'Have we got Awit's number?' he asked.

'No,' replied Joanna, switching off Iron Maiden. 'But I have a feeling we'll find out what's going on even without it.' She tuned the radio to RMF FM, and they waited anxiously for whatever pop rock classic they were playing this time to finish.

She changed stations again and again, but it seemed they had hit a news vacuum. Everywhere was broadcasting either ads or music. Chyłka ceded control of the radio to Oryński, and concentrated on overtaking more vehicles. The entire journey from the bridge over the Netta to Sajenko Lake took them a little over five minutes. And as soon as they drove past the wall of trees screening the Szlezyngiers' home, they saw what the commotion was about.

Four police cars were parked on the road outside, while uniformed officers were in the process of escorting the couple out of the house. Chyłka slammed on the brakes, and as its wheels locked, the X5 continued to churn up earth for a second or two.

She and Oryński shot out of the car. 'Hey!' shouted Joanna. 'What do you think you're doing?'

A number of police officers, who had so far been standing around watching, suddenly sprang into action. They raised their hands almost simultaneously as if in response to some sort of signal.

'Please stay back,' one of the women began.

'No, you stay back!' shouted Chyłka without breaking step. 'I'm their lawyer. Get out of my way!'

The officer showed no intention of moving, so Joanna reached for her phone and held it up, as if ready to take a picture.

'Smile for the camera,' she said.

'Please put that down . . .'

Chyłka swept past the officer, and repeated the same procedure with the others. Kordian followed, albeit less gracefully, until they were both on the other side of the barricade, where they should have been in the first place. Meanwhile, the first news vans were already pulling up.

'What in God's name do you think you're doing?' asked Joanna, stopping in front of the police car.

'Please don't make things difficult . . .'

'Are you arresting my clients? What fucking right have you to do that?' The Szlezyngiers were completely surrounded by police officers, still walking, but totally confused.

'The prosecutor made a request for custody pending investigation,' one of the officers said, 'and the court approved it.'

'On what charge? This is preposterous!'

'The suspects have the right to make a formal complaint.'

Joanna glared at him. 'I know exactly what they have a right to do. So where's the warrant for this temporary arrest?'

'One of the officers read it to them earlier.'

'Isn't the prosecutor here?' The officer shook his head.

'When were they charged?'

'Today.'

'And what was the charge?'

'Ask the prosecutor in charge of—'

'I would, but he's not here.' Chyłka spread her hands and looked around. 'And I'd add a few choice words about how this is completely out of order.'

The officer stood by silently while his colleagues manoeuvred the Szlezyngiers into the waiting police car. Joanna realised there was no point protesting. If anything could be done, it would have to be through the official channels.

'I'll get you out,' she called out without thinking as the car door started to close.

It was a promise she would regret as soon as her adrenaline had subsided. The prosecutor's office often made requests for temporary custody pending investigation, but they were only granted when there was either genuine fear the suspect would obstruct the enquiry, or there was irrefutable evidence.

8

They walked into the empty house in silence. Oryński slammed the door shut, leaving the swarm of reporters outside, then leaned back on it.

'Szrebska will be sorry she handed the story over,' said Joanna, heading for the living room.

Kordian followed her.

'We're fucked,' he said.

'Shut up, Zordon.'

'I'm just stating a fact.'

Chyłka opened the bar and leaned over to make her choice. Kordian didn't want to dull his thinking with anything too strong, so he went to the fridge for a beer. Then they both sank heavily onto the sofa.

'So they must have some concrete evidence,' said Kordian.

'Looks like it.'

'But what?'

'Maybe someone else saw Awit that night. Someone apart from that old codger. Maybe they recognised him.' Chyłka took a sip of her drink.

Oryński opened his beer and was about to take a sip too, but stopped, feeling his supervisor's gaze resting heavily on him. He turned to look at her.

'Oh no you don't,' she said.

'Huh?'

'No alcohol for you today.'

'Why not?'

'Because you're about to drive my car.'

'I didn't know I was going anywhere.'

'Well now you do. We need a copy of that warrant,' she said. 'We'll get the prosecutor's note, and that'll tell us everything we need to know. Then we'll file a complaint, and whoever did this will be sorry they were born.'

Kordian nodded, but wasn't convinced. Even a complete rookie in the prosecutor's office would have avoided pulling a stunt like this. Unless, of course, they had new information.

A few hours later, it was done. Having submitted documents to prove they were officially handling the Szlezyngiers' defence, the lawyers were entitled to see the arrest warrant, but had to drive to the town of Suwałki, some forty kilometres away, to do so. This murder case was beyond the jurisdiction of the local courts, and was to be tried in the regional court on Waryński Street, in the province's former capital.

As soon as they had the paperwork, they made their way to a nearby pizzeria and sat down to inspect it. The interior décor was predominantly red, which didn't put Oryński in an optimistic mood, but Chyłka seemed to like it. It probably reminded her of the Hard Rock Café. She ordered a mexicana – unsurprisingly – while he went for a vegetariana.

'Now, let's have a look,' said Joanna, spreading the paperwork out over the table.

There was far less of it than Kordian had expected. He'd thought the court would give them everything they had, an entire opus explaining why their clients had been arrested. But the documents they had took up less space than two pizzas.

'Is that it?' he asked.

'So far.'

'But they arrested two people. Surely we should have a full explanation as to why.'

Joanna looked up from the page she was studying. 'Our next step will be to request the basis of the charges and a full justification in writing.'

'So we haven't got that here?'

'No. The suspects don't have full access to their file at this stage in the game, and neither do we.'

'Right.'

'They don't get them until pre-trial proceedings are about to close, and that's when we can review the file in its entirety.'

'OK, that's something I'll learn in practice, no doubt.'

She looked at him, then pointed to the papers on the table.

'This is practice.'

'OK,' he said. 'So tell me what they've got on them.'

Chyłka skimmed the papers. 'In order to ensure the smooth running of the proceedings blah, blah, blah ...' she read, '... there is legitimate reason to fear obstruction ...'

'What?' Oryński cut in. 'Who would they be buying off, or putting the frighteners on, or encouraging to lie?'

'Some witness, clearly.'

'Does it say who?'

'No,' said Joanna, looking up. 'It just says the prosecutor's office thinks that, on the balance of probabilities, the suspects committed the crime of which they're accused.'

'And that is?'

'Article 148.'

'Murder? But there's no body, and no evidence that the girl is even dead.'

'The case against them is circumstantial,' Joanna answered, lost in thought.

'But that's ridiculous!'

'Zordon, they don't need to find the body or provide any direct evidence.'

Kordian watched the waiter carrying pizzas back and forth, as if that might save him. He'd never heard of anyone being charged with murder without any direct evidence that the victim had even died.

'But the child could simply have disappeared.'

'Stop it, Zordon. We both know that's not what happened, and the court knows it too.'

'So they'll try them without evidence?'

Chyłka pulled out her phone, switched on her data, typed something into Google and turned the device to Kordian. The case she'd found hadn't been high-profile enough to make Wikipedia, but it was a good summary. Oryński read that the accused had been sentenced to twenty-five years, although the victim's body had never been found and the evidence was all circumstantial.

'Didn't they teach you this sort of thing at university?'

'Maybe they did, but . . .'

'But you were too busy planning to lose your virtue.'

He scowled. 'That happens a bit earlier now than it did in your day,' he said. 'The sexual revolution in the sixties took care of that.'

Joanna muttered something under her breath. Just then, the waiter appeared with their order.

'Vegetariana?' he asked with a smile, looking at Chyłka.

'For this chinless wonder,' she said, indicating Kordian. 'I need meat to keep me going.'

'Confirmed carnivore,' Kordian agreed.

'I'm nurturing the traditions of my ancestors,' she said. 'The earliest homo sapiens fed on big game.'

'Not true. Faecal samples from fifty thousand years ago found in Alicante show they ate tubers, nuts and berries, and a lot of other things.'

The bemused-looking waiter set the other pizza down.

'Enjoy your meal,' he muttered as he hurried away.

Chyłka cut a piece off her mexicana and shook her head. 'I don't want to hear another word of pro-vegetarian bullshit.'

'But it's all been proved by scientists at MIT.'

'I'm willing to concede they may have added a few berries to their cheetah meat, but that's it.'

Kordian took a slice of pizza and bit off the end. Chyłka looked at the vegetable toppings with disdain. 'You might not have the strength to pick up a pen after this.'

'Me?'

'Who else? You're not expecting your supervisor to write a simple letter of complaint, are you?' she asked, her mouth full. 'You do it. I'm sure you'll take it to the heights of erudition, and if not, I'll take you by the hand and help you get there. Who knows, you might even learn something.'

He soon found that the educational content of the task was pretty much zero. As soon as they'd finished their pizzas, he got his laptop from the car and set to work. He appealed against the court's decision, arguing that, according to the Court of Justice of the European Union, Poland was excessive in its use of pre-trial detention, almost to the point of abuse. He went on to stress that their clients had no previous convictions, enjoyed unblemished reputations, and that there were no grounds to accuse them of possible obstruction. He finished by emphasising there was no evidence to say they had even committed a crime.

He typed the final full stop, and turned the screen to Joanna. She was glued to her phone screen.

'*Ground control to Major Jo,*' he said.

'What?' she asked without looking up.

'I'm paraphrasing David Bowie. I thought you liked that kind of . . .'

'Go to the NSI site, Zordon.'

He turned his screen back and switched to the browser. He didn't have to search long for the news Chyłka was so interested in: the headline on the homepage told him everything he needed to know.

FATHER KILLS CHILD. MURDER WEAPON FOUND IN WOODS.

9

Chyłka and Oryński rose as one, hurtled back to the car and drove straight to the remand prison where their clients were being held. Visiting wasn't a problem. Although suspects didn't have the same rights as those already accused or even convicted, there were no restrictions on seeing their lawyers. In other circumstances, they'd have had to apply for a visiting order.

They entered a large room with a row of white cubicles, the prisoners' and visitors' sides separated by a plexiglass screen. Each cubicle held a small, white phone.

They sat in one of the booths and waited for Awit. He appeared within minutes, looking exhausted, although he'd only been behind bars for an hour or two. He slumped into the wooden chair and reached for the phone. Chyłka did the same.

'Tell me you've got something,' he said.

His voice was piteous and pleading, not at all in keeping with the tough businessman image Szlezyngier had been cultivating since the times of political change.

'We're working on it.'

Awit looked down. He was deathly pale, the network of fine blood vessels beneath his skin clearly visible. For a moment he was silent.

'They told me to give them the paperwork,' he said weakly.

'They what?' asked Joanna, looking at Oryński. Kordian shrugged. He hadn't heard either. Joanna gestured that he should put the phone closer to his ear.

'When I went into the cell, the other guys in there demanded I give them the paperwork.'

'What paperwork?'

'The warrant, the one that says what I've been charged with. They said they needed to know what they were dealing with.'

Chyłka had a sudden urge to hang up. She knew what he meant, and she knew what was coming next. Prisons usually separated paedophiles, rapists, homosexuals, former law-enforcement officers and child-killers from other prisoners; on the inside, all these groups had a similar status, and a few minutes in the wrong place could be fatal for them. They tended to be kept apart even on remand, but sometimes, for whatever reason, they were put into an ordinary cell. And if a new prisoner didn't have a warrant with them, if there was no record of their alleged offences, it was usually taken to mean one thing.

'What did you tell them?' she asked.

'That the screws took it away because I was getting aggressive.' The emptiness in his eyes told Chyłka he hadn't convinced his cell mates.

'There are four of them. All serious criminals. They said they'd . . .' he stopped and shook his head. Joanna could scarcely believe that this broken figure on the other side of the plexiglass screen was the same man who, according to Zordon, had been on the cover of *Forbes* a few short weeks ago.

'Can you get me moved?' he asked, looking up at Joanna at last.

'You'll be out of there by tonight.'

'Are you sure?'

Chyłka nodded. The formalities wouldn't take long, and the Szlezyngiers of this world were quickly put where they belonged.

'Thank you.'

'You can thank me once we've made some progress,' she said. 'At the moment, everyone seems to know more than we do.'

'What do you mean?'

'They've searched the forest east of Sajenko.'

'And?' pleaded Szlezyngier. 'My God, they haven't . . .'

'If the media are to be believed, they've found some sort of rod with blood on it. About fifteen kilometres from the Belarusian border,' said Joanna, watching her client's face carefully. 'It's got your fingerprints on it too.'

Awit opened his mouth, but nothing came out. The mesh of tiny blood vessels beneath his skin seemed to spill over into two huge purple patches on his cheeks.

'Did you hear me?'

It wasn't a rhetorical question. The sound quality of the prison phone system left a lot to be desired. Voices became distorted, and Szlezyngier had been speaking quietly in the first place. Now he sat motionless, staring at Joanna.

She leaned towards the plexiglass screen. 'You've got to cooperate,' she said. 'If you've got any more surprises in store for us, you'd better tell us now, because I swear—'

'What about Angelika?' Awit interrupted.

Chyłka sighed, leaning back in her chair. 'They've charged her with being an accessory.'

'Where is she?'

'She's in the women's wing. Don't worry, conditions are a bit better there.'

Szlezyngier leaned his elbows on the countertop and covered his eyes with his hand. For a moment he was silent.

'How's that possible?' he said weakly. 'What rod? What fingerprints? What blood?'

She knew he wasn't expecting an answer. It was Nikola's blood, but so far Joanna had no idea how much of it there was. One report said there was only a drop or two, another that the rod was saturated.

'Tell us now, quickly, while there's still time,' urged Chyłka. 'In a minute they'll ask us to go, and we'll be left with nothing.'

'But I don't know anything about a . . . I don't understand what's going on.'

'Tell me about the rod, Awit.'

He was thinking furiously, and Joanna could hear his shallow, ragged breathing through the phone. He looked genuinely shocked, but then as a shark in the business world he probably had the play-acting game down to a tee.

'Come on, think. What sort of rod have they found?' she asked again. 'And how come it's got both your fingerprints and your daughter's blood on it?'

'For God's sake, I don't know. I don't know!'

Joanna swore under her breath and looked at Oryński, who shrugged helplessly.

'I . . . I . . . some time ago I bought some posts. I was planning to build a balustrade, but—' He stopped again and looked up. Joanna thought she saw a glimmer of hope in his eyes. 'Nikola must have cut herself.'

'How? When?'

'We were always telling her not to play in the workshop.' Szlezyngier went on as if he hadn't heard the question. 'That must be where the blood came from.'

'I need the truth, Awit.'

He shook his head and pressed the phone to his ear. 'You said before that you didn't care about the truth,' he said.

'The situation's different now. Tell me what happened. Was there an accident?'

'I'd never raise a hand to my daughter!' he shouted. Immediately, a warden in a blue uniform shirt appeared at his side. He looked at the prisoner, then at the lawyers. Joanna gestured that everything was fine.

'You need to tell us the whole story,' she said after he'd gone.

'My God, this again! How many times! When we went to bed, our daughter was in her bedroom. When we got up, she was gone! Which part of that don't you understand?'

'Calm down.'

'For God's sake, I'd never hurt my own child!'

'Calm down, or they'll take you away.'

Awit looked at her with rage. She knew she'd get nothing more out of him now – and as if to prove her right, Szlezyngier slammed down the phone, stood up and walked away without a backward glance.

Chyłka massaged her temples, still holding onto the receiver.

'Shall we go?' asked Kordian.

'Yes, let's.'

They left the remand prison, walked to the car in silence, then sat inside, motionless. Finally, Joanna hit the start button.

'I believe him,' said Kordian.

'What?'

'I don't think he did it.'

'What, because he looked shaken? I would be too, if I were him.'

'I don't think he killed the child, Chyłka. In fact, chances are nobody killed her.'

'You reckon? Care to tell me your reasoning, oh great master of speculation?'

'I've got a few theories.'

'Anything that will stand up in court?' she asked, turning into Waryński Street.

'I don't think so.'

'Then don't even bother.' She took a deep breath. 'Because let's take a look at it. First, it could have been Angelika. Second, it could be kidnapping for ransom. Third, abduction. Fourth, maybe she just got lost, fifth . . . well, we could both carry on speculating forever, but none of it would stand up in court.'

'OK, OK, I get it.'

'And none of it explains how she actually disappeared without leaving any traces whatsoever,' Chyłka went on. 'Did someone stand the ladder on a board so it would leave no marks? Did they tunnel into the house? Or blow a hole in the wall then plaster it over? They're all theories, just like yours. But in court, you might as well talk about how the moon landing was a hoax.'

For a moment, Kordian was silent.

'I still think the Szlezyngiers are innocent,' he said at last.

10

Chyłka and Oryński's complaint was only partially upheld. The court changed Angelika's custody conditions and she was allowed to leave prison – but only under police supervision, which Chyłka saw as abuse.

The lawyers picked her up as soon as she was released and drove her back to the summer house, where the access road was still teeming with TV news vans. Since the bloodied weapon had been found in the woods, the case had been given nationwide publicity. The whole of Augustów was plastered with posters of Nikola, while the media made daily appeals for her return.

It was now a week since she had gone missing. Kordian had read enough thrillers in his time to know that the first seventy-two hours were crucial; after that, the chances of ever finding her decreased drastically.

Angelika sat in silence all the way to Sajenko. Only when the front door was closed behind them and the shouts of the reporters had let up a little did she speak.

'Someone's got it in for us.' She walked over to the bar and grabbed the nearest bottle. 'No, it's more than that. Someone's hell-bent on destroying us.'

Oryński believed her, just as he'd believed Awit. Chyłka disagreed, which didn't surprise him – she was never keen to give anyone the benefit of the doubt.

'Who would want to do that?' he asked.

'How many names do you want?' answered Angelika, sitting down on the sofa. She twisted round, stretched her legs out on the seat and tilted her head back. 'Awit's made countless enemies over the years.'

'So have you,' said Joanna, taking a seat on the armchair.

'Maybe I have. But not enough for someone to kidnap my child and make us look guilty.'

'Where did that rod come from?' Chyłka asked.

'Awit bought it some time ago. He was planning to build a balustrade.'

'Himself? Surely he's got enough money to hire someone to do it.'

'He used to be a locksmith before ... you know, in communist times. He goes on and on about how he can do that sort of thing better than anyone else. And now he's got his comeuppance.'

Angelika shut her eyes and put her glass down. Kordian guessed she hadn't been given an easy ride in prison either. Things might not be as bad in the women's block as they were in the men's, but as a potential child-killer, they wouldn't have let her off lightly.

'Nikola cut herself on one of those rods,' Angelika continued quietly. 'It was nothing. I didn't even mention it to Awit. He'd told her over and over again not to go into his workshop, but what can you do?'

'A three-year-old went into the workshop by herself?' asked Joanna.

Angelika sighed. 'I'm guessing you don't know many little children,' she said.

'Not really.'

'Nikola started walking when she was eighteen months old. She's three and ten months now, and if she could, she'd walk the length and breadth of the world.' Angelika opened her eyes again and reached for her glass. Oryński noted that she had no qualms about her liver – she was drinking her vodka neat. Joanna walked over and took the glass from her.

'When did she cut herself?' she asked.

Angelika frowned. 'Two days before she went missing.'

'Did you put a plaster on the cut?'

'Of course.'

'And where did you throw it away?'

All three looked towards the kitchen, and a small gleam appeared in Chyłka's eye. She ran out of the room, opened the cupboard under the sink, pulled out the bin and tipped the contents onto the floor.

Kordian looked with faint disgust at the leftover food, used condoms, vegetable peelings, beer bottle tops and other debris.

Angelika opened another cupboard and took out three pairs of rubber gloves, and the three of them started to pick through the rubbish. It wasn't long before they found the plaster, complete with a patch of dried blood.

'Hallelujah,' said Joanna. 'This will tip the scales in what's become an unequal battle. Now give me a bag to put it in.' She packed the evidence into a bag and gave it to Oryński. 'Put it somewhere safe, Zordon.'

'Like where?'

'The glove compartment in the X5.'

'Wouldn't it be better to—'

'No,' she cut in. 'Given the circumstances, I trust the BMW's alarm more than I do the one here. Just don't forget to lock the car.'

Kordian did as he was asked, checking twice that he'd locked up as instructed. If someone really had framed the Szlezyngiers, this little plaster could prove they weren't guilty of kidnapping their daughter. Before returning to the house, Kordian checked yet again that he'd set the car alarm.

Back in the living room, he saw that both women had a drink in their hands. This time it was Joanna who had poured Angelika a glass.

'I know it must be hard for you to believe we're innocent,' Angelika was saying, 'but there's no way Awit did this. I sleep very lightly, and I'd have woken up straight away if he got up in the night.'

Oryński looked at his supervisor, who was nodding. He could see she wasn't taking Angelika's words particularly seriously. Wives defend their husbands, that was nothing new – in court their testimony was about as much use as a meat cleaver to peel an orange.

'And besides, what motive could he possibly have?' she asked, spreading her hands. 'We're not on the breadline, we're not eking out an existence, we could afford to support a whole bunch of children.'

Joanna sighed. 'The prosecution could argue that you wanted to get back to the way things were before, when it was just the two of you.'

'What?'

'A child changes a relationship completely. Children can be draining, and—'

'Jesus, you really don't have any idea about children, do you?'

'And please God, I'll never have to.' Chyłka took a long pull on her drink. 'Or they might say it was an accident – that the child died because of your negligence, and you wanted to cover it up.'

'What? By taking her out through the chimney?'

'I don't know. But they're treating you as suspects, so they must have a plausible theory. No prosecutor wants to shoot themselves in the foot, whatever it sometimes looks like.'

'But now we've got the plaster.'

'Yes, we have,' Joanna said happily. 'And if we can just persuade the judge, we might be able to make something of it. But remember, it's not exactly a cast-iron defence. It all depends on how we argue it and which judges we get.'

'When's the trial likely to be?'

'First they have to formally accuse you.'

'Haven't they already done that?'

'No, at the moment you're prime suspects, but the investigation's still ongoing. When that's finished, they'll make their formal accusation.'

'How long will that be?'

Chyłka looked at Kordian.

'There's no time limit,' he explained. 'Some people are suspects for years. In theory, no one should be in remand for longer than three months, but it can be extended to twelve months. After that, the prosecutor can apply for a further extension, then another. There really is no limit. That's why we sometimes call it the confessional – the suspect is held until they admit they did it.'

Chyłka nodded, satisfied with his explanation. 'And who holds the record?' she asked.

'A man called Kowalczyk. Twelve and a half years. It wasn't until the European Court of Justice got involved that he was released.'

'And it's worth adding he was acquitted,' said Chyłka with a wry grin. 'So you can see it's not going to be easy. One plaster doth not a summer make.'

69

Angelika looked down. 'Surely it can't go on that long in our case. We've got a business to run.'

Kordian would have thought the pain of a long separation would have been Angelika's main worry, but values were clearly different in this family.

'We'll do everything we can,' said Chyłka.

'But surely it's as clear as day.'

Oryński would have said nothing about this case was clear, but he maintained a strategic silence.

'Someone planted that rod,' Angelika said at length. 'All we have to do is find out who. There must be footprints, or even witnesses, other than . . .'

She broke off, and looked to Chyłka for help.

'You mean besides Antoni Ekiel.'

'That's the one. And maybe even he didn't even see anyone. From what you say, he's not a very credible witness.'

'In this instance, he's pretty credible,' said Joanna.

'Whatever. But he definitely didn't see my husband in the middle of the night, because Awit was with me, fast asleep in bed.'

Angelika repeated the same thing over and over again, in several different ways. Not once did she give the impression she was lying. She seemed completely convinced that her husband had nothing to do with their daughter's disappearance.

A theory Oryński shared. So he stopped listening to her repeated justifications, took the printouts they'd been sent by the security company and went upstairs, sat down on the floor and spread the papers out around him. The computer had meticulously recorded the exact times the alarm had been activated and deactivated, and he'd been assured by the company that it was impossible to falsify the data. Although to Kordian, that seemed absurd. There was no electronic system in this world that couldn't be manipulated; it didn't even make headline news anymore. He took out his phone and rang Kormak. At this time of night, he'd probably be sitting in his den pretending to work, but in reality flipping through the pages of a book he already knew by heart. Kordian was afraid this would stop him answering, but Kormak picked up the phone after only a few rings.

'What do you want this time?' Kormak asked.

'Just to talk.'

'I've got better things to do right now.'

'You also owe me a load of favours,' Oryński reminded him. 'I haven't called in half of them yet.'

'What on earth for?'

'Actually, it's more of an insurance. Don't you remember you gave me drugs? Gandalf the White, as you called it?'

'Yeah, but I didn't make you take them.'

'And I'm not making you help me now. I'm merely making a gentle suggestion.'

Kormak muttered something, which Kordian took as agreement.

'Tell me, how reliable is the statement from a home security alarm system?'

'The statement?'

'You know, a list of times it was activated and deactivated and . . .'

'Mate, you mean a log.'

'A log, whatever. Are they easy to falsify?'

'As easy as running a fake promotion on the Lidl website,' said Kormak. He paused. 'I've been following your case online,' he said, 'and it's not looking good. Chyłka's finally getting her arse handed to her, isn't she?'

Kordian turned back to his papers. He could hear Angelika sobbing downstairs, and thought how Joanna was probably going out of her mind down there.

'We've got some new information,' said Oryński, 'but it's still early days. What can you tell me about the logs?'

'The prosecutor will call in an expert who will already have checked the system and established that everything's hunky-dory. If there'd been signs of a break-in, Szlezyngier probably wouldn't be in the slammer. Familiar name though. I think that's what my squash racket's called.'

'That would be Slazenger, not Szlezyngier.'

'Whatever. We could have a game sometime.'

'I haven't had a lot of time recently, Kormak.'

'You have time to go running. Quite regularly too, from what I see on Endomondo.'

Kordian closed his eyes, sighed, and reached for his ersatz cigar-ette to calm his nerves. It was supposed to taste like a Marlboro, but it was more like a wet sponge. He took a drag, then put it down.

'How good is this expert likely to be?' he asked.

'Complete arsehole, probably.'

'You IT experts all talk about each other like that.'

'Well, you can trust me, because I'm not an IT expert.'

'I detect a hint of contradiction here,' Kordian muttered, rubbing his forehead. Then more loudly: 'If someone tried to hack the log, would they have left tracks?'

'Obviously. The internet is like a playground for hackers. Set up a tiny, insignificant website which no one visits, and I guar-antee that within weeks hackers will have tried to log in, and there'll be hordes of botnets.'

'And when they've done what they set out to do, can they clear their tracks?'

'Of course.'

'So where does that leave us, Kormster?'

'Stop it. You know I hate it when you call me that.'

'I know. Sorry.' Kordian heard his friend heave a sigh.

'Where it leaves us is that it all depends on what the hackers did and how they did it. They won't have got in through ports twenty-one and eighty, because those are always secure, even in a small company like this. If the rest of the TCPs and UDPs were set up properly, the hacker might have left tracks. Of course, you'd have to take a close look at the SSH – that's port twenty-two – because that's where someone might have tried a brute force attack. I can't tell you anymore, but make sure you ask the professional expert who checked it all the right questions.'

'Will do. I'll tell them everything you've just said.'

'Just tell them there could potentially be loads of traces. If they use a fairly primitive algorithm to crack passwords, they could have left a trail of breadcrumbs, or been detected by the network monitoring tools.'

'OK.'

'You haven't taken any of this in.'

'No, but I'll get Chyłka to call you before the trial. If the worst comes to the worst, we'll call in our own expert.'

'Well don't count on it being me. I don't work for peanuts. Thirty zlotys an hour? Forget it.'

He wasn't the first to complain about the rates. Many of the top specialists refused to give expert evidence simply because it wasn't worth it financially. And that wasn't set to change – although it was precisely in the courtroom that the best expert witnesses were needed.

'Give the old fart a run for his money,' said Kormak. Then he said goodbye and abruptly hung up.

Kordian went back to studying the security company's logs. He reckoned if he was going to find something, that was where he'd find it. Antoni Ekiel was a red herring.

An hour later, he realised he'd been right.

'I know what the prosecutor's got on him,' Kordian said, coming downstairs. Chyłka looked up from her laptop. She was comfortably settled in the armchair, her feet on a footstool and her computer on her lap. Beside her was a drink and her e-cigarette. All she needed to complete this picture of bliss was Zordon to come to her with good news.

'Well?' she said.

He sat down on the sofa and looked around.

'Angelika's fast asleep,' Chyłka explained. 'So what have you found?'

'The log from the security company. It tells us when the alarm was switched on and off.'

'And?'

'The Szlezyngiers switched it on at seven p.m.'

Chyłka put her laptop on the table. 'So?' she said.

'Nobody puts their alarm on that early.'

She looked at him.

'Maybe in winter, when it gets dark at four. But in August? I don't think so.'

'Any statistics to support your theory?'

'No, just common sense,' he said, leaning towards Joanna. 'Imagine you were here on that day. It's a scorching hot evening. You'd probably be sitting out on the terrace, or maybe by the lake. Anywhere not to be inside the house. Why would they turn the alarm on so early?'

'Maybe they just felt like it.'

'Or maybe they'd already killed the child and buried her in the woods, then they came back here and turned the alarm on so they'd have an alibi.'

Chyłka nodded her head approvingly. 'I thought you thought they were innocent?'

'Oh, I do,' he assured her. 'I'm just saying what the prosecution might allege.'

'Maybe you'll make a quick-witted lawyer after all. Not a brilliant one, but quick-witted all the same.'

'Quicker than you, given you hadn't even thought of it.'

'I had, I assure you.'

'Yeah, right,' he said, craning his neck to see her laptop screen. Joanna smiled, gratified, as she watched his face fall.

'What is it, Zordon?'

'Nothing.'

'Admit it – I've stunned you with my superior intellect.'

'You do it all the time,' he muttered, getting up. He walked over to Joanna and began examining the more detailed, electronic version on her screen of the papers he had on the floor upstairs.

'And what do you deduce from this data?'

'That they normally switched the alarm on just before midnight.' Oryński swore under his breath.

'I checked the whole of last year,' she said. 'There was only one other occasion when they set it so early. I'm afraid you'll have to start looking at them from a different angle.'

Kordian was silent.

'At least we know what the prosecution will start with,' said Chyłka.

'I still don't think they did it.'

'Great. So we've got one person on our side. Now we just have to convince the rest of the world.'

'Those records can easily be doctored.'

'OK, for argument's sake, let's say they have been. But we'd still need another suspect for the abduction. If we want the court to consider the possibility the Szlezyngiers might be innocent, we have to give them someone else to latch onto. And who would that be? Ekiel's out.'

'Plenty of people know who lives in this house and how much money they've got.'

'But would any of them do something like this?'

'There's always one. Someone desperate.'

Joanna looked at him. She wasn't sure if he was baiting her, or if he actually believed their clients weren't guilty. For her, the case was clear. She closed her laptop and got up.

'Go and talk to the neighbours if you want. You might find there's a connection to the Belarusian gangsters across the border.'

'That's not as far-fetched as you may think.'

'You think not?' she asked with a yawn.

'How far's the border? Thirty kilometres?'

'About that.'

'These forests are the perfect place for smuggling kids. And not only kids. Have you ever seen what the border looks like?'

'You mean those little signs warning you not to cross or else?'

He nodded. 'Exactly. Ideal conditions for someone from over there to abduct a child.'

'Why would the Belarusians want to abduct this particular little girl?'

'For the ransom, of course.'

'Great theory, Zordon,' Chyłka scoffed, wandering over to the bar. 'There's only one problem. There's no ransom demand.'

'Maybe there is, and we don't know about it.'

'Right,' she said, adding more vodka to her drink. She gave Oryński a fleeting smile and headed off towards the stairs. 'You can go out and harass the neighbours, I'm going to bed.'

'Too right I'm going out.'

She waved towards the door, then climbed up to the attic and lay down on the bed, expecting to fall asleep in seconds. It was unlikely, she knew, that Kordian would get anything from the locals. The Szlezyngiers probably had minimal contact with them. In this sort of village, people mostly kept themselves to themselves. They might as well be investigating the child's disappearance on a desert island.

She closed her eyes and rolled onto her back. Sleep should have been beckoning by now, but instead Chyłka was struggling to still her mind. Oryński's words echoed in her head.

A Belarusian kidnap plot had been the first thing she thought of when all this started; just being here made you suspect something of the kind. God knew there were plenty of people on the eastern side of the border willing to risk everything they had to make big money. And if one of them knew who lived in the summer house just thirty kilometres away . . .

Joanna turned onto her side. But with no ransom demand, there was little chance that the court would be interested. She lay in bed a moment longer, wrestling with her thoughts, but eventually gave up on the idea of sleep and sat up. She looked around the room, wondering what to do. In the end she reached for her phone to ring Kormak, and one short conversation later, she knew exactly what her next step should be.

She crept downstairs and sneaked into Angelika's bedroom. The woman had had a skinful, and was well out of it. Joanna looked around for her mobile, eventually spotting it on the bedside cabinet. A moment later she left the room, phone in hand, closing the door gently behind her.

In the kitchen she picked up a charger, took it into the living room, sat down and fired up her computer. Then she plugged the cable into the USB port and rang Kormak again.

'I've connected her phone to the computer,' she said. 'Have you got remote access?'

'Of course, as always. I've got to get my kicks somehow.'

'Don't even joke about online stalking. I know you're kidding, but I want to feel safe using my laptop. Even now I can almost feel you staring at me through that little lens above the screen.'

'OK, I get it,' said a slightly bewildered Kormak. 'And I can see the phone. The latest Samsung, no less. Nice.'

'Will you be able to get into it?'

'No problem. You can do anything with an Android. Did you look through her inbox? Is there anything we need to delete?'

'I did, and there's nothing there.'

'In that case, I'll get to work.'

Joanna watched the black terminal that appeared on her laptop screen. Strings of characters and numbers scrolled by at a furious pace, but they meant little to her. Kormak, meanwhile, was silent. All she could hear from his end was a rhythmic tap-tapping on the keyboard.

'You've got a good machine,' he said.

'It's the company's.'

'It'll take me a while to retrieve all the data. Although if I was doing this on Zordon's computer, you'd have time to drive to Warsaw, have a bite to eat at the Hard Rock Café and then drive back,' he continued. 'Are we looking for anything in particular?'

'You know very well we are.'

The minutes seemed to drag on forever, and Chyłka couldn't keep up with all the information appearing on her screen. She didn't understand much of it anyway.

But when Kormak finished, she knew precisely what she was seeing. He'd restored all Angelika's deleted text messages.

12

Kordian wandered gloomily around Sajenko. He'd called at a few dozen houses, but the distances between them were enough to deter even the most enthusiastic hiker. And now it was dark. Very, very dark. Street lamps were few and far between, and the only light came from the windows of the houses. As luck would have it, Oryński had forgotten his phone, which could have served as a torch.

The search had been futile anyway. Everyone was adamant that the Szlezyngiers kept themselves very much to themselves, and even went to Augustów for their shopping; although they could sometimes be seen boating on the lake. The good thing was that he'd got to know the neighbours a little better. They were generally polite and helpful and were happy to answer his questions about the village, the Szlezyngiers, the state of the local tourist industry and the Sajenko area. But the minute Kordian mentioned Antoni Ekiel, they stopped being quite so forthcoming. Clearly the old man was already under a cloud. One of the local papers must have got wind of his crimes. And there was one other person they all seemed reluctant to talk about – a nineteen-year-old living off the beaten track, both of whose parents were dead. A year ago, on their way back from a family funeral in Białystok they had collided with a truck on the main road. Instant death, fifteen kilometres from home. The young man had been left on his own, and he wasn't coping well. Allegedly. Because all Kordian knew was what the residents told him, and even that was based on speculation. Aleksander Soboń, they said, rarely left his house.

Oryński wondered whether he should turn up there unannounced at this late hour, but seeing lights on in two windows, decided it would be fine. Late evening was, after all, when most nineteen-year-olds started their day.

He stood at the door, but where the doorbell should be, there was only an empty space where the paint was cleaner and brighter. So he knocked and waited, listening for the sound of footsteps. When none came, he knocked again, and then a third time. Eventually, the door opened.

'What?' asked the fat, greasy-haired youth who'd opened it. His eyes were glassy, and it was clear he'd been drinking. The smell of cheap beer was unmistakable.

'Aleksander?'

'Alek,' said the young man. 'What do you want?'

'Just to talk. I'm one of the lawyers representing—'

'Szlezyngier. Yes, I know. I saw you on TV.'

As well as alcohol, Alek smelled strongly of stale sweat. He clearly had little use for personal hygiene.

'Can I come in?' asked Kordian.

'What the fuck for?'

'I'm trying to find out about—'

'About who? Me?'

'No,' answered Kordian patiently. 'I wanted to know more about the Szlezyngiers. What they do when they're here, who their friends are, that—'

'Not me, anyway.'

Kordian nodded. He was finding it hard to keep his temper in the face of the young man's constant interruptions, but so far, he was doing fine.

'Anything could be useful, no matter how ludicrous you think it is,' he said, moving half a step closer. Straight away, Alek made as if to shut the door, so Kordian backed away again. 'Because they didn't do it,' the lawyer said. 'They didn't kill their daughter.'

'Well, to me it looks as if they did.'

'Why?'

Soboń shrugged, then puffed out his lips. 'They've got so much money they think they can do what they want.'

'They're not particularly well-liked, are they?'

'I wouldn't know.'

'Do they think they're better than everyone else?' Kordian went on. 'Maybe they had a run-in with someone?'

'I don't know why you're asking me.'

Oryński decided he had to try a different tactic. The gap between the door and the doorframe was getting smaller and smaller, and might soon disappear altogether if he didn't watch out.

'Why, have you got better things to do?' he asked. 'Do you have to get back to the basement and play Minecraft for the twelfth hour in a row? Wearing the same sweaty clothes?'

'Go fuck yourself.'

'The Szlezyngiers' whole future is hanging on a thread.' The door slammed shut.

'Go on then, off you go. You carry on building little pixel-lated houses, and let the Szlezyngiers rot in jail!'

Alek didn't answer, although that was hardly a surprise. Kordian knew he'd get nothing more from him now, but hoped things would be different in a day or two, and that Aleksander would get a sudden surge of empathy when he read the newspaper headlines or saw another news item on TV.

He'd started to walk away when he heard the door opening. He turned and looked over his shoulder.

'Talk to Ekiel,' said Alek.

'We've already spoken to him and—'

The boy disappeared into the house again, slamming the door. Oryński stood there for a while longer, then set off back to the Szlezyngiers' house.

13

Chyłka was waiting for him on the doorstep. 'Where have you been?'

'I went—'

'We've had a breakthrough,' she said, looking at him. It was clear from his face that he had news too. 'What is it?' she asked.

'I don't know. Could be something, could be nothing,' he said, and shook his head. 'You go first.'

Joanna took him by the arm and led him back out onto the veranda.

'Kormak found Angelika's deleted texts,' she whispered.

'Deleted texts?'

'That's what I said.'

'But how . . .'

'I borrowed her phone and connected it to my laptop, then Kormak did what he does best,' she explained all in one breath. 'But that's not important. You'll never guess what I found.'

'A ransom demand.'

'Not quite,' she said with a smile. 'Although I was hoping to. That's why I took the phone in the first place.'

They went down the steps and headed for the jetty. The photocell on the veranda lit up only the surrounding few hundred metres; everywhere else was in darkness, the nearest light being on the other side of the lake.

'I couldn't stop thinking about what you said,' she began.

'Wow.'

'Mainly because it was naïve and monumentally stupid, which made it difficult to forget.'

'You still went with it though.'

'I tested the theory, just in case,' she said, stepping onto the jetty, 'and discovered some new facts.'

'What facts?'

'Angelika had a passionate exchange of texts with some guy called Sakrat.'

'Sakrat? What's that, some sort of weird nickname?'

'It's a real name, I checked. It's Belarusian.'

Oryński gawped. 'You're joking,' he said. 'So I was right? The Belarusians are involved?'

'I'm not sure,' she answered, sitting on the edge of the little pier and dangling her feet over the edge. Kordian joined her.

'But what I can tell you is that those texts were pretty spicy. In one, Sakrat wrote that as soon as Szlezyngier left, he would rip her clothes off and have her there and then on the kitchen counter.'

'What about her?'

'Her fantasies are just as explicit, if not more so. I'll give them to you to read later. I tell you, *Fifty Shades* has nothing on this.'

Oryński gazed at the lights opposite. 'And she didn't say a word. It's a bit strange, isn't it, given Awit's behind bars and she's in danger of ending up there herself. And suppose this Sakrat abducted the child? I'd have been honest about the affair from day one if I were her.'

'Me too.'

'So what do we do now?'

'What the CIA do to Al-Qaeda.'

'What, waterboarding? Eleven days without sleep? Sensory deprivation?'

'Yes, each in turn. But first we'll find out who this Belarusian is.'

They fell silent, and Chyłka reached for her e-cigarette, promising herself that if they found anything that would stand up in court, she'd buy herself a packet of real Marlboros and smoke them all, one after the other.

'Let's hope it doesn't get us into even deeper shit,' said Kordian after a while. 'Maybe Angelika is hiding this guy for a reason.'

'Or maybe she's so in love she can't imagine him having anything to do with the kidnapping,' said Joanna. 'You can speculate all you want, for as long as you want.'

'But that's not why you dragged me here, is it? To speculate?'

She turned and blew the steam from her cigarette straight at him. 'No, I felt like a romantic evening by the lake.'

'I thought as much.'

'I know.'

'But we haven't had a chance to properly be together like this for so long.'

Chyłka shook her head and got up. 'Come on, Zordon. Let's get a few hours' sleep, then we'll set to work. And the minute we've got something, we'll set up a meeting with the prosecutor.'

Kordian got up too. 'Why, so he can spit facts at us while we hurl speculations at him?'

'Sometimes speculation is stronger than fact.'

'Sometimes, maybe. But in this case? I'm not sure.'

She put her e-cigarette away into her jacket pocket and set off towards the house. 'Except that our speculations don't contradict the facts,' she said. 'Quite the opposite, in fact. And we'll present them in a way that'll make the prosecutor think he holds all the cards.'

'What does that mean?'

'It means we'll do everything we can to speed things up, Zordon.'

'What's the point of that?'

'Because we're beginning to fill our sleeves with aces the prosecution has no idea about. And I intend to pull them out in the courtroom and not before.'

She knew she might be being overenthusiastic, but on the other hand, the element of surprise was key. And that's exactly what those text messages gave them. The prosecutor would assume the alarm, set for 7 p.m., would be his trump card. But Chyłka was prepared for that particular argument.

'What was it you wanted to tell me?' she asked as they stepped off the jetty.

'Compared to your news, it pales into insignificance.'

'Come on, spit it out. Did you find anything when you were out doing the rounds?'

'Nothing much, to start with. People were polite, they invited me in for tea and cake, but mostly knew nothing about the Szlezyngiers.'

'Get to the point.'

He nodded and took a breath. 'The last place I went to, at the back end of Sajenko, belonged to a young man, an orphan, who lost both his parents in a car accident a year ago. He's not coping well.'

'Would anyone?'

'He's hugely overweight, and his hygiene standards are like something out of nineteenth-century France.'

'Is that when a light stench was supposed to be attractive?'

'Correct,' said Oryński. 'Napoleon, on winning his battle and setting out to return to Paris, is said to have sent a letter to Josephine telling her not to wash, as he was on his way home.'

'He must have been as romantic as you, Zordon.'

Kordian ignored the jibe. 'The boy didn't want to talk, but eventually said I should speak to Ekiel.'

'Why?'

'I don't know, but it sounded serious. As if Antoni knew something.'

'He definitely knows something. He saw Awit with the girl that night.'

'I think there might be more to it than that.'

Joanna was loath to speculate further. They would speak to the old man the following day; it was unlikely he'd be going anywhere.

As she made her way upstairs, Chyłka was sure her second attempt at getting to sleep would be no more successful than the first. She was even more confused now than she'd been then, and the case was taking an unexpected turn. Not that she hadn't anticipated something like this. Things were rarely as they seemed, and as a lawyer, she knew she had to dig deep, find whatever she could. The more doubt she planted in the judges' minds, the better.

'Stay out here on the landing,' she said as they got to their attic room.

'Why?'

'Because that's where you're sleeping,' she said, closing the door. She waited a moment, then added, 'I'm joking, Zordon, I need to get changed.'

Needless to say, he tried the handle, but she held it firmly in place.

'Childish,' she said through the closed door.

'It was worth a try.'

She was asleep within minutes. And with sleep came dreams – restless dreams full of vague connections and figures with two faces.

14

They were up at the crack of dawn, having had only as much sleep as they needed to function. A quick shower and two strong coffees took care of the rest. As they were leaving, Angelika got up, completely unaware of what they had found.

Chyłka considered confronting her, but decided in the end that she wouldn't. All clients lie if they get the chance, and if they didn't discover the facts for themselves, she'd simply keep telling them what she wanted them to hear.

They went outside, and Oryński stretched. 'New day, same old shit,' he remarked.

'Your usual sunny outlook, I see.'

'It's being with you. You inspire me to love life.'

'You'll love it even more after our morning run.'

'We're going for a run?'

'Yes, to see the neighbours. Now that you've built up such a good relationship, we'll see if we can squeeze any more information out of them.'

'About Sakrat?'

'No Zordon, about the Doronbo Gang.'

He glared at her, but she just pointed to the nearest house, and they set off together towards it. They could hear roosters crowing in the distance, and the mist was just beginning to rise from the lake. Dewdrops still glistened on the grass, reflecting the rays of the rising sun. Chyłka looked on uneasily. Give her the queues of morning traffic on Wybrzeże Gdańskie any day, or even the jams on Marszałkowska Street. She missed the urban bustle and felt uncomfortable here.

Kordian looked at his watch. 'Isn't it a bit early to be knocking on people's doors?'

'This is a village. People get up when the cock crows.'

'Actually, it's part of the city.'

'Really?'

'Yes, it became part of Augustów in 1973. One of the neighbours told me about it yesterday. Apparently, the city is more forests and lakes than buildings.'

'Well, Zordon, isn't that riveting.'

By now they were at the first door. Joanna pressed the button on the right, and a mechanical chime rang out. Almost immediately, a little old lady appeared, her head swathed in a flowery, coloured scarf. City, my arse, thought Chyłka.

'May God bless you and keep you,' she said. The woman eyed her uncertainly. 'I believe you know Zordon, my protégé.'

'Good morning,' said Oryński with a polite bow.

The old woman looked at him with a frown; then her face lit up.

'Ah,' she said. 'You were here yesterday!'

'That's right.'

'Come on in then, welcome, welcome. And you too,' she said to Joanna.

The pair followed her in. Chyłka elbowed Kordian, whispering that they didn't have all day.

'I'll put the kettle on,' said their host.

As she went off into the kitchen, Kordian began to ask his questions. 'We're looking for information about—'

'Speak up, son.'

'We're looking for information,' he said again, more clearly this time. 'About a Belarusian named Sakrat. Unfortunately, we don't know his surname.'

'Tatarnikov,' she said. 'Sakrat Tatarnikov.'

Chyłka felt her heart start to race.

'Of course. I know the one.'

The old lady stopped in the doorway as her guests gaped at one another. She leaned against the dresser and turned to them.

'Why are you looking for him?'

'We just want to ask him something.'

She shook her head. 'He doesn't take kindly to strangers.'

It was like pulling teeth. Joanna felt like hurrying her up, but thought better of it. Zordon was the one the old lady knew; it was best she left it to him. She looked meaningfully at Oryński.

'Sakrat left as soon as all those cameras appeared,' the old woman continued. 'And who could blame him? They'd only hassle him.'

'Why would they want to do that?'

'Oh don't be naïve. It's obvious.'

'Because he was Belarusian?'

'What do you think?'

'What was he doing here?' asked Kordian.

The woman looked down, then moved off towards the kitchen again. Joanna and Kordian followed.

'They said he was fleeing Belarus to escape persecution,' she said after a while. 'But who knows? Few of us tell others the whole truth about ourselves.'

She was right there, Chyłka acknowledged.

'What did he do?' Oryński continued.

'Odd jobs mostly. He liked looking after gardens. He used to travel into town a lot and he'd always find something there.

He'd repair things, do a bit of welding, mow the lawn . . . he did what he could.'

As far as Joanna could see, the only lawn around here worth mowing was Angelika's. She nodded to Kordian. He got the message.

'Did he look after the Szlezyngiers' garden?'

'Yes, I'm sure he did. He helped me too, sometimes. When the sink was leaking or a light bulb needed changing. He was a good man.'

'Where did he live?'

'Anywhere he could lay his head, to start with. A night here, a night there . . . Sometimes he slept in a barn with the animals.'

'Was it really that bad?'

'Well, how did you think it would be?' she answered, pulling out a chair. She was so focused on the conversation she'd completely forgotten about the kettle on the stove. 'He came here without a penny to his name.'

'He must have had something.'

'Nothing. He was as poor as a church mouse. He came here, dressed in his rags, asking for bread. Not money, you understand; a crust of bread. That's how you recognise a good person,' she said, holding onto the table and sitting down slowly.

'Did he live here, with you?'

'Yes, in the beginning. Then he told me he didn't want to be a burden.'

'Where did he move to?'

'I don't know. He did tell me, but I can't remember,' said the old woman, frowning. 'I don't leave the house these days, so I never visited him. Although he sometimes came to see me, as I say.'

The lawyers exchanged glances.

'When was he last here?'

'Just before that poor child went missing. Maybe a day or two before.' She looked up at Chyłka. 'But why are you asking all these questions? Has he done something?'

'No, we're just gathering information,' said Joanna.

'He was a good lad, he never bothered anyone. People say that Belarusians are a problem, but if there were more Poles like him, this would be a better country.'

She carried on talking about the magnificent Sakrat for a while, skilfully encouraged by Kordian. He didn't press her, although there were times when he could have done. Eventually Chyłka decided she'd heard enough. It was time to leave the old woman's kitchen and focus on other things.

'Do you have a photo, by any chance?' she asked as they were leaving, not particularly hopefully.

'Of Sakrat? Yes, I should have, somewhere. He spent Christmas here one year.'

It took her quarter of an hour or more, but eventually the old lady found a picture, which she handed to the lawyers.

With a bit of luck, Sakrat Tatarnikov would turn out to be a prime candidate to take Awit Szlezyngier's place as suspect.

They said their thank yous and left the house. The village of Sajenko was slowly waking up: dogs were starting to bark, cats were skulking around and people were beginning to come out of their houses.

'Good God, he looks like Brad Pitt,' Joanna said, handing the picture to Oryński.

'The East European version maybe.'

'Good-looking, anyway.'

'Enough to risk an affair when you could be looking forward to a quiet retirement with your own personal Croesus?' he asked.

'Looks like it.'

Chyłka pulled out her e-cigarette and drew the smoke deep into her lungs.

'Do you think this'll give us anything?' asked Kordian. Joanna looked at the cigarette.

'I don't know. Cancer?'

'I meant Tatarnikov.'

'I'm sure it will,' said Chyłka. 'If we introduce the evidence in the right way, then together with the story of the plaster we should manage something.'

'Shouldn't we do that ahead of time?'

'What?' said Joanna, looking around. The residents of Sajenko were showing a keen interest in the two lawyers. One man had opened his living room curtains and was glaring at them, while a woman nearby was hanging around in front of her house, surreptitiously glancing at them every now and then.

'If we want our evidence to be considered, don't we have to present it before the trial?'

'What kind of world do you live in, Zordon?'

'One where the rule of law applies.'

'You should drag yourself away from it from time to time,' she said, only half to herself. 'I KZP 54/99.'

'I don't know what you mean.'

'It refers to a resolution by the Supreme Court. Anything a witness says in court is treated as "evidence mentioned in the initial charge sheet".'

'I can't see how us finding the plaster fits in with that.'

'It's enough for Angelika to mention that her daughter cut herself and that she stuck a plaster on the wound. Then we can request to supplement the evidence,' Joanna explained, and turned to Kordian. 'Leave it to me. We need to move on.'

'So, to Ekiel?'

'If you believe that what that loner-boy said was a tip-off, then yes, let's go and see Antoni Ekiel.' Kordian had no objections, so they went off to Gwiezdna Street. Joanna held out little hope. Although Oryński was sure Aleksander Soboń had mentioned Ekiel for a reason, Joanna had already seen and spoken to him for herself. And while it might look suspicious that he'd gone out in his boat while the divers were searching the lake, and then that he'd come to sit with her, she didn't see any cause for alarm. The old man was simply looking for something to do.

Even so, it seemed he had no intention of opening his door for them, although Joanna and Kordian knocked again and again.

'Maybe he's still asleep?' Kordian ventured.

Chyłka hammered on the door for what was probably the fourth time.

'Or he's passed out?'

'He didn't seem that much of a drinker to me,' she said, looking around the house. She banged on the first window, but there was no sign of the owner. She knocked again, perhaps a little harder than she should have done.

They circled the house, but Ekiel was clearly not at home, so they sat on the steps by the front door to look out for him.

'Maybe he went out—'

'Where, Zordon?' she cut in. 'To get a paper from the non-existent news-stand?'

'He could be milking cows or something.'

It became increasingly clear that he wasn't coming home any time soon. They sat for a good quarter of an hour, pondering their next move.

'Right,' said Chyłka eventually, getting up. 'Let's go.'

'Go where?'

'To see the boy, the one who said we should talk to Ekiel. You lead the way.'

Kordian got up reluctantly and took her to a building at the very edge of the village, on the boundary of the impenetrable forest. There was nobody there either.

'Great,' said Chyłka. 'If all our potential witnesses disappear, we should start lobbying for the return of the death penalty. It would save Szlezyngier a huge amount of suffering.'

'You're a ray of sunshine today.'

Joanna turned to him, spreading her arms wide.

'Are you surprised?'

'Let's see if I can't cheer you up a bit,' he said.

'You're not going to try any of your legendary moves on me, are you?'

'I didn't know they were legendary.'

'I'm sure they are in some circles. Among fans of *Beverly Hills 90210*, for example.'

'That was a good programme.'

'Like hell it was.'

'But no, I wasn't planning any moves,' said Oryński, pointing towards the forest. Chyłka turned to look. The boy they were looking for was weaving his way unsteadily through the trees.

Suddenly, they both realised there was blood pouring down his face.

'No!' shouted Kordian as they rushed towards Aleksander and grabbed him under the arms. He scarcely noticed them: he was clearly in shock and could hardly support his head, which was drooping onto his chest.

'Get him into the house,' ordered Joanna.

It was only at the front door that Soboń seemed to see they were there. He looked with terror at Joanna, but when he saw Kordian, his eyes almost lit up with relief.

'You . . . you came to my house before,' he managed.

Chyłka tugged on the handle and the door opened, which didn't surprise her unduly. The boy had been dragged from his home and beaten; of that she had no doubt.

15

Oryński wasn't expecting Alek to recover quickly, but within half an hour he seemed more or less himself again. They looked him over carefully and gave him painkillers, but other than that there was little they could do, especially as Soboń refused to go to hospital. He wouldn't let them call a doctor either, and judging by the way he was failing to enunciate his words, a visit to the dentist was probably in order. His face was a jumble of cuts and bruises, but they wouldn't leave many visible scars. Even the damage to his jaw could have been worse.

'This is all your fault,' Alek said quietly.

'How?' Chyłka asked. 'Who did this to you?' She'd kept her questions to herself until now, to give the boy time to settle down. Oryński was impressed she'd held out for so long.

'I didn't see, but I know who was behind it.'

Kordian was half-expecting to hear his own name.

'Ekiel,' said the boy. 'That fucking old shitbag, Antoni Ekiel.'

Joanna frowned and leaned over Soboń, whose eyes were immediately drawn to her cleavage. Oryński wasn't surprised; he wouldn't have passed up an opportunity like that either.

'Why would Ekiel send someone to beat you up?' Chyłka asked.

'Because I mentioned his name,' he answered, looking straight at Kordian. 'I told you he might be able to help you.'

'All you said was that we should talk to him,' said Kordian. 'And nobody even heard you say it.'

'They obviously did.'

'And now Antoni's disappeared like the morning mist,' Chyłka added.

Oryński took a step back and shook his head. 'I don't get any of this,' he said, in growing bewilderment. The case was getting too convoluted for them to continue seeing the Szlezyngiers as suspects in their daughter's disappearance. Whatever was eating away at this small community was more serious than he'd originally thought.

He studied the boy, who was now lying on the sofa, then turned round and walked out to the kitchen. Within moments he was back with a cold bottle of Żywiec, which he opened and handed to Alek.

'Start talking,' he said. 'Now, before it's too late.'

Soboń downed his beer with gusto, looking from Joanna to Kordian and back again. Finally, he put down the bottle and took a deep breath.

'Sometimes I go out in the morning for a walk in the forest,' he began. 'Believe it or not, I want to shed some of this . . .' He looked down at his belly with distaste. 'I didn't see who attacked me, but it couldn't have been anyone but that Tartar.'

'Sakrat Tatarnikov?' asked Kordian.

'Got it in one.'

'But why?' Chyłka asked.

'He and Ekiel were close. That's why I suggested you talk to Ekiel. I think if anyone knows anything about the missing girl, it'll be Tatarnikov.'

'What makes you say that?' Joanna asked.

'Call it intuition. A child goes missing, and the same day, this guy vanishes into thin air.'

Joanna sat down on the edge of the sofa. 'You say they were close?'

'Sakrat had been living with Ekiel for some time. Instead of paying rent he cleaned, did the gardening and looked after the boat. That sort of thing. Neither of them ever left the house, except to go fishing on the lake. They gradually saw less and less of other people, and rumours began to circulate.'

'Not that different to your situation, really.'

'Except that I don't know what else to do.' Alek looked down. 'Everything reminds me of my parents – every face, every voice, every glance. But these two chose to close themselves off.'

'Not completely,' said Chyłka. 'Because Tatarnikov used to visit the Szlezyngiers' house.'

'Those rich bastards?' said Soboń, his disapproval evident. He wasn't alone in feeling that way, but he was the first to be honest about it.

Kordian realised how incredibly naïve they'd been, coming here from their big law firm in their big city, assuming they'd easily navigate the affairs of this small rural community. There were untold demons lurking here, and all the courtroom skills in the world wouldn't help them.

'Sakrat did their gardening,' said Joanna.

'Maybe. I never followed him, so I don't know.'

'How come you know anything at all?' she asked. 'Everyone tells us you never leave your house.'

'I still keep in touch with my friends,' he answered. 'I haven't deleted my Facebook account.'

Joanna and Kordian stayed for another hour to make sure Alek was OK. In that time, he told them everything he knew about Ekiel and Tatarnikov. Apparently, the latter had a poor reputation among the locals, and even his Hollywood-star good looks didn't help – the community saw something disturbing in Sakrat. He'd once been reported to the police for threatening behaviour, and although no charges were brought, the misgivings remained.

Some time ago, a few residents had got together to check out Sakrat's past. It was no distance from here to the border, and the further east one went, the more common it was to find Polish and Belarusian families living along the same road. They tried to find out more about Tatarnikov, but, according to Alek, they found nothing. Nothing concrete, anyway, although there was speculation that he'd fled Belarus not to escape persecution, but to avoid the consequences of some crime or other. But no one could say what it was he'd done.

At last, the two Żelazny & McVay lawyers had what they wanted.

'You're worth your weight in gold, Alek,' said Chyłka, patting him on the back. 'But Sakrat and Antoni know that too, and that's why you got beaten up. To silence you.'

'Yes, probably.'

'And next time, it'll be to show you that talking to us was the wrong thing to do.'

'Next time?' Alek whimpered.

'Yes, unless you change things.'

Soboń frowned, and looked Joanna straight in the eye. 'What do I need to do?'

'First, let's go to the police station. You can make a statement, then we'll arrange protection.'

'What sort of protection?'

'Police and media.'

'Do you think they'll protect me? Just like that?'

'Think about it. How many times have you been beaten up in, say, the last twenty years?' asked Joanna. 'Even a blind man could see a connection between this and the disappearance of that little girl. It'll be enough.'

He gazed at her for a while, but eventually nodded his agreement. Kordian brought the car around, and they set off for the police station on Brzostowska Street, where they'd been fobbed off earlier by the sergeant with the unpromising name. This time, Satanowski was nowhere to be seen, and the case of the boy and his beating got the officers' sympathy. Chyłka and Oryński made sure Alek was in good hands, then decided it was high time to speak to the prosecutor. Time was beginning to work against them – not to mention the missing child.

They climbed into the X5, and Joanna drove to the district prosecutor's office on Młyńska Street. Kordian had expected a shabby, dingy little building, and was surprised to see it looked more like a modern hotel. 'Why are they handling the case?' he asked as they got out of the car. 'Shouldn't it go to the regional court?'

'If it were up to me, it would,' said Joanna. 'But it's not, it's up to those clowns in parliament. It is what it is. Even Amber Gold were tried at district level, which is a complete farce.' Amber Gold was a Polish financial institution, a pyramid scheme suspected of money laundering and other financial irregularities. It went into liquidation and its founder was sentenced to fifteen years in prison.

'I suppose that works in our favour, doesn't it?'

'Why would that be?'

'Aren't district prosecutors less capable?'

'It depends.'

'Damn, that's your answer to everything.'

Chyłka shrugged. 'The one assigned to this case is no Einstein, though,' she added, 'locking up our client instead of looking for a missing child.'

'That worries me.'

'It worries all of us, Zordon.'

'No, I mean I'm worried about Nikola. No one seems to be looking for her anymore.'

'What are you talking about?'

'They're looking for a body, not a little girl.'

'Don't exaggerate.'

'But it's true,' he said, walking off towards the building. 'Somewhere out there, a child has been abducted, Christ alone knows why. The authorities are busy chasing their tails, and we're just sitting here.'

'We are not just sitting here,' Joanna protested, opening the gate.

'What I mean is we're not looking for her.'

She stopped and grabbed him by the arm. 'That's not our job,' she said. 'Do you understand?'

They looked at one another.

'Yes, OK, I understand.'

'Our job is to make sure the Szlezyngiers emerge from this unscathed,' she continued.

'I know.'

'You're not the prosecutor leading the investigation, or a police officer, or even a private detective. And if you tried searching for Nikola, your efforts wouldn't amount to shit. So leave it to the people who know.'

'Like Satanowski? Or the prosecutor who locked up the wrong person?'

Chyłka looked around carefully, then whispered, 'I'm not so sure it was the wrong person.'

'You still think Awit and Angelika had something to do with this?'

105

'I don't know. But I'm a long way from thinking they're as blameless as they say,' she said. 'But now, end of discussion. Let's go and chase up our esteemed law enforcers.'

They entered the building, and found that their case had been referred to the district prosecutor's office in Suwałki. They also learned that it would be handled by a particular individual widely perceived as a living legend. As soon as his name was mentioned, Kordian noticed a look of uncertainty cross his supervisor's face.

16

Prosecutor Zbigniew Aronowicz welcomed the two lawyers with a beaming smile. Chyłka had let him pick a meeting place, and he had opted for a pierogi restaurant in the centre of town.

Joanna parked in a small car park right by the restaurant and spotted Aronowicz in the garden, sitting underneath a Coca-Cola-branded parasol and already heartily tucking in.

They walked up to him, but he seemed not to notice them.

'Enjoying your meal?' Chylka asked.

The prosecutor carefully cut off a piece of dumpling and popped it into his mouth. Only then did he look up. Still chewing, he pointed to the bench on the opposite side of the wooden table. Chyłka hadn't expected to be greeted with enthusiasm, but she had hoped for manners at least. How wrong she was.

She and Zordon sat down. Both fixed their eyes on Aronowicz.

'So, Zbigniew,' she said. 'Tasty, are they?'

Aronowicz put down his fork and glared. 'I didn't realise we were on first-name terms already.'

'And I didn't realise you were an arbiter of good manners. After all, you didn't even look up from your plate when we arrived. So how are the pierogi here?'

He opened his mouth to speak, but Chyłka waved him away and reached for the menu.

'Get me a portion with bacon, Zordon,' she said. He looked at her incredulously. 'You can have ... I don't know. There's nothing here that once had gills, so you might have to settle for spinach or some other abomination.'

Kordian looked at her in silence, as if expecting her to change her mind. But she didn't, so he nodded and went inside.

'That boy has my sympathy,' said Zbigniew.

'Oh, sod off.'

'I beg your pardon?'

'Eat up, before Zordon gets back, because as soon as he does, we're getting down to business. You've only got a minute or two to clear your plate, so come on now, chop chop!'

He looked as if he'd like to get up and walk away, but he stayed seated. He must have realised that Joanna wouldn't have called this meeting without good reason, and might even have been hoping she'd make some sort of offer that would save him a lot of time and trouble.

Chyłka quickly sized him up. He was wearing a cheap suit, but his tie was in a perfect Windsor knot; and although his shirt had seen better days, it was immaculately ironed. His cologne smelled unpleasant though, and he had probably had the same hairstyle since communist times. Meanwhile, the wrinkles on his face and dark circles under his eyes bore testament to many years of experience.

An archetypal, seasoned prosecutor. A perfectionist, without the money to take his perfectionism any further. If he earned as much as Żelazny or McVay, he'd probably have looked like an older version of Harvey Specter. But here he was, looking more like a grim veteran of the war in Kosovo, happy to destroy any newcomer to the courtroom.

He wasn't well-liked in the legal community, which meant he was clearly doing a good job: Joanna had heard of him even though he rarely ventured outside his own district.

He'd quashed a number of cases on which Żelazny & McVay had been working, although in theory, they'd already been won, and one of the eponymous partners had mentioned him to Joanna in passing, saying that he wouldn't wish a court-room run-in with him on anyone, not even his competitors at Dentons.

And now Chyłka scrutinised him carefully, trying to ascertain how much truth there was in the myths surrounding him. Her sources were credible, so it was fair to assume he wouldn't be giving them an easy ride.

Meanwhile Zbigniew Aronowicz ate in silence, staring at his plate, looking up only when Kordian came out with two portions of dumplings.

'Bacon for you,' he announced, placing a plate on the table in front of his supervisor, 'and courgette for me.'

'Congratulations.'

The prosecutor coughed, his face still stony.

'Shall we get down to business then?' he asked indifferently, pulling a single napkin from the holder.

'Yes, let's,' answered Joanna. 'Zbigniew, you're probably expecting—'

'It's Mr Aronowicz to you, and always will be.'

Chyłka and Oryński exchanged glances. 'No problem,' she said. 'I keep forgetting that the prosecutor's office still runs on communist-era etiquette, and that you have no idea what Western corporate culture even looks like.'

'I know all about it, believe me,' Aronowicz retorted, 'and seeing you with your trainee simply confirms my impression that a great deal of time is spent on extramarital relations.'

Joanna smiled broadly.

'You've hit the nail on the head there,' she said. 'Zordon and I – just leave us alone after-hours and . . . Well, you can imagine.'

Kordian looked confused, and she patted him on the thigh. The prosecutor gave an exaggerated sigh and wiped his mouth.

'Is there a point to this meeting?' he asked.

'Of course,' Joanna replied. 'I wanted to give you a chance to settle out of court.'

'Is that right?'

'Yes, because if you don't, you'll get your arse handed to you for detaining an innocent man,' she retorted. 'Oh, I'm sorry, where are my manners? I mean your delicate, communist-era backside.'

Zbigniew carefully placed his knife and fork together and pushed his plate away. Kordian busied himself with his food, but Chyłka seemed to have no objections to letting hers go cold.

'He doesn't look innocent to me,' said the prosecutor.

'No one looks innocent to you though, do they? You see two people together and the first thing you think is that they're having illicit sex. What a sad job you must have, that you see nothing but perversion.'

'And your point is . . .'

'No point really, just an observation. What I wanted to say is that we have a new lead that could help catch the real culprit.'

'Oh?'

'But I'm sure you don't give a shit.'

'On the contrary.'

'Because for you, it's all about the statistics, isn't it?' Chyłka went on. 'You've got a suspect, you've already put him behind bars, so now all you have to do is get a conviction, isn't that right? You don't give a toss that there's a little girl out there, being held against her will, maybe starving, beaten or raped. But—'

'That's enough!' Aronowicz cut in, getting to his feet. 'If you've got a concrete proposal, I'm all ears. If not, I'll see you at the trial.'

'I've got a concrete proposal all right, Ziggy. Either you do your job or I'll wipe the courtroom floor with you.'

'I've heard enough.' This time he didn't bother saying any more, just picked up his plate and went inside. He shambled a little, but his bearing was impeccable – like an actor on the stage.

'That went well,' said Oryński, his mouth full of dumpling.

'Didn't it just? You can always rely on my natural elegance and finesse.'

'So what now?'

'Nothing. He'll be leaving in a minute, won't he?' she said, smiling as she cut herself a piece of dumpling.

As predicted, Aronowicz soon left the restaurant, heading for the car park. As he was about to exit the garden, Joanna and Kordian blocked his path.

'Was there something else?' he asked.

'Yes. We found a sticking plaster, with blood on it, that Nikola's mother used for her daughter when she cut herself on that rod.'

The prosecutor said nothing, but his face visibly fell. Kordian twitched uncertainly, and Joanna wondered if she should have warned him. Never mind, this way it would be a lesson he'd never forget.

'The rod you're presenting as primary evidence,' she added, looking Aronowicz straight in the eyes. 'The evidence on which your whole case is based.'

'And you're telling me this because . . .'

'Because I want you to find the real offender.'

'Not true,' said Zbigniew. 'You want to get a nice, fat cheque and add another win to your statistics. You want to be the media darling again, like you were in the Piotr Langer case, don't you?'

'No, I want someone to look for the girl instead of trying to take the moral high ground.'

'We are looking for her.'

'You're looking for a body,' said Kordian, 'not for Nikola.'

Zbigniew didn't respond, but Joanna could see he was upset. Maybe, deep down, he wasn't the corrupt prosecutor people took him for. Maybe even this cynical legal maestro was moved by the thought of what might have happened to the little girl.

'The plaster will undermine your main argument,' said Chyłka.

'No such evidence has been submitted,' returned the prosecutor.

'We'll be submitting it today,' Oryński assured him.

'And there's more. We've got aces up our sleeves to beat whatever cards you play, Ziggy,' Chyłka added.

They smiled and headed back to their table. Neither looked round, but Joanna assumed Aronowicz had returned to his car, realising there was no more to be said.

She waited a few moments, then turned her head towards the car park. A Mercedes, a good few years old, was just driving away.

'Now we can say it went well,' she said.

'Do you think they'll make the formal accusation more quickly now?'

'I'm sure they will.'

'But apart from the plaster, there really isn't much,' said Oryński. 'He's got Ekiel's statement that he saw Szlezyngier with his daughter by the lake that night, but Ekiel's disappeared now, and it'll be hard to prove who he actually saw.'

'There are the printouts from the alarm system,' said Chyłka, 'and the usual reasoning, that says only the parents can be responsible for their child's disappearance. Don't worry, they'll have a pretty coherent strategy. I'm sure they feel a bit threatened now, but not so much that they're scared they'll lose the case. They'll bite, Zordon, I'm sure of it.'

17

Kordian hadn't been at all convinced that Chyłka's plan would speed the prosecutor up, but he was forced to change his mind. The guitar solo from 'Afraid to Shoot Strangers' rang out while they were still in the car on the way back to Sajenko.

'Yes?' Joanna called cheerily, switching the phone to loud-speaker.

'What was that all about?' It was the prosecutor.

'Good question. Where did you get my number?'

'Artur Żelazny gave it to me.' Zbigniew spoke quickly, clearly shaken, which was music to Kordian's ears. 'I'm ringing because you might not realise—'

'Realise what?' Joanna cut in.

'That threatening witnesses is a crime.'

'I know. Article 230 of the Criminal Code.'

'And that the penalty is—'

'Three months to five years in prison,' said Joanna. 'And what's that got to do with us?'

'Antoni Ekiel didn't just vanish into thin air.'

'Into thin air? No, I doubt very much he did that.'

'So?'

Kordian had the impression the prosecutor's teeth were firmly gritted.

'So any prosecutor worth their salt would be taking an inter-est in his sudden disappearance,' said Chyłka.

'If you had anything to do with this . . .'

'We didn't. We've been looking for Ekiel all day, and I suggest you start doing the same.'

Before he had a chance to reply, she pressed the red handset icon on the screen and turned to Oryński, smiling.

'We've got him,' she said.

'Do you think so?'

'No,' she admitted, 'but I thought it would sound good.'

Kordian shook his head and gazed out at the idyllic landscape. They were already outside the town, in the more sparsely populated area, and would reach their destination within twenty minutes. He wondered how they should approach Angelika. Chyłka would probably want to lay all her cards on the table, telling her everything. But given their mutual past, plus the media coverage the case was getting, that could end in tears. It wasn't Angelika footing their bill, but she could easily have them removed from the case.

'How are we going to play this?' he asked as they drove past the turn-off to the surrounding villages.

'What?'

'With your old friend.'

'Do you mean should we confront her with the truth? Ask her why she was giving Tatarnikov one?'

'That's one way of putting it.'

'I'm still wondering if we'd be better off putting pressure on her under cross-examination.'

'You're joking.'

'I'm not.'

'But she's our witness.'

'The fact remains, a witness who's genuinely surprised is better than one who just pretends to be,' said Chyłka, overtaking a car exiting to the right.

'What if she blurts out something that could get her in trouble?'

'Like what?' asked Joanna, surprised. 'Weren't you the one insisting she's innocent? If she is, the only thing she can admit is that she had an affair. And that'll work in our favour.'

Kordian thought for a moment. In principle, Joanna was right. But only in principle. She was assuming that Angelika was simply cheating on her husband with Tatarnikov. But supposing there was more to the relationship?

'Are you sure?'

'No, I'm still thinking.'

'If she tries to pull some sort of stunt,' Oryński began, shaking his head.

'I'm more worried about something else.'

'What?'

'If we reveal the affair, the court may decide there's a conflict of interest.'

'What, and appoint another defence lawyer for her?'

'It's not quite as simple as that,' she said, as if it were obvious. 'They'll issue an order to appoint a new legal representative within a certain timeframe. But whatever the details, we'll end up losing one of them.'

'Is that a bad thing?'

'Given that we started out defending both of them, yes, it could be bad. If either one of them is found guilty, it'll tarnish our reputation.'

'I think they're both clean.'

'We'll promote you to crystal-ball-gazing expert shall we, Zordon?' retorted Chyłka, then fell silent, fully focused on her driving. Which was unusual, to say the least. Whenever

Kordian glanced her way, he could see she was still wondering how to play it.

Even when they parked in front of the house, she remained silent. She climbed out of the car and slammed the door shut, probably for the first time since he'd known her. And still without a word, she walked up the steps and onto the veranda where Angelika sat.

Seeing her, Angelika got up and waved, but her face soon fell.

'What the fuck do you think you're doing?' were the lawyer's first words.

It wasn't what Kordian had anticipated, but with Chyłka he'd learned to expect the unexpected. Chances were she'd been thinking it all through, and had got so wound up that she couldn't keep a lid on her emotions a minute longer. Or maybe she'd decided this was the best way to handle things.

'What are you talking about?' asked a bewildered Angelika.

Joanna stood face to face with her client, and for a moment, looked as if she might strike her. Kordian quickly positioned himself beside them, thinking it best to take the initiative himself.

'We've discovered . . .' he began, but stopped when he saw the look Chyłka gave him. So much for taking the initiative.

'Sakrat Tatarnikov,' said Joanna. 'You stupid, stupid cow.'

'What do you mean?'

'Your affair.'

'But . . .'

'But how did I find out? I just did, damn it,' said Joanna, measuring her words carefully but without raising her voice. 'This is the sort of thing you tell in your brief right at the start, for God's sake.'

'But how . . .'

'Especially if the affair's with the prime suspect in the case of your daughter's disappearance.'

Chyłka slumped into the wicker chair, eyeing the steaming mug of coffee Angelika had poured for herself. She picked it up, took a long swallow, and set it back down.

'Prime suspect?' Angelika looked confused.

'Not formally,' Kordian explained. 'It's only that he seemed to disappear just after Nikola did.'

Angelika pressed her lips together, frowning. 'You think I don't know that?' she said. 'I've been trying to contact him ever since. But how come you know about him? About us?'

'We have our sources,' said Joanna. 'But now it's confession time, so sit down and start talking.'

Angelika looked at her for a moment, as if weighing up whether it was better to stay or to make a run for it. Eventually she sat down at the table. Kordian leaned his back against the beam and folded his arms.

'Have you gone out of your mind?' asked Chyłka.

'I . . .'

'Didn't it even occur to you he might be the kidnapper?'

'But there's no ransom demand!' Angelika's voice rose. It didn't take a psychologist to recognise that was exactly what she'd feared from the start. 'Plus, he would . . . he would . . .'

'For fuck's sake!' said Joanna, spreading her hands and looking helplessly at Oryński. 'Just listen to her! For God's sake, Angelika, don't make yourself look even more of an imbecile than you already are.'

Angelika ran her fingers nervously through her hair. She didn't look close to tears, though – more like she was about to explode, like a drug addict who'd snorted too much snow and didn't know what to do with the energy pulsating through their body.

'It's not like that.'

'Of course it's not. It's never like that. He's never like that. Have you got anything else to add before you run out of clichés?'

'You don't understand.'

'I understand perfectly. I've seen the pictures.'

Angelika reached out a trembling hand for her coffee, but Joanna whisked it away and took a sip herself, then glared at her friend. Angelika nodded.

'You win,' said Angelika. 'If you really want to know . . .'

'Want and need are two different things.'

'We met during our first holiday here,' continued Angelika, undaunted. 'Sakrat's Polish wasn't very good, but he was a quick learner. I used to help him with the more difficult stuff.'

She stopped, clearly expecting one of the lawyers to interrupt, but they simply waited for her to continue.

'Awit and I used to come up here quite often, but he's got a business to run, so sometimes he'd go back to Warsaw early.'

Chyłka lowered her gaze. Angelika could have spared them the details, but she'd clearly decided there was no point holding back.

'One day, when Sakrat was here working in the garden, I suggested we have a Polish lesson, you know, sit on the veranda, have a drink . . . I didn't plan for anything to happen. I didn't even think there was any chemistry between us, not then.' She broke off, took a breath and looked over to the jetty. 'We drank more than we should have.'

'Did you get drunk?' asked Chyłka.

'Drunk? Understatement of the year. I hardly knew what was going on,' said Angelika quietly. 'I mean, I get flashbacks.

I know that one minute I was on top of him, then he was on top of me, and you know, we ended up . . .'

'Thanks. I can imagine,' said Joanna.

Angelika bowed her head. 'I don't know how much time passed, but eventually we went back to the house. He stopped in front of the veranda, turned me around and told me to bend over. All I remember is that I was clutching hold of the railing, and that it felt wonderful. Don't get me wrong, I've nothing against Awit, but this was different. Feral. Primal, even.'

'Spare me the bullshit,' sighed Chyłka. 'Where was the child all this time?'

'You mean when we . . . Jesus, Chyłka, you don't think I'd have done it if Nikola was home, do you?'

'I don't know. I'm asking.'

'You know nothing about parenthood, do you? Nikola was with her grandparents in Warsaw. Sometimes Awit and I would go away for weekends and . . .'

'Never mind that now. Did you and Sakrat get together again after that?'

Angelika nodded.

'How often?'

'Whenever we got the chance. When Awit went shopping, or . . .' She stopped and shook her head while Joanna gaped in disbelief. Mind you, Angelika had never been prudish, not even in school. Chyłka had been very different. No one would have predicted her future as a hot-shot lawyer in a major, globally renowned legal practice. She was quiet, dressed simply, didn't listen to the latest music and rarely raised her hand in class. But she excelled in exams, tests and term papers. She wasn't a swot, though, and didn't cram just to get good grades: it was pure ambition. Joanna always wanted to be the best. Meanwhile,

Angelika was busy chasing boys, and despite what Chyłka had told Zordon, she really had stolen Joanna's boyfriend. So no, a steamy affair with Eastern Europe's answer to Brad Pitt shouldn't come as a surprise.

'What was his take on it?' asked Kordian, if only to break the silence.

'In what sense?'

'What did he expect from you? Did he want you to leave your husband?'

'No, absolutely not. He knew it would be impossible.'

The lawyers looked at her expectantly, so she took a breath and continued.

'Because of Nikola, mainly. But there were other reasons too. We have a separation of matrimonial assets arrangement, so what's his is his and what's mine is mine. And, you know, we got married straight after I finished college, so I've got no work experience. If I applied for a job now, my CV would go straight in the bin. Sakrat knew that.'

'So you discussed it?'

'A couple of times. But only casually.'

'How long has it been going on?' asked Kordian.

'A few years.'

'And in all that time you haven't tried to change things?'

'No, definitely not. Of course, we talked about it from time to time, about how things could have been – but it was just in the heat of the moment, if you know what I mean.'

Kordian looked down, and Joanna reached for her e-cigarette. Her head was beginning to ache from it all, and although nicotine certainly wouldn't help, it might calm her racing mind.

'Where is he, Angelika?'

'I don't know.'

'You must have some idea.'

'He lived with Antoni Ekiel for a while,' she said, 'but apart from that, he didn't really have anywhere to go.'

'Could he have gone back to Belarus?' asked Oryński.

'No, absolutely not. He's got an unspent criminal conviction there.'

'What for?'

Angelika stared silently at the end of the e-cigarette, so Joanna deliberately put it down on the table and looked her in the eyes. She could see Angelika was about to drop a bombshell.

'Murder?' she asked.

'Manslaughter.'

'You are fucking joking!' said Chyłka through gritted teeth. 'You're telling me lover-boy was a wanted criminal?'

'I just . . . he . . .'

'And you didn't think to mention it?'

'He would never hurt my daughter!'

Joanna sprang to her feet and strode off the terrace. She'd had just about enough of Angelika. From now on, she knew, they'd be going round in circles. Angelika would tell Joanna that Tatarnikov was Prince Charming and would never hurt her, then Joanna would counter that that was a pile of bullshit.

'Chyłka?' said Kordian, coming after her.

'Fuck her.'

'Right,' he said with a smile, catching her up. 'But have we got a plan?'

'I know everything I need to know. Now it's time for Arono-wicz to make his move.'

And make it he did. Seeing his arguments in danger of melting away, Aronowicz sent the charge sheet to the court the very next day.

The Szlezyngiers were charged of co-conspiracy under Article 148 of the Criminal Code, accused of being jointly responsible for the murder of their daughter. The prosecutor recommended life imprisonment.

Chyłka was thrilled. It was time for a courtroom showdown.

Part 2

1

Before the trial began in earnest, the presiding judge ordered a fifteen-minute recess. A crowd had already gathered in the small room where the case was to be heard. There was also to be a second judge and three jurors, so to 'uphold the solemnity of the law' the presiding judge announced that the case would move to a larger room, whereupon they would all be called again.

Kordian kept a close eye on Zbigniew Aronowicz, trying to determine whether the prosecutor had uncovered something in the last few days of which the defence was unaware. If the expression on his face was anything to go by, the answer was yes: he looked sure of himself, smiled at his aides and seemed not to notice the defence team at all.

Awit Szlezyngier, meanwhile, was cuffed hand and foot, his demeanour the polar opposite of the prosecutor's. He seemed to have aged years. He sat hunched over, shoulders pulled forwards, staring blankly at the floor.

The police officers led him outside and escorted him upstairs to the new courtroom. The defence team followed, Angelika in tow. Camera operators lined the walls, a guard of honour for the solemn procession.

'Ziggy looks like he'd like to crush us.'

'Tough, Zordon. We're the ones who'll crush him.'

Oryński would have loved to see the prosecutor looking unsure of himself and Chyłka smirking in anticipated triumph, but it was the other way round.

'He's got something,' said Kordian.

'Too right. The realisation that he's fucked.'

'Shh,' whispered Kordian, pointing discreetly to the cameras and a microphone from one of the local radio stations. 'Don't make a scene.'

'I'm not, I'm simply talking in a corridor in the court building.'

'It reminds me of the newbie burrow in the Skylight.'

The newbie burrow was the passage between the lifts and the main workspace, where Żelazny & McVay's interns and trainees used to sit. Manoeuvring through it was a real challenge; it had taken Oryński a good few weeks to find a foolproof way to negotiate the swarms of junior lawyers. It was similar here, the difference being that these crowds were vying for his attention.

'How much do you think we'll get through today?' he asked as they climbed the stairs to the second floor.

'Depends how sluggish Ziggy is with the experts.'

'Will we get a chance to question Angelika?'

'I hope so. We need a good, strong attack.'

Kordian wasn't sure they had the wherewithal to achieve that; from Chyłka's tone he decided probably not.

They stood outside the appointed room and the case was called again. The presiding judge appealed for calm, and invited everyone to take their seats. This time there were enough seats to go round.

'I see no reason for anyone to stand,' he said, 'other than the defendants and the cross-examiner.'

Kordian took a seat next to Chyłka and leaned over to her.

'What do we know about this guy?' he whispered.

'Not a lot. Kormak checked him out, but all he came up with was that he'd be happier in the UK system, where he could sit all day with a wig on his head, basking in his own majesty.'

'A wig? They really wear those?'

'Yes, but sadly it's increasingly rare,' she whispered back. 'Until 2007, every judge and barrister, both prosecuting and defence, wore a robe and a wig. Now it's only for serious criminal cases. But judges are still treated with great deference.'

'Quite right.'

She looked at him sceptically. 'Any idea how you'd address a High Court judge, or a designated Senior Judge?'

'None at all.'

'"My Lord" or "my Lady". It's a bit more formal than our "Your Honour", isn't it?'

'Quite possibly.'

'And in Ireland, you'd say "the Honourable Mr Justice". Same in Canada. Maybe in other English-speaking countries too for all I know. Can you imagine us saying something like that in Poland?'

'Everyone would laugh.'

'But it gives you an idea of how much respect they have for their judges. Here, not so much.' Chyłka pointed to the journalists standing by the panel of judges, who were mostly in jeans and T-shirts. One, Kordian noticed, was chewing gum.

'Horses for courses, I suppose,' he said.

'People don't respect the legal profession here because a whole generation associates it with the repressive justice system of the communist era.'

'That's quite some digression,' said Oryński, but didn't think she'd registered his words.

'And in the British Isles, you're not allowed to take photographs in court, let alone make recordings,' she continued. 'There's an official court artist who's allowed to make sketches.

That's all. It's a great tradition, and also ensures proceedings stay calm.'

'So no cameras at all?'

'No, none. There are warnings everywhere telling you photographs are only permitted outside the building, and if some joker takes a selfie with their phone, it's straight to prison. I'm not kidding. They take it really seriously.'

'But that's daft.'

'Why?' Chyłka shrugged, and gestured towards the journalists again. 'If it were like that here, we wouldn't always have to wait for the courts and media to agree terms.'

'And the public would have no idea what goes on in their courtrooms.'

'You really think the British don't know?' she asked with a smile. 'They get a comprehensive report, believe me, they just don't make a song and dance about it.'

'You were trying to make a song and dance yourself a minute ago.'

She snorted. 'That was before the trial, not during it. And not in here.'

The journalists were beginning to set up their cameras, as directed by the presiding judge.

'You know the O.J. Simpson trial?' whispered Joanna.

'I think I've heard of it.'

'The actor and football star. Accused of killing his wife and her friend, of stabbing her over and over in the head and neck. It was the trial of the century. You must have read something at least.'

'Possibly.'

'The media went crazy. Coverage went far beyond the US. The public were divided, and the pressure was immense. A complete circus.'

'Did they lock him up?'

'No. All the DNA evidence was against him, but a guy named Shapiro managed to establish reasonable doubt, and the jury acquitted him.'

The judge cleared his throat and adjusted his microphone.

'Just like this lot is about to acquit Szlezyngier,' added Chyłka quietly.

Kordian couldn't buy into her analogy, as he was still convinced Awit had nothing to do with his daughter's disappearance. He looked at the judges, trying to determine how each one saw their client, but their faces were inscrutable.

Finally, the presiding judge rose to open the trial. He presented the details of the case and introduced the different parties, starting with the defendants, then the defence lawyers, prosecutor, witnesses and finally his fellow judge, all in a flat, official monotone.

'Will the defendants please rise.'

Szlezyngier stood, but didn't look at the judge. Angelika stood beside him, checking out the jury.

'Your names, please.'

'Awit Szlezyngier.'

'Angelika Szlezyngier.'

The next question was simple – the names of their parents – yet the businessman took a moment to answer. His voice shook, and his eyes darted around as if he wanted to take in the whole floor at once.

'Are there any formal requests before we begin?' the judge asked.

The prosecutor rose. 'No, thank you,' he replied almost reverently.

Chyłka said the same, but without the ingratiating tone.

'Then I declare the hearing open,' he announced, 'and give the floor to the prosecution.'

Zbigniew Aronowicz rose and assumed a pose worthy, Kordian thought, of a classical statue. With an almost imperceptible use of body language, he delivered a lengthy monologue, finishing by accusing the Szlezyngiers of murdering their daughter and hiding her body. He then looked at the judge with affected deference, and sat down.

'Would the defendants please rise,' said the judge. 'You have heard the charges against you,' he said. 'Do you understand the accusations?'

'Yes,' they replied in unison.

'Do you plead guilty to these charges?'

'No, Your Honour.'

The judge then proceeded to instruct them that they had the right to provide a reason for their plea if they wished, or to decline to do so without the need for explanation.

'So would the defendants like to explain their plea?' he asked in conclusion.

Awit and Angelika chose to give a fulsome explanation, recounting the events of the evening Nikola went missing. As instructed by Chyłka, they made sure to include that they'd set the alarm at 7 p.m.

Kordian noticed the prosecutor's grimace of disappointment. The alarm had been one of Aronowicz's main arguments and he'd intended to milk it; the fact that the Szlezyngiers had handed it over on a platter undermined his strategy somewhat.

'We just want our daughter to be found, Your Honour,' Angelika finished, then they both took their places to the left of the adjudicating panel. Joanna nodded to let them know they'd done well.

The first expert called to the stand was from the forensics lab. He confirmed that the fingerprints on the rod found in the forest matched Awit's, and that the blood was his daughter's. The prosecutor asked only if there was anything on the rod indicating the presence of a third party. The expert confirmed there wasn't, and Zbigniew sat down.

The judge turned to Joanna. 'Any questions?'

Chyłka rose, smiling faintly. She looked at the man on the witness stand and took a deep breath.

'Can you confirm how old the blood is that was on that rod?'

'I can give you an estimate.'

'And how accurate would that estimate be?' she asked before the expert had time to elaborate. 'To the hour? The day? The week?'

'It all depends on—'

'Just give us a rough idea.'

'Accuracy would range from one to several days.'

'Can't you be more precise?'

'It depends how long the blood was on the murder weapon. The longer it was there, the—'

'If it's a murder weapon at all,' Joanna cut in. 'Because there's no way we can determine that.'

The expert nodded uncertainly.

'Am I wrong?' asked Joanna. She wanted an unambiguous answer.

'No, in this case it's simply—'

'Thank you,' she said. 'So, if the traces of blood were from a month ago, how accurate would your estimate be?'

'As I said, it would be to the nearest few days,' answered the expert, a little irritated now. 'If the sample were fresher, we'd be able to tell with significantly more accuracy. But in this case, the blood had already dried.'

'I see,' said Chyłka, leaning her hands on the desk in front of her. 'Have you heard of the method developed by Meez Islam of Teesside University?'

'I'm afraid I haven't.'

'Really? It was quite the discovery – the Holy Grail of forensic science.'

'I'm sorry, I don't know.'

Aronowicz looked furiously at Chyłka. If the criminal procedure bore even the slightest resemblance to the ones seen on American TV, he'd be on his feet objecting for all he was worth. But in the Polish system, that wasn't possible.

'Islam developed a new hyperspectral imaging device,' Chyłka continued. 'Perhaps that's something you know about?'

'Of course.'

'Can you explain to the court how it works?'

The expert shifted from foot to foot. This clearly wasn't what he was expecting, and he looked to the jury for help, but no one obliged.

'Well,' he said uncertainly, 'the device in question is a prototype developed in 2013. It scans the haemoglobin spectra, and on that basis determines the precise age of a bloodstain. A sample dating from a month ago can be determined to within a day. The age of a fresher sample can be pinpointed to the nearest hour.'

'Exactly,' said Chyłka. 'I've read Professor Islam's work, and he claims that without this new development, blood testing is less than ideal, often compromising the whole process of delivering justice.'

'I wouldn't say that . . .'

'He claims we're currently using methods from a good century ago. Is that true?'

'Well, they may have been developed decades ago, but—'

'The professor's method is based on colour, isn't that right?' she cut in.

'Yes, essentially. Yes it is.'

'Can you tell us any more?'

He nodded. 'The device contains a liquid crystal filter, which assesses the colour of the blood. We know the rate at which blood colour changes from bright red to brown, providing a mechanism to quickly determine the age of a bloodstain.'

'How quickly?'

'Almost immediately.'

'And how long did it take you to reach your estimate?'

'A few days.'

'I see.' Chyłka straightened up and took her hands from the benchtop.

Kordian recognised that the exchange was intended to lead the jurors to assume the expert witness was not the top man in his field; which, in this case, could well have been true. Because if he'd really been a leading expert, he would have been quicker to gain the upper hand in what turned out to be an uneven battle.

'Do we know how the blood got onto the rod?' she asked.

'No.'

'Do the blood traces indicate in any way that some sort of impact took place?'

'No.'

'So the sticking plaster recently admitted as evidence could work in my clients' favour?'

'Ms Chyłka . . .' warned the presiding judge. 'Please limit your questions to those that can be answered objectively.'

'Of course, Your Honour,' she replied, bowing slightly. She shifted her gaze to the man on the rostrum, who looked as if he'd like to get it all over with and go home. 'Did you also examine the blood on the plaster?' she asked.

'Yes, we carried out the same examination.'

'And?'

'The samples came from the same person.'

'And they were the same age?'

'They were.'

Chyłka allowed herself a small smile, shrugged, and sat down. 'No more questions, Your Honour,' she said, folding her arms and observing their opponent on the opposite side of the room.

2

Joanna didn't expect any problems from the experts and witnesses who were being questioned. The evidence against the Szlezyngiers was purely circumstantial, and the jury would need more than that. Now if Ekiel had been on the witness stand, that could have been problematic – if he'd testified he'd seen Awit and his daughter on the night in question, the defence would have been sunk. But all the prosecutor had was what the police had recorded – a witness who wasn't sure whether it was Szlezyngier he had seen or not.

The trouble started when Awit took the stand. Given what Chyłka wanted to achieve, he made a good first impression: the picture of a victim, unjustly convicted, broken by his time in prison and now past caring. Not many businessmen would have been prepared to adopt the same stance, but luckily, when Joanna had stressed how important it was for both judges and jury to see him like that, he'd readily agreed.

Rising slowly and avoiding the defendant's gaze, the prosecutor began his questioning.

'What time did you switch on your alarm?' he asked.

'From the agency's records, it seems that—'

'I'm asking you, not the agency.'

Szlezyngier nodded meekly. 'I apologise,' he said. 'As far as I remember, I set the alarm earlier than usual that night.'

'From the security firm's records, it seems the time was seven o'clock.'

'That's right.'

'From the same records, I can see that this was unusually early for you. In fact, it seems you never turned your alarm system on this early.'

'That is correct.'

'So why this particular day?'

Awit lowered his head and remained motionless.

'Does the defendant wish to exercise his right of refusal to reply?' asked the presiding judge.

'No, Your Honour.'

'Then please answer the question.'

'Yes,' said Szlezyngier, nervously jiggling the chain binding his hands and feet. 'That was the day I discovered my wife was having an affair.'

Chyłka looked thunderstruck, while Oryński sat with his mouth gaping open, as if struck by a bullet.

'Was that planned?' he whispered.

'Absolutely not,' Joanna answered through gritted teeth.

Awit knew about the affair – and the deleted texts – only because Chyłka had told him. She'd figured it was the only way to avoid a run-in in the courtroom when Angelika introduced it as new evidence under cross-questioning.

But this could torpedo her entire plan. She looked daggers at her client, but he pointedly refused to look back at her.

Zbigniew, meanwhile, stood like a pillar of salt, the expression on his face an echo of Oryński's.

'I beg your pardon?' he said.

'That day we had a . . . confrontation.'

Joanna was consumed by black thoughts about her client. He was playing by his own rules, and dropping his wife in it at the same time. If this carried on, she and Kordian would be left looking like idiots. Angelika too, probably. Chyłka looked at her, but she didn't seem the slightest bit perturbed, as if her husband's testimony hadn't surprised her at all.

'What's going on?' Kordian whispered.

'I don't know.'

'Are they taking the piss?'

It certainly looked like it, although there was no way the two could have communicated before the hearing. Angelika was, of course, still free and could do as she pleased, but she'd had no opportunity to see her alleged co-conspirator.

'Your Honour, please forgive my confusion,' said Aronowicz, 'but this is the first I've heard of any affair. Or even argument, come to that.'

'The court too,' said the presiding judge.

The prosecutor turned to Awit. 'Please elaborate.'

'Certainly,' said Szlezyngier, deferentially. 'It's about time it was in the open.'

The courtroom was silent, everyone in it equally stunned. Except the journalists, who eyed Angelika like hunters homing in on their prey. They knew they'd have some excellent material to file that evening.

'Something evil was hanging over us that day, right from the word go,' Awit began. 'We'd argued about something trivial just before bed, so by daybreak we were sleep-deprived, angry and spoiling for a fight.' He stopped and looked at his wife. Angelika smiled slightly, as if to encourage him. 'We ate breakfast in silence, but then started arguing again. One thing led to another, and eventually we got to the core of the problem.'

'The defendant's affair?' prompted Aronowicz.

'Yes. My wife admitted she was having a relationship with the Belarusian we had working for us as a gardener.'

'His name?'

'Sakrat Tatarnikov.'

'How long had the affair been going on?'

'A few years. It started just after we built our summer house in Sajenko.'

The prosecutor exchanged a knowing look with the judge, and seeing it, Chyłka cursed inwardly. They were both surprised, which seemed to hearten them both. And that was not a good sign.

'Please go on,' said Zbigniew. 'What happened that day?'

Szlezyngier took a deep breath.

'Our emotions got the better of us,' he began, 'and it got out of hand pretty quickly. We started yelling at one another, but at a certain point Angelika decided she'd had enough. She got dressed and went out, while I stood on the terrace, still yelling, calling her every name under the sun.'

Angelika looked at him, again giving the impression she wanted to reassure him. Remorse and honesty would do neither of them any harm, but Chyłka had no idea where all this was going. Or why they were doing it without consulting her.

'Angelika was gone for hours, she didn't get back until around six o'clock. I was convinced she'd been with Tatarnikov, and that they were making plans to run away together.' Awit looked at the judges. 'How foolish I was. Yes, we'd both made mistakes, but that aside, I was simply foolish. That day, my wife had been to Tatarnikov to say she wanted to end their relationship. He hadn't taken it well, but she'd given him no choice. She told me as soon as she got home, but I didn't believe her.'

His whole monologue sounded like a pre-rehearsed script, Joanna thought. Szlezyngier was trying to make it sound as if he was speaking straight from the heart, but there was something stilted about it.

'I started to shout at her, threaten her . . .' He broke off and shook his head. 'I almost hit her. She wanted to go out again, but I locked all the doors, and around seven o'clock I set the alarm. My wife doesn't know the code, so she couldn't turn it off.'

The businessman attempted to shrug his shoulders, but the chains prevented him. Nevertheless, everyone in the courtroom saw him try. Silence fell.

'Mr Aronowicz?' said the judge. Aronowicz coughed, straightening his robe.

'Where was your daughter while you were arguing?' he asked.

'In her room.'

'Even after the alarm was on?'

'Yes.'

'So how did she disappear?'

'That's the question the detectives are trying to answer,' said Szlezyngier, nervously. 'Or were. Until they shifted their focus to my wife and me.'

'Do you know why they shifted their focus?'

Awit moved nervously from foot to foot. 'I don't want to comment on how the police do their job.'

'It was because there was no way your daughter could have gone missing after the alarm was set. Therefore the only logical conclusion is that she was missing from home before seven o'clock in the evening.'

'Not true.'

Aronowicz adjusted his lapels and sighed.

'You've fed us a nice, neat story, intended, I'm sure, to cast suspicion on a third party,' he said. 'But in reality, it adds nothing to the case.'

Awit took a breath, ready to reply, but Aronowicz didn't let him.

'Do you still maintain your daughter was home when you switched the alarm on?'

'Yes.'

'Then I have no further questions, thank you.'

'Ms Chyłka?' said the judge.

Joanna exchanged a confused glance with Kordian. She'd prepared herself to lead Angelika by the hand, not her husband, and she wasn't happy about suddenly having to improvise in court.

She got up slowly, staring straight at Awit. 'Can you tell the court where Sakrat Tatarnikov is now?'

'Not in Sajenko, I know that much.'

'Has he run away?'

'As far as I know, yes.'

Aronowicz spread his hands, looking pleadingly at the judge. The judge noted his disapproval, but didn't interrupt Chyłka.

'Why would he run away just when your daughter went missing?'

'I don't know. Maybe he was here illegally.'

Joanna nodded, unconvinced. 'You said that on that day, Tatarnikov and your wife argued.'

'Yes, he didn't want to give her up. He vowed he'd never let her leave him.'

Chyłka glanced at Angelika.

'No doubt we'll find out more from your wife,' she said. 'Thank you, Your Honour, I have no further questions.'

Joanna took her seat, satisfied. She'd managed to plant that first seed of doubt, although not in the way she'd planned. She still couldn't work out why her clients had taken matters into their own hands rather than stick to what they'd agreed. It didn't bode well, but on the other hand, as long as it still went in their favour . . .

'Does the defendant have anything to add?' the judge asked.

'No, Your Honour.'

'Then you may sit.'

The officers escorted Szlezyngier back to the defence table and sat him down next to Chyłka. Joanna expected at least a modicum of whispered explanation, but she got nothing. Awit sat in silence, staring straight ahead.

3

Angelika took her place on the rostrum, looking infinitely better than her husband. She stood up straight, and looked confidently at the judges and jury. The effects of many nights of broken sleep were visible on her face, but her demeanour sent out a clear message: *I may be beaten, but I am not broken.*

She gave her name, then took a deep breath. 'I'm not going to repeat what my husband said,' she declared. 'But I would like to add a few words of my own.'

The judge nodded.

'Sakrat Tatarnikov is not a violent person,' she began, 'and he stayed calm throughout our conversation. I never once felt I was in danger. But when I made to go, that's when he started threatening me. He said I couldn't just leave, that what we had, he and I, was far more than I'd ever had with Awit.'

Kordian listened with growing concern. Although first impressions had been good, this was beginning to sound disastrous – like a speech she'd learned by heart and was reciting because her lawyers had told her to.

'I didn't think he'd carry out his threats. Dear God, I still don't think he would.'

'What threats did he make?' the judge asked.

'Sakrat said he'd ruin my life,' she said. 'He kept telling me that ending our relationship would be the worst thing I ever did. He swore I'd regret it.'

'Did you have any further contact with him?'

'No, Your Honour.'

The judge settled himself more comfortably in his seat. 'Is there anything else you wish to say?'

'No, Your Honour, that's all.'

'Mr Aronowicz?'

Zbigniew pushed away the notebook in which he'd been scribbling and rose to his feet.

'Why did this man disappear?' he asked.

'I beg your pardon?'

'You'd known him for a few years, hadn't you? And better perhaps than any of the other residents.'

'Possibly.'

'So maybe you can tell us. Why would he disappear? In your opinion, of course.'

'I've already said I don't think he kidnapped Nikola.' Only now did Angelika lower her gaze. 'And I don't know why he's gone. Maybe he'd just had enough?'

'I think you can do better than that.'

Angelika looked at the judges. The presiding judge sent the prosecutor a warning glance.

'I beg your pardon, Your Honour,' said Aronowicz. 'I just want to establish one thing.' He looked back at Angelika. 'I'm asking you this because it doesn't exactly cast him in the best light, does it?'

'No, probably not.'

'But of course, we must presume innocence.' She nodded. 'So if he's innocent, why would he run away? He must have realised it would make him look suspicious.'

'You're right.'

'There must have been a reason.'

Angelika looked around, clearly annoyed.

'Can't you think of one?'

'Not just like that, no.'

'Maybe the fact that he was here illegally?' suggested Aronowicz. 'If Mr Tatarnikov heard that your daughter had gone missing that morning, he must have realised he'd be one of the first to be questioned, that his papers would be checked and that he'd probably be deported back to Belarus. He has a criminal conviction there, doesn't he?'

'Yes, but—'

'You know him,' Zbigniew interrupted. 'You know if he's got the wit to work all this out himself.'

Angelika was silent.

'Do you think he did?'

'Yes, of course . . .'

Kordian couldn't get his head around what was happening in this courtroom. Chyłka had devised a neat plan for them, which would make things go in the defendants' favour, but they had completely turned their backs on her and were busy creating their own misfortune.

'Thank you.' The prosecutor finished his questioning and sat down, sending Joanna a defiant look.

'Ms Chyłka?'

Joanna got up and straightened her robes. 'What crime was Mr Tatarnikov convicted of in Belarus?' she asked.

'Manslaughter.'

A murmur ran through the courtroom. The judge looked carefully at the gallery trying to find the source, but the sound died away immediately.

'Can you tell us more?'

'I'm afraid that's all I know.'

Joanna grimaced. 'How come?' she asked.

'Sakrat didn't talk to me about his past, so I don't know the details.'

'You mean you never asked him? Your lover of many years' standing?'

'I asked him, but he wouldn't talk about it.'

'Did it make him uncomfortable?'

'Yes. Whenever I mentioned it, he said I was opening up old wounds just to hurt him.'

'I see,' said Chyłka, looking at the jury and nodding slightly. Then she faced the defendant again. 'Soon after Mr Tatarnikov disappeared, someone else in Sajenko went missing, didn't they?'

'Yes, Antoni Ekiel,' Angelika confirmed.

'Do you know anything about that? Have you any ideas why they might run away together?'

The question was tantamount to an accusation, but neither of the judges overruled it. Maybe they too were interested in getting new information in a case that was becoming more enigmatic by the minute. Or maybe it just didn't bother them that the defence lawyer was starting to manipulate the jury.

'I can only assume that Antoni Ekiel helped him disappear.'

'What makes you say that?'

'They'd been close for years.'

'How close?'

'Sakrat lived with Ekiel. He even said that Ekiel treated him like a son.'

'And did he treat Ekiel like a father?'

'Not really,' she admitted. 'They were close, but Antoni Ekiel was definitely more committed to the friendship.'

'So he could have helped Sakrat disappear?'

'Yes, possibly. I think so.'

Joanna was silent for a moment, and regarded her client. Then she took a deep breath.

'Was it Antoni Ekiel who saw your husband by the lake the night Nikola disappeared?'

'It was.'

The prosecutor protested, looking disgruntled. The presiding judge was also not keen to let this go.

'Please,' he said. 'I would appreciate it if you did not go back over evidence we've already heard. Especially as it doesn't concern the defendant.'

'Your Honour,' Joanna replied politely, 'in the light of my client's explanations, Antoni Ekiel's evidence has become questionable, to say the least.'

'That's for the court to decide.'

'Of course.'

'Any more questions for the defendant?'

'No, Your Honour. Thank you,' she said, sitting down next to Oryński, who smiled at her discreetly. She smiled back. On the other side of the room, on the prosecution bench, the mood was very different, which was hardly surprising. Once the link between Tatarnikov and Ekiel had been revealed, it was clear something wasn't right. Kordian could see they'd managed to convince the jurors, and sow a seed of doubt in the judges' minds. The Szlezyngiers definitely had grounds for optimism.

The presiding judge sighed, looking from one side of the room to the other.

'Thank you. The defendant may return to her seat.' Angelika hurried down from the rostrum and sat beside Chyłka.

They didn't speak.

'Well,' began the judge, 'this is taking longer than anticipated. I hereby call for a half-hour recess.'

Oryński left the courtroom with relief. A few months ago, he and Chyłka would have rushed straight downstairs to satisfy their nicotine cravings; now they simply stood in the corridor, looking at one another. As the media and other interested parties gathered round them, the corridor started to become too noisy.

'Follow me,' said Joanna, heading towards the stairs. Kordian didn't protest. He followed his supervisor, who manoeuvred her way through the crowd with a skill born of many years spent negotiating the twenty-first floor of the Skylight.

Outside, Joanna looked around.

'We need a kiosk.'

'Not for cigarettes, surely?'

'No,' she retorted, '*Men's Health*. I want you to see what a real six-pack looks like.'

He gave her a withering stare.

'Of course for cigarettes,' she said.

'No way.'

'What are you, my guardian angel?'

'We made a pledge.'

Chyłka snorted.

'Why don't you look at it as a competition with your better self?' he asked. 'You hate losing, and if you give in now, you'll be the loser.'

'Shut up, Zordon.'

If she was that determined, there was no point even trying. For a moment, Oryński thought she'd ignore him, but Joanna rolled her eyes and pulled out her e-cigarette. He did the same and they smoked for a few minutes in silence.

'What happened in there?' said Kordian eventually.

'I don't know.'

He could count on the fingers of one hand the number of times Chyłka used those words.

'They're up to something,' he said.

'You don't say.'

'So what do we do now?' he asked.

'I'm going to give them the bloody third-degree, that's what,' she said. 'But in the privacy of their own home, with no witnesses. But right now, we'll file a motion for Szlezyngier's immediate release.'

'Do you think the court will approve it?'

'They'll have to. We've shown that the blood could be quite a few days old, and that the only witness has links to the person who's beginning to look increasingly like a prime suspect. And what does Aronowicz have left?'

'Sod all.'

'Exactly,' replied Chyłka, cheerfully. 'We'll get Szlezyngier out of prison, then we'll start looking for Tatarnikov and Ekiel. And as soon as we find either of them, it's in the bag.'

Oryński looked at her in disbelief. 'Now there's a turn-up for the books,' he said. 'It's almost as if you think they're innocent after all.'

'Maybe.'

'So maybe you were wrong,' he added with a low whistle. 'That'll be a good story to tell them back at the office.'

Joanna looked at her watch and put the e-cigarette back in her jacket pocket.

'I think you're misinterpreting my "maybe",' she said. 'All I mean is that once I had Antoni and Sakrat in my sights, I could make them look guilty of dropping the bomb on Hiroshima and Nagasaki. I'm not interested in who really took that child, but I can promise you, I'll make everyone think it was those two.'

'OK.'

'And spare me the lecture about how we should look for the child.'

'I wasn't going to . . .'

'The hell you weren't. I can already hear you whining about how heartless we are, and how we only care about winning the case.'

'I wouldn't have used the plural there myself, but—'

'It's the police's job to find the girl,' Joanna interrupted him, 'and as soon as the Szlezyngiers are cleared, they can do just that, which they should have been doing all along. If you're OK with that?'

'Sure.'

They went inside, paying no attention to the cameras around them. Kordian had to admit she might be right – although what she hadn't mentioned was that if they found Sakrat and Ekiel themselves, they might uncover a trail leading to the child.

Various reporters tried to ask them how the case was going, but they skilfully picked their way through the throng, ignoring their presence. They entered the courtroom a few minutes before the hearing resumed.

A few more witnesses were questioned, including Aleksander Soboń, who, from the defence perspective, acquitted himself perfectly. The marks from his beating were still visible, and he testified that he'd been assaulted the day after he'd told Chyłka and Oryński about Ekiel. He also confirmed that the old man and Sakrat Tatarnikov were friends.

Tatarnikov's name was coming up again and again, mentioned by various residents even when they weren't asked specifically. Chyłka's plan seemed to be taking shape, and the jurors looked ready to mount a search for the Belarusian straight away.

All was going swimmingly – until Sergeant Satanowski took the stand.

4

Chyłka expected that Aronowicz and the police officer had agreed every detail of his cross-examination in advance. Satanowski looked at the judges confidently, as if he had some secret piece of information which would solve the case in a trice.

She was surprised. The Szlezyngiers' testimonies, along with those of Sajenko residents, should have cast doubt on everything the Search and Identification Team had established so far, but it was as if Satanowski had been elsewhere for the last couple of hours.

He introduced himself, giving his age and rank, then described to the court what he and his team had been doing as part of the investigation. The prosecutor started steadily enough, repeating all the findings. But when he came to the part about the alarm system, Chyłka noticed a gleam in his eye.

'Let's assume that everything the defence has said is true,' said Aronowicz with a beaming smile.

'Yes, let's,' Satanowski parroted.

'How could Tatarnikov have taken the child?'

The police officer shrugged.

'Doesn't the witness have anything to say?' asked the judge.

'I . . .' began Satanowski, shifting from foot to foot. 'Your Honour, I don't know what you want me to say. We've established that the alarm was turned on at seven p.m., and both parents testified that the child was in the house at the time. It would be physically impossible for anyone to abduct her.'

'So what happened to her?'

'We're still trying to establish that.'

'What would be the most likely scenario?' asked the prosecutor.

'I'm afraid it implicates the parents,' Satanowski replied, glancing at the defendants. 'We've basically ruled out the involvement of any third parties.'

'But let's say a third party *was* involved,' Zbigniew went on, his smile undimmed. 'Let's say this Tatarnikov took the child. How would that fit in with what we know?'

'There's no evidence to suggest it,' the police officer said confidently, straightening up even further. His expression changed. 'If someone had kidnapped the child, they must have done it before seven p.m. I find it difficult to believe that if the child was gone, the parents would simply switch on the alarm and behave as if nothing were amiss.'

'Unless, of course, they did it themselves.'

'That, in my opinion, is the only logical conclusion.'

'So they hid the child, then set their alarm?'

'The child, or the body, yes.'

The Szlezyngiers lowered their heads as if they had been struck.

'How else could you explain the child's disappearance?' asked Aronowicz, looking at the judges.

'I can't. In my opinion, that's the only way.'

'Thank you. No more questions.'

'Ms Chyłka?' said the presiding judge. Chyłka rose, and rolled her eyes.

'I certainly do have a few questions, Your Honour,' she began, 'and I'll try to make my facial expressions as eloquent as the prosecution's, but I'm not confident I'll succeed.'

'Ms Chyłka, please . . .'

'I beg the court's pardon,' she said with a thin smile, turning to the police officer on the rostrum.

'Sergeant Satanowski, if the alarm was switched on at seven p.m., what does that prove, exactly?'

It wasn't a tricky question, but the police officer had clearly been expecting to discuss more obvious issues.

'It shows that no doors and windows were opened until the following morning.'

'Does that include all the windows?'

'Except the rooflights.'

'Because they aren't alarmed.'

'That's correct,' he confirmed.

Chyłka folded her arms, tilted her head to one side and simply observed him for a moment or two. As the silence went on, Satanowski became nervous, and started to fidget.

'Ms Chyłka?' prompted the judge. Joanna uncrossed her arms.

'So someone could have come in and gone out again without triggering the alarm.'

'In theory, yes.'

'Why only in theory?'

'Because we found no evidence on the outside. No tracks, no forensics, nothing. Other than those left by the defendants.'

'Those could have been there already.'

'You're right, they could have,' admitted the sergeant. 'But that doesn't alter the fact there was nothing else.'

Chyłka smiled again.

'How long have you been in the police force?' she asked.

'Five years.'

'And in that time, have you ever come across a case where the perpetrator leaves not a single trace behind?'

Satanowski's brow furrowed as he thought. The pause was long enough for the remark to produce the effect intended, and before the sergeant realised what was happening, Chyłka had sown another seed of doubt.

'No, I've never seen it before,' he said. 'There's always something.'

'I understand,' she said. 'So how long have you been with the Search and Identification Team?'

'Three years.'

'And how much of your work involves search, and how much is identification?'

'I don't keep statistics.'

'More or less?'

'I'd say it's mostly identification.'

'The vast majority, would you say?'

'Yes. Yes, I think so.'

'And what about abductions? What's your experience?'

'They're mostly family abductions.'

Chyłka spread her hands almost imperceptibly, but even her subtle gesture was hard to ignore, and the judge sent her a disapproving glance.

'Forgive me for asking, but how many crime scenes have you investigated personally?'

'Me? Well, let me think.'

That reply alone was enough for Chyłka. She'd won. Deservedly so, in her opinion.

'I'm not in a position to give you a number at the moment.'

'You're not in a position to give us a number.'

He shook his head, clearly uncomfortable.

'And yet you speak as if you're a world-class expert.'

The judge tutted his disapproval. 'Ms Chyłka,' he said. 'I appreciate that a hearing of this kind implies a certain amount of confrontation, but I would be grateful if you could limit yourself to asking questions only.'

'Of course, Your Honour,' she replied sweetly. 'So if I may ask the witness, is it possible for a perpetrator to leave no traces at all?'

Satanowski looked to Aronowicz for help, but the prosecutor was engrossed in his notes, avidly crossing something out. Nothing was lost on the jurors though – they saw exactly who the police officer turned to in his hour of need.

'We need an answer,' said the second judge. The presiding judge gave him a sidelong look.

'What can I say? There's always something.'

'But it's not always found by the investigators, is it?'

'No, I suppose not. Not always.'

'Especially when they think they already know who did it,' Chyłka said, gesturing towards her clients. The judge rebuked her immediately, but it made no difference. She'd said what she had to say, and got the result she wanted.

'Thank you, Your Honour,' she said. 'No more questions.'

5

As the hearing drew to a close, the Żelazny & McVay team were on a high. Although Chyłka had had to improvise, she had managed to salvage something from what had initially seemed a hopeless situation. Kordian was sure this would put them in an unassailable position for the next hearing.

He sat in the back seat of the X5, hands behind his head. Angelika sat in the front passenger seat, and despite her lawyers' obvious delight, her face was like thunder. She had no doubt been expecting a tirade of abuse, but Chyłka didn't say a word, simply inserted the key fob and pressed the start button. The BMW purred into life.

'So what happens about temporary custody?' Angelika asked.

Joanna gestured to Oryński, who swallowed nervously, not sure he could remember how to deal with this specific situation.

'Come on, Zordon, let's hear it. Could we lodge a complaint?'

'We could.'

'A second complaint? Against the same decision?'

'No.'

'Then what can we do?'

'Do you have to put me through this now? In public?' he said.

'I'm your supervisor.'

'And I'm your trainee, who graduated a long time ago.'

She looked at him in the rear-view mirror. 'So what would my trainee, who clearly has some form of dementia, do in this situation?'

'He'd appeal.'

'Think again. Where would you appeal to? The district court has already ruled that Awit needs to be in jail.'

'The appeal court?'

Angelika turned round. 'Aren't they going to let him out?' she asked. 'Surely there's so much uncertainty now, they have no right to keep him in there.'

'They won't, as soon as Zordon comes up with an idea.'

'Damn it!' he hissed, dredging through the depths of his memory. He couldn't remember anything specific – but improvisation had served them well that day, so he decided to give it a go. 'The person detained can ask for the ruling to be overturned.'

'Hallelujah! The synapses are firing at last,' said Joanna. 'He or she could also ask for the ruling to be modified, not just revoked.'

'So Awit will get out?' Angelika asked again.

'Yes.'

'Are you sure?'

'If I wasn't, I wouldn't have said it,' Chyłka replied coldly. She still refused to look at her passenger. Clearly she felt indifference was a better weapon than rancour.

For a moment, the only sound in the car was Bruce Dickinson singing about fear of the dark. Kordian thought he could feel electricity in the air, like just before a storm.

He soon realised he was right.

'You miserable old cow,' said Joanna all of a sudden.

'I beg your pardon?'

Oryński felt it best to stay out of the conversation.

'What did you just say?' asked Angelika.

'That you stink of old people and piss.'

'Oh really? Stooping that low, are we?'

'If I want to talk to an idiot, I have to get down to their level.'

Angelika shook her head. 'I refuse to indulge in a playground scuffle with you. We're not in school now, you know.'

'You should have thought of that before you tried to make fools of us in the courtroom.'

'I didn't try to make a fool of anyone. Awit and I are defending ourselves as we think best.'

Joanna let go of the wheel and spread her hands wide. The BMW drove unerringly forwards as if some hidden stabiliser had kicked in. Nonetheless, Kordian suddenly felt hot.

'Well, I guess it makes sense. You're experts in criminal law after all.'

'It's not that, but—'

'We only got off because Satanowski proved a pretty undemanding opponent,' Chyłka cut in. 'But if you ever pull a stunt like that again, I'll ask the judge for a recess, and I'll terminate our relationship. Is that clear?'

Angelika nodded almost imperceptibly.

'What on earth were you thinking?'

'We were acting in our best interests. That's what it's all about, isn't it?'

'Yes, but it's also about the fact that you should be relying on us,' Joanna said. 'We're on your side, for God's sake.'

'Sometimes I wonder about that.'

'What the hell are you talking about?'

Angelika turned to face her. They glared at each other briefly.

'You think we did it,' said Angelika.

'So? I've defended some of the very worst criminals knowing they were guilty.'

'But we're not.'

'Who the fuck cares?' she asked, spreading her arms wide again. 'Because I don't. How about you, Zordon?'

Kordian coughed, and straightened his tie. This, he thought, might be a good time to join the conversation. He could try to calm his supervisor down.

'As far as I'm concerned—' he began.

'I'm your best shot at avoiding jail,' Chyłka went on, ignoring him. 'You made that decision yourselves, and you're going to scupper your chances if you keep up this ridiculous farce.'

Angelika said nothing, and they drove the rest of the way to Sajenko in silence.

Oryński had to admit he understood his clients' point of view. If they truly had nothing to do with their daughter's disappearance, it couldn't be much fun knowing your lawyer thought you were guilty. Also, Awit was a businessman, and used to being in control. He probably couldn't bear to sit idly by, and had to take matters into his own hands. Either way, it had all ended well. This time anyway. Now it was a matter of waiting for the next – and final – trial.

Chyłka parked in front of the house, and Angelika left the car without a word. The lawyers also got out.

'Wait here,' Joanna said. Kordian looked confused.

'Just wait here a minute,' she repeated, and turned towards the building.

He thought at first she was heading indoors for a private chat with Angelika – old friends face to face – but then saw she had slipped past her client and disappeared into the house.

Seconds later she emerged, a bottle of Heineken in each hand.

One had already been started – and that was the one she handed to Oryński.

'Thanks a lot,' he said.

They strolled over to the jetty and sat at the end, legs dangling down over the water. For a moment they didn't speak, simply gazed at the surrounding woodland.

'I detect a hint of gloom,' said Kordian eventually.

'And you'd be right.'

'But it went well,' he said, turning towards her.

'It was good. But not perfect,' replied Chyłka sombrely, taking a long gulp of beer. 'In the end, it'll come down to two things: there's no evidence of abduction, and the only witness has disappeared.'

'That's not so bad for us.'

'It's hopeless for us,' she said. 'If Ekiel had been on the rostrum, I'd have questioned him to within an inch of his life. In the end he'd have admitted he couldn't be sure who it was he really saw on the lake shore that night with the little girl.'

'True,' Kordian murmured.

'We might still find him.'

'How?'

'I don't know. We'll look for him.'

'A plan brilliant in its simplicity.'

'Drink up and stop talking rubbish.'

He couldn't argue with that.

'The lack of evidence is more of a problem,' she went on. 'The court isn't likely to swallow our version, unless we can show it was possible for Nikola to be abducted when the alarm was already set.'

Oryński put down his bottle. 'How are we going to do that?'

'I don't know that either. Do you have to keep asking questions?'

'Yes, it's that sort of situation.'

'I'd rather you gave me some answers,' said Chyłka, pointing at him with her bottle. 'You've been at Żelazny & McVay for a year, you should have learned something by now, especially from your supervisor.'

'My supervisor spent the best part of the year ridiculing any input from me.'

'That's more than the average trainee can say.'

She was right, and Oryński was reluctant to let the subject go. Not now he'd got the conversation where he wanted it. They had grown apart after the Langer case, and he wondered, absurdly maybe, if it was because they'd become too friendly. Grown too close to one another. Chyłka, he was sure, wasn't the type to have hundreds of friends. She found it difficult to build close friendships, and as soon as she realised what was happening, she backed off.

'Still, we could sometimes . . .'

'What? Go out to the cinema?'

'Not necessarily the cinema, but occasionally we could . . .'

'See this?' she asked, shaking her bottle at him. 'I know we're sitting by the lake, dangling our feet over the water, and you're getting all amorous, but this green glass receptacle should tell you what I think of that.'

'Huh?'

'I came down here to drink beer, not to get all loved-up over a bottle of wine,' she said. 'Do you get the subtle difference?'

'Not really,' he said, 'but maybe it says something about you as a person.'

'I think it does.' She took another swig, then focused on the headland opposite. 'Listen to me, Zordon,' she said. 'I know that a year ago you were getting your hopes up, but you should have realised by now it was just a pipe-dream.'

'Yeah, right.'

'I beg your pardon?'

'I said, "Yeah, right".'

'I heard what you said.'

'And what I meant was that you're talking rubbish,' he went on, taking another pull on his beer. 'We both know what your feelings are towards me, and it makes no difference that you're my supervisor. I know we can't let anything happen for another two years, but after that?'

Chyłka opened her mouth, but nothing came out.

'We could be at it like rabbits.'

'I'd rather stick pins in my eyes, Zordon.'

'See?' he smiled. 'The spark's there already.'

'And that spark's about to ignite and make your crown jewels explode,' she said. 'Now focus on the case.'

'I've spent the whole day in the courtroom focused on the case. I've had enough now.'

Chyłka gazed at the treetops in silence, and Kordian accepted that this was as far as the conversation was going to go. He wasn't wrong.

'You believe the Szlezyngiers are innocent,' she said at length.

'Correct.'

'Then prove it to me. How was their daughter abducted? And why?'

'Give it a rest . . .'

'No, prove it to me. Why and how?'

Oryński had been expecting the question to come up sooner or later, but had nothing rational to suggest. He'd been looking for answers since the beginning, and had no reason to think he'd suddenly have an epiphany that evening.

'I don't know,' he said after a while.

'In that case, I'm surprised you still believe them.'

'If you did the same, maybe they wouldn't have made fools of us at the hearing.'

'What makes you think they're innocent?' she asked, as if he hadn't spoken. She sat cross-legged and turned to face him. 'Is it just a feeling you get?'

'Possibly.'

'Well, feelings have no significance when they clash with facts.'

'True.'

'Then why are you so stubborn about it? Maybe you want them to be innocent so much that you're bending your inner voice to fit your narrative? You don't want to be seen defending child-killers?'

'I don't think anybody would,' he said. 'I know that one day I'll probably have to represent paedophiles, perverts and cold-blooded killers, but that's not what the Szlezyngiers are.'

All the same, he had his doubts as they walked back to the house. Chyłka's words echoed in his head, and for the first time he began to think the prosecutor might be right. But as he lay down on his mattress in the attic, he tried to dismiss the thought.

He couldn't sleep. After two hours of trying, he gave up. He got up and headed for the door, turning for a moment to look at the sleeping Chyłka. Then he quietly left the room, closing the door behind him.

Downstairs, he grabbed a beer, threw on his jacket and went outside to look around the house. The motion sensors kicked in, flooding the area with light, and for the next two hours, he combed every inch in silence. Then he went in, helped himself to another beer and returned to the jetty, where he sat until dawn.

He'd realised the people they were defending were guilty.

6

Chyłka spent the time before the second hearing honing arguments she'd already made. Having had to improvise, she'd thrown everything she had into the ring, and thus lost the element of surprise – although the prosecutor was in the same boat, so she shouldn't have anything to worry about.

First and foremost, she had to prove that Ekiel and Tatarnikov had really gone underground, and that Aleksander Soboń's beating was connected to the case. The first task wasn't too onerous, as both men were being hunted by the police. They'd left no clues, and no one knew where they might be. Kordian nevertheless intensified his own efforts to find them, going from door to door and refusing to give up.

Joanna knew this went far beyond what his job required, and that he was searching for the men in the hope of finding a clue to the missing child's whereabouts. Only then could he be sure their clients hadn't committed any crime. Chyłka wasn't expecting him to succeed, so was all the more surprised to see Kordian's jubilant face when after several days of searching he hurtled onto the terrace. She eyed him from over her laptop.

'Watch yourself, you'll break something,' she said as he raced up the steps.

'I've got it!'

'Eureka!'

'Stop it,' he said, trying to catch his breath. 'I've got a lead.'

Joanna closed her laptop and looked at him doubtfully. 'Tell me,' she said.

He sat down at the little table and took a sip of her coffee, looking around for Angelika. But she was nowhere to be seen – she had taken the boat out to the other side of the lake. She'd seemed withdrawn for days, and had been going off like this more and more frequently, so much so that Joanna had started to worry. Though not enough to follow her. Sajenko was small, and there wasn't that much her old friend could get up to. If she carried on, she'd have to talk to her, but she hoped Angelika would sort herself out first.

Oryński put down the coffee mug restlessly. 'You'll never believe . . .' he began, trying to calm his breathing.

Joanna wasn't expecting his discoveries to amount to much. At this stage he was like a drug addict in withdrawal who'd been given glue and was hoping it would satisfy his cocaine cravings.

'No, I don't expect I will.'

He glared at her, noting she didn't share his enthusiasm. 'This will smash all your suspicions to smithereens!' he declared.

'Then shoot, Captain Zordon.'

'Tatarnikov left a clue.'

'Did he now?'

'Ekiel was more careful, which isn't surprising,' said Kordian, picking up the mug again. 'He had a bit more time to plan his escape. Sakrat had to leave in a hurry. He knew what would happen if he stayed in Sajenko.'

'So where did he make his mistake?' asked Chyłka.

'He'd have had to stop at some point, wouldn't he?'

'I expect he would. Unless he's the next Dean Karnazes.'

'The next who?' asked Kordian, frowning.

'The guy who can run for three days and three nights without a break. You should know about him. You're a runner too.'

'Yes, ten kilometres in the morning. Not exactly a marathon.' Oryński stopped, dismissing the subject with a wave of his hand. 'Anyway, I figured Sakrat couldn't have gone far when he first disappeared. He was probably waiting for Ekiel to get his savings together, organise transport and so on.'

'Could be.'

'But when Nikola went missing, it was several days before we lost track of Antoni Ekiel. So where was Tatarnikov all that time? Where was he waiting?'

Chyłka took the coffee mug away from Kordian and stared at him. He'd clearly come up with something.

'The nights are still warm,' he continued, 'Sakrat could have slept out in the open. It didn't rain, there was no wind, and there's dense woodland all around. Perfect for holing up somewhere.'

'If you're OK with wild animals.'

Oryński pointed his finger at her. 'Exactly,' he said. 'I assumed he wouldn't stay in a house, or even an outbuilding, nearby. That would be too risky. Also, he needed somewhere with a good view of the surroundings, so he could see people searching the woods.'

Joanna had already guessed what he was driving at.

'So I asked the neighbours about hunting hides.'

'Hunting hides? I thought hunting was prohibited in national parks.'

'It is normally, but there are exceptions,' said Oryński. 'I checked the regulations. And of course, culling is still permitted. And the hides are used by birdwatchers as much as by hunters.'

'OK, I get it. Get to the point.'

'One of Antoni's neighbours, a nice woman, by the way, told me he was a member of the Polish Hunting Association.

Apparently, he used to go into the forest with Tatarnikov. She even knew which part they went to.'

'You found the hide they used.'

'Exactly,' said Kordian happily. 'And that's where Sakrat spent those few nights. He took food with him, or maybe Ekiel brought it to him. Either way, there's plenty of evidence. I didn't touch anything so I wouldn't contaminate the scene.'

'What exactly did you find there?'

'Empty peanut shells, crisp packets, beer cans . . .'

'They could have been left by bona fide hunters.'

'Poachers, more like.'

'Whatever. You know what I mean.'

'I do, but I'm sure this was Sakrat,' said Kordian, straightening up, 'because he'd left some empty packs of Belarusian Camels.'

He pulled one from his pocket and gave it to her proudly. 'One of the neighbours told me he used to buy from Tatarnikov at least once a week. L&Ms used to go for 4.50. Not a bad price, eh?'

'Quite,' said a bewildered Joanna, holding up the packet. 'So Sakrat was trading illegal goods? Even though he already had one conviction from a Belarusian court?'

'He wouldn't be the only one. Just look at the statistics.'

'What are you talking about?'

'Approximately fifteen per cent of cigarettes smoked in Poland come from across the eastern border.'

'And how might you know that?'

'From data published by a company called Almares, who analyse excise duty labels on the packets people throw away.'

'Not bad going,' Joanna complimented him. 'But I still find it difficult to believe he'd take the risk.'

'He didn't, not really,' Kordian said. 'He was just the middle-man. He'd get the goods from a mule . . .'

'A mule?'

Oryński nodded.

'For years, anyone over seventeen has been allowed to bring two packets of cigarettes over the border. The mules spend the whole day going backwards and forwards, and by the end of the day they're able to hand forty packets over to the middlemen on the other side.'

'And Sakrat was part of it?'

'Looks like it,' said Kordian. 'He received the goods, then drove them somewhere in the south. I don't know where. But I'm guessing Ekiel helped him.'

'How do you know all this?'

Oryński pointed to the L&Ms. 'I showed these to a few of the residents, and as I told you, one of them said he used to buy them from Tatarnikov. He didn't get huge quantities, but it was still worth buying them from him. The statistics say that in some of these border villages, pretty much a hundred per cent of cig-arettes come from the East. The border guards are beginning to treat it as organised crime, because a good proportion seem to go further, across our western borders.'

Chyłka pulled out her e-cigarette and took a deep drag. All that talk about smoking had given her the urge to find the near-est petrol station and buy herself a pack of Marlboros. Maybe even two.

'OK,' she said. 'This is all very interesting, but not really help-ful. In fact, it could work the other way, and give Aronowicz a stick to beat us with.'

'How?'

'It shows that Sakrat and Ekiel had a reason to run.'

Kordian's face fell, but he shook his head.

'That's not relevant,' he said.

'I think it's very relevant.'

'If we find those two, we'll find the girl, and that'll be it.'

'And where were you thinking of looking?'

'Don't you see, Chyłka, we've got a lead now.'

She didn't need to ask what he meant – she just needed a few moments to think. Basically, Oryński was right. The fact that Tatarnikov was involved in an organised crime ring meant that there must be some trace of him, somewhere.

'Mules,' she said.

'Exactly.'

'Where's the nearest border crossing?' she asked, grabbing her jacket from the back of the chair.

'Kuźnica-Bruzgi. At the speed you drive, it's about forty minutes from here.'

A bit of an underestimate, Zordon, thought Chyłka, walking to the X5. She realised the young man wasn't behind her.

'What are you waiting for, a round of applause?' she asked, turning around.

'No.'

'Then why are you standing there?'

'Are you going to drive there? Just like that?' he asked.

'Why? Any objections?'

'No, as long as you tell me what I should say to these people. Or even how you intend to find the mules who've been passing stuff to Sakrat.'

'I have my ways.'

'Which will take time we haven't got. And may turn up nothing.'

She stopped and looked at him, intrigued. He'd done a decent job, she had to admit, and she liked the new determination in his voice.

'All right, Zordon,' she said. 'What do you suggest?'

'I know which car he used. Ekiel's.'

'And?'

'And I'm going to borrow it. It's a Passat estate, dark blue. Older than dirt.'

'You want to steal a car from one of our potential suspects?'

'Not exactly steal . . .'

'*Hola, hola, señor*, I'm not asking for justifications,' said Chyłka with a grin.

7

Kordian wasn't sure what he should do next, but noticing the approval in Chyłka's eyes, he decided to go for broke. The idea of breaking into Antoni's house came to him unbidden, and had he had time to think about it, he'd probably have backed out.

Which didn't mean, of course, that Chyłka would have, too.

He presumed it would be relatively easy to break into the old building. They both put on latex gloves, more for their own comfort than to hide any potential forensics they might leave, and made their way around the house looking for an open window, or at least one that had been left ajar. But there was nothing. The house was locked up like a fortress.

'I'll create a disturbance, Zordon,' whispered Joanna. 'And you break a window.'

'What?'

'You've taken the first step. Now it's time for the next one. I'll take care of the rest.'

Oryński glanced around.

'Have you gone mad? Someone will hear us.'

'Don't worry, I'll drown out any noise you make. Get to it.'

'How are you going to drown it out?'

'I'll think of something. Now go! *Banzai!*'

Kordian looked from his supervisor to the window and back again. When he saw how serious she was, he took a deep breath, stepped towards the house and took a swing at the window. Looking round, he could just see Chyłka's back as she hurried away.

'Zordon, you're unbelievable,' she called, raising her hand.

'But where—'

'You tell me where,' she cut in. He rushed after her, pulling off the gloves. 'Did you really think we were going to break in through a window?'

'No, I guess not.'

'Where does that guy live, you know, the one who bought the cigarettes?'

It took Kordian a moment or two to get his bearings, but eventually he worked it out, and they walked off. After a couple of hundred metres and round two corners, they came to a clearing, with a small building and courtyard against a backdrop of trees. The area wasn't fenced off. There were clothes drying on the line, and beside them, a dog kennel from which an old mutt emerged, barking to let its owner know he had visitors.

An old man appeared in the doorway, unhurried, squinting to get a better look at his visitors.

'Good morning Stanisław,' Kordian greeted him courteously.

'Who's there?' asked the old man.

'Kordian Oryński.'

'With his own personal Cruella in tow.'

'What? Who?' said Stanisław, scratching his head. 'That young lawyer?'

'That's right,' said Kordian.

'And we need your help,' added Joanna, looking suitably earnest. 'We've found a possible lead on the missing girl, but without your help we can't check it.'

Stanisław hissed at the dog, who barked once or twice more then slunk back into his kennel.

'If there's anything I can do to help ... Why don't you come in?'

'I'm sorry, we haven't got time,' said Joanna. 'We have to move fast.'

'Yes, I can understand that.'

Chyłka looked hard at the old man, her hands on her hips.

'You know Antoni Ekiel, don't you?'

'Of course I know Antoni. I know him well. We grew up together in Sajenko, before it became part of Augustów. Let me see, that must have been 1973. Or was it '72? Jaroszewicz was prime minister. I remember it as if it were yesterday. And our local council—'

'This is Antoni Ekiel we're talking about,' Chyłka cut in. 'He didn't move here until 1999.'

'Oh yes, now I remember. I know him.'

The old man's tone changed. He became cold and distant, possibly because rumours about Ekiel and Sakrat were already circulating around the village.

'Are you on good terms with him?'

'Oh yes, we're good friends. We go fishing together.'

Chyłka took a breath. 'It was more than just fishing though, wasn't it?'

'What?'

'Did you play cards?' she suggested, 'and talk about old times? Maybe had a drink or two?'

'Possibly.'

'And was it Antoni who told you about the cigarettes?'

'I beg your pardon?' He took a step back.

'The cigarettes. The ones you bought illegally from Sakrat Tatarnikov.'

'But I—'

'I'm not surprised he told you. He's your friend, isn't he, and 4.50 is a pretty good deal compared to what you'd pay in the shops. What kind do you smoke? Camels? You'd normally pay about fourteen zlotys for a pack of those, wouldn't you?'

'But I've done nothing wrong—'

'You've been involved in handling smuggled goods.'

'I haven't,' he protested, but turned deathly pale. Kordian didn't like the way Joanna was scaring the old man, but the end would justify the means. At least that's what he hoped.

'It's all right, we're not the police,' Chyłka said, raising her hands. 'I tend to buy at street markets too, because I think there's no way on earth to justify such high prices. If I want to poison my body, that's got nothing to do with the state, has it? It's my decision. But it doesn't mean I want to poison my wallet as well. One should have nothing to do with the other.'

'Yes, I—'

'We need to get into Antoni's house, and fast.'

'But—'

'It's for his own good,' Joanna assured him. 'We're not digging for dirt, I'm sure you can understand that. Antoni is a key witness, you may have seen me paying him a visit.'

'Yes, he said you'd spoken. On the jetty.'

'Exactly. Now we need to get into his home.'

'But why?'

'Because we need to find his car keys.'

Kordian felt sorry for the old man. Chyłka had been pretty aggressive, and was now moving closer and closer, invading his personal space. Oryński assumed he'd agree, but instead, Stanisław shook his head. Then he promptly changed his mind when Chyłka quoted him an imaginary law about fines for persons importing goods without paying duty. He threw on his jacket and took them to the house, where the Passat was parked. He opened the letter box, pulled out the spare key and opened the front door. Shame they hadn't tried that themselves, thought Kordian.

'The car keys should be in the top drawer,' said Stanisław, gesturing towards a chest of drawers in the hallway. Chyłka looked inside, and smiled broadly. They thanked the old man, telling him how grateful Antoni would be. As they were leaving, Stanisław begged them not to breathe a word about the illegal cigarettes.

'How did you know?' asked Kordian when they got to the car.

'A blind guess. If I'd got it wrong, I had another trick up my sleeve.'

'Quick work.'

'Quick and effective,' she agreed. 'Now you get into this old banger, and I'll follow you in the X5.'

'Wait, what? You mean alone?'

'A few minutes ago you had balls as big as Jupiter's moons, Zordon. Dig deep and find a bit more courage.'

'It's just that . . .'

'You get in, you drive to the border crossing,' she said. 'Then you get out and lean on the bonnet and wait. Then you wait some more. Until someone comes up to you. Or until your homie steps to you, as you hipsters say. Then you say that Sakrat sent you, and that he's indisposed.'

'But maybe someone's taken his place by now.'

'Possibly.'

'I'm worried about the potential conflict of interest.'

'Fear not, my child. Chyłka will be right behind you.'

'Is that supposed to make me feel better?'

'Just get in the car and drive.'

'But . . .'

'We'll worry about it later,' she said, patting him on the back. 'They're mules, Zordon, not dangerous gangsters. OK?'

He got into the car, not at all convinced he was doing the right thing.

8

Kordian parked on a muddy road close to the Kuźnica-Bruzgi border crossing. A few dozen metres away, the first group of mules were rooting through their rucksacks, while behind them, along the fence, stood a long procession of smugglers. The ground was covered in cardboard packets and plastic wrap. It looked like a battlefield.

Oryński got out of the car, took a drag on his e-cigarette and looked more closely at the mules. Most were young men in their twenties, all crouching down or bending over their rucksacks. Their shoes were caked in mud.

Some glanced at Kordian, but mostly they weren't interested. On this side of the border, they were operating perfectly legally – at least that's how it seemed. They certainly weren't trying to hide what they were doing. Meanwhile, the state was losing millions in tax revenue.

Kordian waited for one of the smugglers to notice the Passat. They seemed totally engrossed in their cigarettes, but he'd definitely been spotted, and the news was spreading through the ranks. Eventually one of the men stood up, looked at the car and sauntered over.

Oryński stuffed the e-cigarette back into his pocket and leaned on the bonnet.

'What's going on?' the man asked.

'I'm here for Tatarnikov,' said Kordian, deciding that the less he said, the better.

The smuggler wore a tracksuit with an anorak over it, and an old, worn-out baseball cap. He had clearly helped himself to some of the goods – not alcohol, because there was none of that familiar odour – and was having trouble focusing.

'Who are you?' he asked, looking Kordian up and down.

The young lawyer had had no time to change his clothes; he'd taken off his jacket, but with his expensive shoes, new jeans and tucked-in shirt he stuck out like a sore thumb. This, he realised could either be an asset, or a nail in his coffin. He had to take his chances.

'My name's Zordon,' he said.

'What the fuck? Like in *Power Rangers*?'

'Correct,' said Oryński, looking round. 'You know how it is.'

'No, I don't.'

'My real name's Kordian,' Oryński said, shrugging. 'And as someone once said, Kordon, Zordon, what's the difference. And since then, it's stuck to me like shit to a blanket.'

'OK . . .'

That someone had been Chyłka, of course, but Oryński wasn't about to give details.

'Cool, I get it,' said the man. 'I had a crap street name too, once.'

Kordian nodded.

'Kielecki,' said the man, introducing himself. 'When they heard my name, they called me the Penknife for ages. You know, after the old pocket knife factory in Kielce. Fucking horrible.'

'Are you sure?' said Oryński. 'Don't you think they might have meant the rapper rather than some steelware manufacturer?'

'What?'

'Nothing, it's just . . .'

'Bro, do I look like I listen to crappy provincial hip-hop?'

'I was just saying . . .' began Kordian, then waved his hand. 'Never mind, it doesn't matter.'

Kielecki just stared. Clearly, reminding him of the halcyon days of Polish rap hadn't been one of his better ideas. He sniffed, wondering how to defuse the situation.

'But we need to talk business,' he said in the end. 'Tatarnikov tells me there's stuff missing.'

'Really?'

'He says the packages don't add up.'

'Tell him to talk to his own guys. I pass everything on as I get it.'

Oryński began to feel a little more confident, warming to his role.

'Where is he, anyway?' the dealer asked.

'He had to disappear.'

'I guessed that much. But why the fuck?'

'They're looking for him.'

Kielecki smiled and shook his head. Then he cleared his throat, spat to one side and pulled out a packet of Bonds. He slipped it to Kordian, who shook his head. Had they been Davidoffs, it might not have been so easy. But with these, there was no internal battle to fight.

'Now tell me what's really going on,' said Kielecki, a cigarette between his lips. 'Did he try and trade one package too many?'

Oryński thought it best to say nothing. Of course Sakrat Tatarnikov would have contacts in the world of cross-border smugglers. Maybe he smuggled more than cigarettes. It was a disturbing thought.

'Listen,' Kordian said, 'I can't tell you any more, OK?'

'OK, chill, I'm not gonna push you.'

'But I do need to find out where our stuff is going missing.'

'Then talk to the distributor.'

'When will he be here?'

Kielecki pulled out his phone and checked the time, frowning as he tried to calculate the approximate time he'd arrive. Oryński didn't know a great deal about the cigarette-smuggling business, but he knew there were three basic links to the chain: mules, distributors and suppliers. The supplier was the one he and Chyłka were interested in, as that was probably who had helped Tatarnikov disappear.

'He'll be here in about two hours,' said the Penknife, eyeing Kordian again. 'But are you sure you want to talk to him in person?'

'Why not?'

'He's completely fucked up, man. You only have to look at him wrong and he kicks off.'

'This is about goods going missing.'

'I know, but he's in tight with the boss. Distributing is only a side hustle, if you know what I mean.'

Oryński thought he probably did know. When Sakrat had had to disappear suddenly, the supplier would temporarily have put someone new in his place. From the lawyers' point of view, it couldn't have been better; the closer this new distributor was to the boss, the easier it would be for them to get to him themselves.

When he and Chyłka had come up with the plan, it hadn't seemed like a bad idea. Now, standing beside this guy in his tracksuit, it seemed like suicide.

They stood for a moment in awkward silence, which didn't work out well for Oryński.

'Who did you say sent you?' asked Kielecki, trying to fill the void.

'Tatar.'

'Why would he do that?'

'I told you, some of his stuff was missing.'

'But the Tyrant has to report to the boss himself, how could he skim something off?'

Kordian made a mental note of the middleman's street name.

'Maybe the boss doesn't check all that thoroughly,' Kordian shrugged. 'He trusts the Tyrant, doesn't he, so he probably doesn't double-check every delivery.'

'Maybe,' said the Penknife, taking a deep breath. 'And Tatarnikov always has his finger on the pulse. He always has.'

'True.'

'Let me think.' Eventually, Kielecki decided he was going to believe Oryński, who heaved a sigh of relief. 'Right,' he said. 'I'm going back to distribute my stuff. If you need me, I'll be by the fence.'

'Cool,' said Kordian.

He went back to the car and closed his eyes. He was on his own here, that much he knew. Chyłka wasn't parked far away, but she couldn't actually see what was going on. If something went wrong, by the time she'd cottoned on and called the police, they'd be digging Oryński's grave.

He looked at the clock in the car. If he was to wait here another two hours, he'd have to find something to do, or he might chicken out. He looked over his shoulder, hoping to find a book, or even a newspaper, lying on the back seat, but there was nothing. The World Wide Web it was then.

He switched on his phone and found the NSI news site. Reports from the hearing were everywhere, along with continuous coverage of the search for Nikola. Vigils had been taking place in Augustów, with prayers for her safe return; but the priests said fewer and fewer people were turning up. Not surprising, Oryński thought. Even the police knew they were most likely looking for a body.

Unless, of course, Sakrat Tatarnikov was smuggling more than cigarettes. That would change the whole game. Kordian glanced up at the mules. None of them looked like dyed-in-the-wool criminals, more like a random group of people looking to make a bit of easy money. It would take a good hour to finish sorting the packages, at which point they'd make their way to the car park behind the roadside shops. A few lorries were parked there, but Kordian imagined the drivers wouldn't be unduly interested in the goings-on. Some were probably even part of the operation, stuffing packs of cigarettes into every nook and cranny, drive wheels as well as spares. Some time ago, Oryński had heard about three drivers who had smuggled in three hundred thousand cigarettes. It was a risky business, but worth it financially – the value of that cargo alone had been over one hundred thousand zlotys.

A figure left the throng of mules and started to make his way to the Passat. It was Kielecki. Kordian got out of the car and walked over to meet him.

'He texted. He's on his way.'

'Good.'

'And you want to meet him? Just like that?'

Good question, thought Kordian. 'I don't know yet.'

'If you start getting heavy in front of everyone, there'll be trouble. He'll spark you out, and that'll be it. You'll have to find a better way.'

'I know. I just need a plan.'

The Penknife smiled nervously and hurried off, having no intention of spending more time in the company of this suicidal maniac. Oryński swallowed hard, trying to reassure himself no one was going to kill him. The worst that could happen was that he'd get knocked about a bit.

It would have been a good idea to involve the police, he thought. He'd said as much to Chyłka on the way from Sajenko, but she'd categorically rejected the suggestion, saying the police would screw everything up – and also that they'd let the prosecutor know, and the ace up their sleeves would disappear in a puff of smoke. Now it seemed crazy.

Kordian stopped behind a ramshackle old building and glanced around the car park. Not a bad place to make the exchange, he thought. Just a few lorries parked nearby – and all of those had their curtains drawn – while on the other side, a row of trees shielded the space from prying eyes.

The mules stood in a tight group. Oryński kept to one side. From time to time, one of them would eye him suspiciously, and he realised Kielecki hadn't even mentioned him. Pity, he thought. It would have done him no harm if they'd thought he was in with their boss. After some time, a delivery van pulled into the car park, an old Ford Transit with some sort of advertisement on the side. Perfect for transporting large quantities of cigarettes in sacks. When he saw a man in a leather jacket get out, Oryński suddenly felt hot.

Particularly as the newcomer focused directly on him.

'Who's that?' he asked, moving closer.

The Penknife stepped out of the ranks, and Kordian sent him a silent prayer of thanks.

'A friend of Tatar's,' he explained. 'He says he needs to talk to you.'

'Yeah? What about?'

'Ask him.'

'Did you check him out? Could he be a mole?'

'Not likely. Not if Tatarnikov sent him,' said Kielecki, folding his arms.

'OK,' said the newcomer. 'I'll deal with him later. Now let's get to work.'

Kordian couldn't see them loading their packages into the van. They all stood behind it, so all he could see was the driver leaning out from time to time. Then came a general murmur of approval – the mules had clearly been given their cut. One by one, they began to move away. Kielecki went too.

He didn't even glance at Oryński, which wasn't exactly encouraging.

Kordian nearly jumped out of his skin as his mobile rang. Chyłka wasn't supposed to disturb him, and he didn't get many other callers. Great timing for an unsolicited sales call, he thought.

He pulled out his phone, feeling the weight of everyone's gaze on him. It was Chyłka.

'What's going on?' he asked.

'There's going to be a raid.'

'What?'

'Customs are on their way, Zordon,' she said calmly.

'What did . . . How do you know?'

'I rang them myself, so I know,' she said, clearly enjoying herself. 'Now pass the tip on to whoever's in charge, and help get everyone out of there. Good luck!' She hung up.

Kordian broke out in a cold sweat. He stood for a fraction of a second as if paralysed, then snapped out of it and raced to the van. He grabbed the man in the leather jacket, clearly a distributor, and looked him straight in the eye.

'There's going to be a raid. Customs,' he said.

'What the fuck are you talking about?'

'They're on their way. We've got to get out of here before it's too late.' The mules didn't need to be told twice. Those who hadn't done so yet now crammed their bags and rucksacks into the van and scuttled off. The distributor looked around nervously.

'How do you know?' he asked.

'From a friend. Let's go. Now.'

The man in leather hesitated for a moment, then gestured to the back of the van.

'Get in.'

'What?'

'Get in the back, man. I don't know who you are, but I'm going to find out.' He grabbed Kordian's arm and pulled him inside.

'But . . .'

'Tatar's Passat stays here. Now in.'

Kordian had hoped he'd be driven to the gang's headquarters, out of gratitude for the tip and purely out of curiosity. But he was sorely mistaken.

'Wait a sec—'

The man pulled him in, then held out his hand. 'Phone,' he said.

'But what—'

'Phone. Now!'

Oryński pulled out his mobile and handed it over. The man slammed the door shut.

9

Chyłka pulled into the car park just as customs arrived. Two customs officers climbed out of a Skoda Octavia estate and looked around cautiously. One of them, spotting the X5, elbowed the other and pointed. Joanna got out and hurried over to them.

'What's this supposed to be?' she asked. The men looked at one another, confused.

'Who are you?' one of them asked.

'Who are *you*?' she retorted.

'Junior Customs Officer Tomasz—' The second officer elbowed him again.

'Was it you who tipped us off?' asked the brighter of the two. Meanwhile, his colleague surveyed the all-but-deserted car park, then lumbered over to a pile of rubbish a few metres away. Pity, he was the one Chyłka would have preferred to deal with.

'Yes, I was the one who rang,' she confirmed. 'And I said the place was swarming with mules and dealers. You were supposed to have back-up.'

'We have. We're both here,' said the officer, gesturing towards himself and his junior colleague.

'You couldn't change a light bulb.'

'What sort of light bulb?'

She gaped at him. The two officers, she realised, were probably on a similar intellectual level. If they ever managed to catch anyone red-handed, it would be the fluke of the century.

'Where are all those people you reported?'

'They must have dematerialised.'

He looked at his colleague, who was picking up a ten-zloty note.

'I think your sidekick's found a clue,' said Chyłka. 'We're saved.'

The officer muttered something under his breath which Chyłka didn't quite hear. But she did notice the Passat parked a little further on. Most of it was hidden behind one of the lorries, but it was the right registration number. Joanna moved towards it.

'Where are you going?' asked the older man.

She didn't slow down until she had passed the lorry and seen there was no one in the car. The doors were unlocked. Helplessly, she opened a door and ran her eyes over the seats.

It wasn't supposed to be like this. The plan was that Zordon would follow them in Ekiel's car as they escaped to their HQ. There must have been some complication. Joanna reached into her pocket for her phone, then remembered she'd left it in her car. She rushed back to the X5.

'What do you think you're doing?' one of the officers called.

'Quiet,' ordered Chyłka as she ran. Moments later she was dialling Kordian's number.

An electronic voice informed her that the person she had called was not available. Remembering what had happened when she last heard that message, she shivered.

'She may be batshit,' she heard one of the men say to the other, 'but she was right. You can see they've been here.'

'So what, did they flee, all of a sudden, just like that?'

'Maybe they had a lookout. They got a message, and they bolted.'

'Possibly.'

Joanna looked at them. They'd probably covered up a lot of footprints as they shambled round the car park, but the tyre marks were still clearly visible. Chyłka shook her head and began to walk methodically around the car park, her eyes firmly fixed on the ground.

'I'm telling you, we should call the men in white coats,' said one of the customs officers. 'She could be dangerous.'

For a split second, Joanna looked up. Then she went back to examining the tyre tracks. Eventually she found some that seemed fresher than the others, bent down and took a few dozen photographs. It wasn't something she'd set out to do; she did it out of sheer instinct.

'Good,' she said, straightening up. 'Do you know most of the smugglers working from here?'

'Of course.'

'Which one drives a white van with an advert on the side?'

The two officers looked at one another.

'Come on, chop chop, I need the information.'

'Who did you say you were?'

'The Sword of Damocles, hanging over your incompetence.'

'You what?'

'Who does the white Transit belong to?' she asked again, coming a step closer to one of the officers and looking him straight in the eye. The man automatically backed away, while his colleague twitched nervously. 'Tell me!'

'But you—'

'I'm investigating a case,' said Chyłka, 'and they've got one of my team.'

'They?'

'The smugglers,' she hissed, glancing around. 'That's all I can say.'

They looked at one another again, as if something were burning.

'And whose is the fucking white van?'

'I'm sorry, first I'm afraid we have to inform our superiors,' said the man she'd originally thought was smarter.

Joanna swore under her breath and turned away. She looked in the direction in which the van, presumably carrying Oryński, had disappeared. She'd spotted it in the distance as she was waiting for customs to turn up, and she'd seen the man with the leather jacket as she'd driven past the car park to scope it out. But she'd lost sight of it, just as she had Kordian. And now, she realised, she might never see him again.

While he was only with the mules, or even a distributor, she wasn't too worried. Later on, though, things might change, and she had to be on red alert in case something went wrong. But at the moment, she didn't even know where to start looking for him.

'Give me your commander's number,' she ordered, looking back over her shoulder.

10

They drove for half an hour, maybe even an hour. It was torture for Oryński for two reasons: firstly, he was worried about what might happen to him, and secondly, there were cigarettes everywhere, thousands of them, but no lighter.

At last, the Transit pulled up and Kordian heard the driver's door open. He listened for footsteps, but the driver clearly had things to do before he unlocked the back doors.

When at last they opened, Kordian had to shield his eyes from the sunlight.

'Out.'

'Why did you do that?' he asked, clambering through the door.

'In,' said the man in the leather jacket, gesturing towards the low, rundown building beside them.

Kordian scanned the dilapidated façade and windows, which were so dirty it was impossible to see inside. It was a single-storey house, encircled by a neglected garden. The grass had not been cut for years, and weeds had taken over the beds. Rusty automobile parts lay here and there, and a number of cars stood on bricks next to the building.

'Get inside.'

The thought didn't particularly appeal, but Kordian obediently set off in the direction indicated. As they came closer, he could hear boisterous, booming voices; it didn't take a genius to deduce that the men inside were well and truly plastered; some of them at least. The man in leather sighed and knocked on the door.

The voices immediately fell silent, and a figure appeared on the threshold, struggling to focus his eyes.

'Kabior?' he said to the man in leather. 'What the fuck is it this time?'

Kabior sighed again. 'There was a raid, so we had to wrap up for the day.'

'Did they get anyone?'

'No, we managed to load everything up.'

'And they didn't fuck anything up?'

'No. Thanks to this guy,' said Kabior, gesturing towards Kordian.

The dealer, patently out of it, looked him up and down. And no wonder. If Kordian felt his clothes singled him out in the car park, here he was even more noticeably out of place. He shuffled from foot to foot, looking at his host's bleary eyes.

'So who's this fucker?'

'I don't know. He came up to me and told me there was going to be a raid, so I got everyone together, shoved him in the back of the van and drove off.'

'Good going.'

'Thanks,' said Kabior. 'Has the boss arrived yet?'

'No.'

'Fuck. This guy wants to see him, so look after him until he gets here,' said the man in leather, turning around. 'The fags are in the back,' he added, as he headed off to the old Escort parked by the gate.

Kordian made as if to stop him, but thought better of it. The man at the door called to his mates, who began to saunter out, stretching and yawning. Some gave Oryński a cursory glance, but no one showed much interest. In their world, a potential threat would clearly have bigger biceps, thought Kordian.

'Get over here,' said one of them, 'and help us unpack.'

As Oryński struggled to lift the first package, he realised the man in leather must have taken his phone with him. Oh well. If this was a war, there would be losses. It was a universal truth.

Despite being drunk, the men brought the packages in without any particular difficulty. Then they sank heavily into some old sofas, whose upholstery looked as if it had been chewed by wild animals. Kordian chose a chair.

'What do you want with the boss?' someone asked.

'I need to talk to him about something.'

The guy snorted.

'So what, you've got fucking secrets with him?'

Oryński shrugged, unsure what to do. Lying was pointless, because as soon as the leader arrived, his story would collapse like a house of cards. But he couldn't tell the truth either. Silence seemed the best way forward, for a while at least.

The man who had asked the question poked his companion, who shook his head as if he'd been asleep.

'Hear that, Jordi?'

'No, what?' said Jordi reluctantly.

'This guy's got some sort of secret deal with the boss.'

'What sort of deal?'

Kordian sat up in his chair and looked at the clock. He felt as if the hands had not so much slowed down as stopped completely.

'This posh git says he's got business with the boss.'

Jordi, thankfully, didn't seem all that interested. He took a gulp of beer, and fell back into a stupor. The other man stood up and cracked his neck – a universal sign that the Mr Nice-Guy act was over.

'Take it easy,' said Kordian, 'it's no big deal. I just have to—'

'Yeah?' the thug cut in. 'And when it all goes to shit, we'll be the ones to catch it for letting you in.'

'How did he get here anyway?' A third man joined the conversation.

'Kabior vouched for him.'

'How?'

'The usual way. He brought him in, didn't he?'

'I suppose so.'

Now the other man got up. They stood a few paces from Kordian and looked down at him. Driving the Passat had got Kabior's attention, and the customs tip-off had given him credibility, so up to that point the young lawyer had felt relatively at ease. Now it all depended on how much these two goons trusted Kabior.

'Tell me what you want from the boss, or I'll rearrange your face.'

Clearly not much.

'I'll tell you as soon as he gets here.'

'Who?'

'The boss.'

'Say his name, motherfucker.'

'What?'

It wasn't hard to see through his feeble ploy, but Kordian had hoped that two pissed-up thugs would have better things to do than bother with him.

'Go on, what's his name?'

As Oryński struggled for something to say, the dealers looked at one another.

'Oi, Jordi, wake up!'

'No ...' mumbled Jordi, making himself comfortable on the sofa, happy that his friend had stood up and given him extra space.

'Wake up, damn you! He might be an undercover pig!' one of them roared.

It woke not only Jordi, but the rest as well, and they sprang to their feet as one. No one would have guessed they'd all been half asleep seconds ago.

Someone picked up an empty beer bottle.

Kordian ran through his options, and decided there was only one way to play it. He forced himself to burst out laughing.

'Well done,' he said, shaking his head. 'You've discovered the truth. I'm a cop.'

They didn't look amused.

'I've infiltrated your organisation like DiCaprio in *The Departed* and—'

'What?' asked someone else.

'What the fuck's he on about?'

Oryński felt the heat spread down his back, then take over his whole body. In a moment, he knew, the first drops of sweat would appear on his forehead. He tried to breathe normally, but it was difficult. He kept repeating to himself that he had the situation under control, but had to admit Chyłka would say that was his typical bullshit.

'It's all over,' Kordian went on. 'The Internal Security Agency will be here shortly, along with the Central Bureau of Investigation and any other agency you can think of whose name can be abbreviated to three letters. And that includes ZUS, the Social Insurance Institution. And they're the worst.'

The men looked decidedly unimpressed.

'Kabior took off because he knows you're all about to go to prison.' He looked at the clock and nodded. 'You've got about fifteen minutes, so let's have it.' He spread his arms, smiling broadly.

It had taken a lot of courage, and he hoped his play-acting had done the trick. There was a good reason why lawyers were second on the list of convincing liars – just behind politicians.

Kordian stood frozen in nervous anticipation. In the end, two of the men waved their hands dismissively and sat back down, although the first thug was still looking at him as at a potential victim.

'OK, you can cut the bullshit,' he said. 'But if anything goes wrong . . .'

'Cool,' said Kordian, feeling the heat leave his body. He gave an inward sigh of relief. He was pleased with the way things had gone so far, although he still wasn't sure how it would all pan out. His plan depended on Chyłka not being far away; he needed her to be standing by to intercept the leader of this merry little group as he made his way to the house. She would talk to him, then get Oryński out.

He swallowed, and rose slowly from his chair.

'Where are you going?' asked Tracksuit.

'To get a beer. My mouth's gone dry from talking crap.'

His tone was conciliatory, but the thug didn't smile, just pointed to a portable fridge plugged in in the corner of the room. Kordian helped himself to a can of Keniger. He'd never tried supermarket beer from Biedronka before, priced at a little over one zloty. The first mouthful was . . . interesting. It tasted like the most wonderful drink in the world, which was most likely down to the circumstances. He took another few gulps, then returned to his chair.

He spent the time until the boss's arrival trying to weather the heavy gaze of Tracksuit Man. He wanted to plan what to say, but it was a struggle. It wasn't until after his second beer that he managed to ignore his own personal Cerberus and come with something vaguely useful.

Just then, a new man appeared. There was no mistaking who this was. His clothing was similar to Oryński's, although he hadn't left his jacket in the car. As soon as he stepped in, the men rose. The leader scanned the shabby room, his eyes resting on the unexpected guest.

'Who the fuck is this?'

'He says he wants to talk to you, boss. He won't say what about.'

'What?'

'Kabior vouched for him.'

'Who is he, I said!'

They shrugged, and Tracksuit Man began to roll up his sleeves. Kordian hadn't expected it to be easy, but he intended to take the initiative as soon as he could.

'Just a minute,' the boss said, pointing at him. 'I recognise that mug. I saw you on TV, you son of a bitch!'

11

Chyłka tried her best to explain to the director of the customs service in Białystok that the situation was urgent, not to mention potentially dangerous for her partner. The director didn't seem convinced, and his patronising attitude was getting on her nerves.

'Where did you get this number?'

'From a directory of mentally challenged adults,' said Joanna. 'Please listen to me. I need—'

'What's your name?'

'Joanna Chyłka. J-O-A-N-N—'

'And who are you, exactly?'

'How many times do I have to answer that question?'

There was silence from the other end; the director was probably moments away from hanging up. She was surprised he hadn't – yet. She'd got the senior investigations officer's number not from the officers in the car park, but from Artur Żelazny. And he'd had to call a friend of a friend in the Interior Ministry to arrange it.

'I'm a lawyer, from Żelazny & McVay in Warsaw,' she said, as if it would mean something to the director. 'I'm defending a couple accused of murdering their own daughter, but I have reason to believe the girl is still alive, and may have been abducted.'

'What are you talking about?'

'I'm not asking for much,' Chyłka went on, 'I would just like you to send a couple of officers out to a property used by smugglers as their HQ.'

'Property? Smugglers?'

'I mean the cigarette-smuggling network operating at the Kuźnica-Bruzgi crossing. Commander, please, that child is counting on you.'

'What are you saying?'

Joanna took the phone away from her ear and sighed. She needed a moment to calm down, and her e-cigarette wasn't helping much. Finally she took a breath and put the phone to her ear again.

'Listen to me. We don't have much time.'

'But . . .'

'If you don't do this, it'll be on your conscience for the rest of your life. I could go to the police, but that would take time. Your people are already in place, they just don't want to move their lazy backsides.'

The director said nothing. Joanna looked helplessly at the sky, while the two officers with her nervously awaited their superior's decision.

'Do you have an officer nearby?'

'Yes, that's what I just said.'

'Put him on.'

'Thank you,' said Chyłka, relieved, handing her phone to the customs officer.

The officer nodded as he listened, then disconnected and handed the phone back to Chyłka.

'We'll take mine, it's faster,' she said, pointing to her X5.

'My instructions are to take you to Białystok.'

'I beg your pardon?'

The two officers straightened their uniforms as if it would give them courage.

'The director ordered us to—'

'I heard you the first time,' said Chyłka through gritted teeth. 'Are you out of your minds?'

They glanced at one another.

'Is it because you've got nothing to do since they opened the border?'

'Madam, please calm down.'

'Because the border guards do all your work for you now? I've seen *The Border*, I know all about it. And you—'

'We have instructions to escort you to headquarters in Białystok.'

'Escort this, officer,' Joanna said, flipping him the bird. Then she turned on her heel, and without waiting for them to even think how to reply, she strode to the X5.

'Wait!'

'You'll have to shoot me,' she called, 'because I'm not stopping.'

By the time they reached her, she was in the car with the engine running. They stood in front of the BMW, arms outstretched. She lowered the window and leaned out.

'OK, now what?' she said. 'Should I run you over?'

'Please step out of the car,' one of the officers said.

'You have no authority to give me orders.'

'We are authorised to stop a moving vehicle.'

'I'm fully conversant with the provisions of the Highway Code,' Chyłka retorted. 'I know you can stop me, but only to check my vehicle. There's no way I'm going anywhere with you. You're not even authorised to check my speed. And even if you do stop me, the law requires you to be wearing a reflective waistcoat.'

One of the officers opened his mouth, but didn't speak.

'And now stand aside, because time is pressing and I'm not wasting any more of it talking to you.'

They looked at one another again, but didn't move away. Joanna, however, noted the hint of hesitation, and that was enough. She threw the car into reverse, drove a little way back, turned around and drove out of the car park through a second exit. She figured the officers would rather forget the whole incident than report back to their superiors.

She picked up her phone and dialled Zordon's number. Still no answer. Cursing under her breath, she rang Kormak.

'I need the location of Oryński's phone,' she said.

'Hi. Lovely to hear from you too. The weather's not too bad in Warsaw, the air-conditioning in the Skylight is running at full—'

'Shut up and give me the coordinates.' Her grave tone brought Kormak to his senses.

'What's going on?'

'He's disappeared off the radar. I need to find him, and fast.'

'I can't do it, Chyłka, I can't get the location.'

'You mean legally, or physically?'

'Both.'

She disconnected, and hurled the phone onto the passenger seat. It bounced off and landed on the floor. Great, that was all she needed. She slammed her fist on the steering wheel and stepped on the accelerator. There was no logic to her actions, a fact of which she was all too aware; she was simply driving in the direction the van must have gone, otherwise it would have passed her.

She sped along the narrow country road and through a village, where at times she felt both sides of the X5 were touching the kerb. Worried residents looked on, and someone would no doubt call the police. Chyłka didn't care. She was sure the smugglers' hideout was somewhere on the outskirts, and she had to get out of Kuźnica as quickly as possible.

She hurtled through the last intersection, ignoring the priority-to-the-right rule, into what looked like a vast, neglected factory area. On the left was a seemingly endless cavalcade of freight wagons, on the right used containers and sundry other detritus. She slowed down, telling herself this would be the perfect place to organise the smuggling of illegal goods.

But eventually she drove across a four-track level crossing and left the area. Beyond Kuźnica, the road narrowed even more, its surface cratered as if it were the moon. Ahead of her was a junction: the sign told her that if she turned left, in seventeen kilometres she'd be in the village of Sidra, while the right fork would take her the sixteen kilometres to Nowy Dwór.

She thumped her fist on the steering wheel again.

12

Kordian locked eyes with the man, who looked as if he'd love to rip him apart. The fact that he looked at everyone that way was scant consolation.

'Who let him in?'

'Boss, it's all . . .'

'Who's the fucking idiot?'

'But he vouched for him . . .'

'I don't give a shit who vouched for who,' snarled the man. 'Where are your brains? What did I say about letting in strangers?'

Oryński took half a step back, earning himself a warning look from the boss. He lowered his head and took a breath. This looked like it could end in disaster. Chyłka didn't know where he was, and if the police tracked down his phone they'd only find the man in leather, who would have the dubious honour of being one of the last people to see him alive. He was finding it difficult to swallow.

'Fuck the lot of you!' shouted the boss suddenly, taking a step towards Kordian. 'It's not the first time I've cleaned up after you.'

The men lowered their heads in silence. Oryński felt it was high time he said something.

'I have no—'

'Shut up,' the leader cut in. 'Do you know who I am?'

'I can only guess.'

'Well I know who you are,' he went on, staring at him and moving closer. 'I followed the Langer case, then I saw that you and that bitch were suddenly in this part of the world. You're defending those Szlezyngiers.'

Oryński looked down.

'And I've got no idea what you want from us, but if I even get one sniff of a pig, you're not getting out of here. Do you understand?'

'Yes,' answered Oryński.

There wasn't much else he could do. He had no idea if Chyłka had called the police, or if the plan had changed. Anything could happen, including a whole host of police officers turning up here – if anyone even knew where 'here' was.

'Everything depends on how you answer my questions. Understand?'

'Yes,' said Oryński again, hoping his voice sounded confident.

'So let's start at the beginning. How did you end up here?'

Kordian was still trying to back away, and noticed he was about to hit the wall. He stopped, took a breath, and decided his only chance was to tell the truth. Or at least a half-truth. He told the man how he had found the trail that led him to the car park. The boss listened, seemingly indifferent.

But suddenly, his eyes ignited with rage, and before Kordian realised he was going to attack, it was all over. The man leaped at him and drew back his arm, and all Oryński saw was a fist about to land straight between his eyes. His head rang from the blow, and he jumped back instinctively, his body slamming against the wall.

'Wait . . .'

He shielded his face with his hands and waited for the next punch, but it didn't come. Kordian lowered his guard, and looked at his opponent in confusion.

'Where did you get that tip-off from, shithead?'

'From a friend . . .'

'What friend? That bitch lawyer? Maybe she called the bastards herself?'

'Who?'

'Customs.'

Kordian detected a metallic taste in his mouth. He wiped his hand across his nose and found blood dripping from it.

'Yes, blood,' said his aggressor. 'And there'll be a lot more of it if you keep fucking me around.'

'I won't.'

'OK, I'm listening. So was it that cow who called customs?'

Oryński pressed his lips together and looked at the man. He felt like taking a swing and hitting his adversary so hard he wouldn't be able to get back up. The problem was, he had no idea how to do it. His only previous experience of fighting had been that time with Gorzym – and then he'd been more on the receiving end too.

'Hey,' said the man, turning to his underlings. 'I think I've hit a nerve.'

They sniggered inanely, and the boss's face suddenly clouded over.

'You don't even know what that means, you bunch of morons,' he said, waving his hand dismissively. He looked back at Oryński.

'So, fallen for your older colleague, have you?' he said. 'Because that could be a problem, a big problem. You understand, when someone grasses us up, I don't take it lightly. I take my revenge. And do you know how I'm going to get back at her?'

Kordian wiped the blood from his lips.

'I'm going to have her myself first. From behind, because that's what she deserves. I'll do it over there.' He pointed to the armchair. 'And the others can hold her down. Then they can have her. They can do what they like with her, and you can sit on the floor and watch.'

Oryński pressed his lips together, wishing he could bring himself to retaliate. His hands were itching to punch the man, but first he'd have to switch off his better judgement – or his brain altogether. In fact, at that moment, he envied people driven by impulse, who could take action without thinking.

'At first she'll struggle,' the man went on. 'But soon she'll be squealing like a piglet.' He looked Kordian deep in the eyes and smiled. 'You know very well what I mean. I'm sure you've imagined that bitch in heat more than once.'

'Fuck you.'

The boss raised an eyebrow.

'What did you say?'

Oryński answered him with a hard punch in the stomach. He didn't think about it, he didn't plan it – his body took over, driven by fury. Kordian's clenched fist landed just above his opponent's crotch, and he bent double. He'd have liked to follow up with a blow to the head, but the man instantly straightened up and hit him so hard on the chin that something snapped in Kordian's jaw.

As he staggered backwards, the man hit him again – in the front teeth this time, then the nose. Oryński raised his hands, but the man quickly batted them away.

'You arrogant fucker,' he said, grabbing him by the hair and snapping his head down while raising his knee and hitting Kordian straight in the forehead.

Kordian fell to the floor, dazed. He felt a foot on his ribcage.

'Why the fuck were you looking for me?'

'Sakrat. Sakrat Tatarnikov.'

The words flowed from his mouth unwittingly – like the blood pouring from his face.

'What about him?' asked his attacker, frowning.

'He took the girl.'

'What the fuck are you talking about?'

'He abducted her.'

The man turned to his companions. They rose from their seats, but where they had all been in high spirits a moment ago, they now seemed dejected. Kordian's head was spinning, but not so much that he didn't notice the change. He also realised that despite his beating, he wasn't feeling too bad, and might even get away without facial surgery; although when he opened his mouth and felt the piercing pain, he changed his mind.

'What bull are you giving me now?' said the boss.

'Tatar disappeared along with another suspect,' Oryński went on, 'just as the police started to take an interest. It's no coincidence.'

He closed his eyes and took a breath, hoping he'd said enough and the beating would stop. He heard his attacker move away, then opened his eyes to find the rest of the men sitting around on the sofas looking listless – noticeably so. Something was going on.

He picked himself up off the floor and leaned against the wall. He knew what he had to do. He wanted to wipe the blood away, but his nose was bleeding so profusely there would have been no point.

'The other man's name is Antoni Ekiel. Have you heard of him?' he asked. 'We checked him out. He was convicted of child abuse.'

No one said a word.

'If I'm right, that poor little girl is going through hell as we speak. She's only three years old.'

The boss glanced at him.

'If you know anything at all ...' Kordian stopped, assuming what he'd already told them was enough. If there was anything you could expect from a gang of criminals, it was that they wouldn't look kindly on a potential paedophile, or any form of child abuse.

'You helped him, didn't you?' he asked, standing up cautiously.

Still no one said anything, so he quickly assessed his condition. His teeth were all in place, although he felt as if he wouldn't want to eat solid food for a month. His nose hurt, as did his forehead and chin, but the first waves of pain had passed, and now it wasn't too bad. He was dazed and his legs felt like cotton wool, but he'd be OK. He tottered over to the armchair, held onto the headrest for support and sat down.

'We don't give a fuck about the cigarettes,' he said. 'We're not from the police, or the prosecutor's office. We just want to find the little girl and return her to her parents. For us, that's ...'

'OK, I get it,' said the man they'd called Jordi.

'We all get it,' said someone else.

Oryński stared hard at their leader. And saw he'd managed to get him on side.

The silence lasted for some time. The men pulled out packs of Belarusian cigarettes and lit up, and soon the place was filled with smoke. And still no one spoke; they were waiting for the boss to say something.

In the end he did; he coughed, and looked at one of his henchmen.

'Bring me two beers. Cold ones.'

In no time, Oryński was holding a can of Keniger to his cheek.

'Wito,' the leader introduced himself.

'Kordian.'

The man gestured towards Kordian's face. 'It'll heal. I didn't break anything.'

'I appreciate it.'

'And I didn't know that . . . well, you know.'

Kordian lowered his head, hoping this was really happening. This was where he should have started. If there was any honour among gangs of this sort, it was that they all deplored crimes against children.

'Sure, I helped him disappear,' said Wito after a while. 'But fuck it, man, if I'd known he'd kidnapped a child I'd have rearranged not only his face, but everything else as well.'

'I'll bet.'

'But there was no one with him,' he added, as if to justify himself. 'No child, no Antoni Ekiel – do you understand?'

'Yes, I do.'

'He told me everything was going to shit. He'd been fucking Szlezyngier's wife for years, and that if the cops came sniffing around it would be game over.'

'I don't doubt it.'

'So is it true? Was he shagging her?'

'Quite regularly, as far as I know.'

Wito shook his head and took a gulp of beer. 'I need to make one thing clear; we don't deal in live goods. Not prostitution, nothing. Sure, we let them earn a bit of money when we can, but we don't pimp them out. Too much of a risk. The cigs are good because we can do it almost legally. You just have to be a bit careful.'

'I guess.'

'So if you're stupid enough to think we'd . . . well you can think again.'

'It didn't even cross my mind,' Kordian mumbled, leaning forwards and resting his hands on his knees. 'But I do need to know where he is.'

'That could be a problem.'

Kordian swore to himself. All that effort, just to find there was a problem.

'What kind of problem?' he asked.

Wito pulled out his cigarettes and offered one to the lawyer. Kordian deliberated for a moment – but only for a moment. Then he let the dark mother hug him to her smoking breast. He smoked greedily, as if his life depended on it. He didn't like it, the taste was disgusting, but that numbness, that feeling of bliss, made up for everything else.

'I didn't actually take him anywhere myself,' began Wito, 'but I gave him the keys to our hideout in Lebiedzin and said he could hole up there for a day or two. There was no one there at the time, we were all having a break.'

'Could he still be there?'

'No, the guys rang some time later to say he'd left the keys where I'd said to leave them.'

'And no one knows where he went?'

'No. He vanished.'

Oryński swore under his breath again, then inhaled deeply. He felt as if his lungs were about to explode.

'I need a phone,' he said.

The man looked at him hesitantly, but reached for his mobile. Straight away, Kordian dialled Chyłka. He'd been warned not to call the cops.

'Yes?' he heard Joanna's voice on the other end.

'Which historical figure do Iron Maiden sing about for almost eight minutes?'

'Zordon!' she shouted. 'What the fuck are you doing?'

'I'd have preferred it if you'd asked if I'm still alive, or if I'm OK, or . . .'

'Where are you, moron?'

'In . . . a hideout,' he said, looking around at his new acquaintances. They nodded their approval. 'I can't say any more.'

'Are you insane?'

'You asked me to find these gentlemen.' A few laughed hoarsely. They'd been pouring so much of the golden nectar into their stomachs that anything, said in the right tone of voice, would have been a source of amusement.

'I didn't mean you should go off the radar completely.'

'You were worried, weren't you?'

'Like I'd worry about a lost puppy.'

'You keep telling yourself that,' he said with a smile. 'You might believe it eventually.'

'Shut up,' she said. 'Where should I pick you up?'

'Nowhere for the moment. Wait for instructions. I'm only ringing so you stop worrying.'

'Listen, you miserable s—'

He hung up quickly and gave the phone back to Wito, but he couldn't stop smiling. Until he saw the black look on Wito's face.

'If I see a single pig in here, our whole deal will change.'

'I get that.'

'That bitch won't alert them?'

'Her name's Chyłka,' said Kordian, 'and she doesn't even know where we are.'

'She could have traced the phone.'

'Come off it, she's not the CIA. And she wouldn't tell anyone anyway.'

Wito still looked unsure, but all in all, it had gone pretty well. Now it was time to consider his next move, although the options were limited.

'If you want to help, take me there,' Kordian said.

'What, our place in Lebiedzin?'

Kordian nodded. He'd have been quite happy to give the address to the police, who had the power to shut down the building and gather up any evidence pointing to Tatarnikov's whereabouts, but the problem was, they had no reason to. They still thought the Szlezyngiers were guilty.

Then there was the added complication that it might bring uniformed police to the second hideout, which would derail the fragile relationship he'd managed to establish with the gang. And if Oryński's recent experiences had any bearing on his future, that could make things tricky.

'I need to find this guy,' he repeated.

'OK, chill,' said Jordi. 'If what you say about him is true, we'll help you.'

Moments later, Kordian was in the smugglers' car, on his way to some rundown village thirty kilometres from the first hideout. It occurred to him that if something went wrong, no one would even know where to look for his body.

13

Chyłka returned to the Szlezyngiers' home with her heart in her mouth. If it had been anyone but Kordian, she'd have commanded them to come back, or she'd simply have gone and hauled them back herself. But in Zordon's case, she simply couldn't. The time had come to show she had complete trust in him.

She parked in front of the house, stepped out of the X5 and glanced around. The media were gradually losing interest: Nikola was probably dead, and the trial wasn't giving them anything new or exciting. Joanna listened, albeit reluctantly, to radio analyses of the hearing, given by lawyers specially invited in by the broadcasters. They all seemed to agree that despite a hard-hitting start, the Żelazny & McVay team couldn't expect miracles, and that the unexplained disappearance of two people couldn't be taken as proof that their client was innocent. Although nobody mentioned it, it couldn't prove he was guilty either.

'Where have you been?' Angelika greeted her as she walked through the door. She was wearing yesterday's clothes, her hair was a mess, and no one would have guessed she was the wife of one of Poland's wealthiest businessmen.

'Zordon and I had things to do.'

'We don't pay you to drive around sightseeing, Chyłka.' For the past few days, Joanna had been finding her old friend more and more irritating. Something had changed, although she couldn't put her finger on what.

'We've been looking for leads,' she said, hoping to avoid a quarrel.

'And what did you find?'

'Not much, so far. But we're on the right track.'

'Oh really?' Angelika said, and laughed. 'In that case, you're better than all those people still pretending to look for Nikola.'

Chyłka wasn't about to argue with that. In fact, as she climbed up the stairs to the terrace, she felt silence would probably be her best option.

'You were looking for Sakrat, weren't you?' Angelika asked, coming after her.

'Yes.'

'I told you there was no need. He'd never hurt a child.'

'That's up to us to decide.'

Angelika rolled her eyes. 'You're off chasing your tails, while I'm dealing with calls from the media. I needed you today, Chyłka.'

'What for?' asked Joanna, hanging her jacket on a peg in the hallway.

'To tell me what to say in interviews.'

Joanna turned to her, trying to suppress her anger. 'I think I made it clear,' she said. 'No interviews until after the trial.'

'But I have a duty . . .'

'No, you just want attention,' Chyłka retorted. 'You simply can't let it go, can you, even in the face of personal tragedy.'

Angelika sighed, giving Joanna an exaggerated look of pity.

'Do you know what your problem is?'

'No,' said Chyłka, crossing over to the kitchen.

'You judge everybody by your own standards.'

Joanna opened the fridge and took out a beer. She opened it and was about to take a gulp, when she remembered that she'd need to be able to drive to pick Zordon up when he called. She decided she'd only drink half.

'You'd go to any lengths to promote your own image, so you expect others to do the same,' Angelika went on. 'I know the kind of world you live in. All defence lawyers keep a tally of the cases they've won, not the people they've helped.'

'It's the same thing.'

'No, I don't think it is.'

Joanna sat at the table and took a gulp of beer. She'd have happily told the old cow to shut up or get out, but she had no taste for a fight. And as a client, her friend had the right to vent.

Angelika took a juice from the fridge and sat down opposite.

'You live a hopeless life, Chyłka.'

'Oh well.'

'You're forever suspicious, you plot and scheme, and you see hidden meanings where there are none. And you're always in a rush. What's it all for?'

Joanna tilted her bottle.

'You've got enough money to retire comfortably. Why don't you let it all go?'

'How much longer are you going to sit there talking shit?'

'I just wonder what it's like to be as damaged a person as you are.'

Chyłka took another sip of beer, trying to ignore the whining old bag – which wasn't too difficult, as she was thinking about Zordon and what he might be doing. So he had found a way to get through to these smuggler people, and even discovered a trail which might lead them to Sakrat. But how safe was he? And how little would it take for his new friends to change their minds about him?

'Are you listening to me?'

'Of course.'

'Bullshit.'

'If you know, why are you asking?'

'Because I want to set you straight.'

'Good luck with that,' said Joanna.

For a moment each tried to stare the other down, then Angelika shook her head and rose from her chair, scraping it against the floor.

'You're forgetting yourself, Chyłka. Remember our current relationship.'

'Oh, I do,' said Chyłka. 'It's called a listen-to-me-or-you'll-go-to-prison relationship.'

'You're on my payroll, Chyłka.'

Joanna laughed. 'Careful,' she said. 'Any more of this and you'll be looking for a new lawyer.'

Angelika muttered something under her breath and left the kitchen. Joanna wasn't particularly concerned. Angelika would spend a bit of time swearing and complaining, but in the end, she'd realise there was only one logical conclusion: the Żelazny & McVay team were the best chance she'd get to save her own future.

Chyłka downed the rest of her beer. She gazed at the window despite the fact it was completely dark – or perhaps because of it.

Then she opened another bottle. If Zordon wanted to meet up tonight, she was sure she'd be able to find some other form of transport. He wasn't on foot, after all, and she didn't need to mother him.

She took a third beer out onto the jetty, constantly checking her phone as she went. It was getting cold now, and she wished she'd brought more than just a light jacket. In the distance she could hear crickets, and every now and then a fish would swim up to the surface. Chyłka sat down on the end of the creaking pontoon and listened to nature.

Suddenly the peace was shattered by the piercing sound of electric guitars.

She grabbed her phone.

'At last,' she said. 'Did you get anything?'

'You could show a bit of interest in whether—'

'You're calling me, idiot. I know you're alive.'

'But this isn't my number.'

'Who cares? Tell me what you've found.'

'Have you been drinking?'

'Is the Pope Catholic?'

Kordian fell silent.

'I'm in a village called Lebie . . .' He stopped, and Joanna could hear a booming voice in the background telling him to shut the fuck up. 'I'm in some godforsaken backwater,' he said instead. 'In a shitty hovel where Sakrat and Ekiel must have stayed before moving on.'

'OK, spare me the minutiae. Did you find any leads?'

'Yes.'

Chyłka sighed.

'From your tone of voice, I take it it basically gives us sod all?'

'I don't know, we'd have to check things out.'

'Could you be a bit more enigmatic, Zordon?'

'I'll tell you everything when you get here.'

She sighed again, rolling her eyes in the darkness.

'Do you know what time it is?' she asked.

'Not really. Time works a bit differently here.'

'It's past beer o'clock.'

'Ah, I get it. Have you had much?'

'Not enough to forget you, but too much to drive.'

'That's kind of romantic,' he said with a grin. 'I always knew there was a soft heart in there somewhere.'

'Kiss my arse, Zordon.'

'I'd like to get back to Sajenko first. Has Angelika been drinking as well?'

Chyłka looked over her shoulder, stood up and reluctantly headed back to the house.

'I'll check,' she said. 'Where do we pick you up from?'

Oryński was silent for a moment as one of the men gave directions; his speech was so slurred that Joanna only just understood. They'd clearly had a great time while looking for clues.

'In Korycin, on Route 8, there's a petrol station. They're taking me there.'

'Orlen? BP? Shell?'

Kordian asked, but they didn't know.

'Just a petrol station. Run by a guy called Zdzichu,' he said. 'Best come with a full tank.'

Joanna snorted. 'Too right. I'd rather drink from the pump myself than put any of that poison into my X5.'

'Makes sense.'

'And from your voice, I take it you've been imbibing similar substances yourself. Borygo, maybe?'

'What's that?'

'Antifreeze. Haven't you tried it?'

'I can't say I've had that pleasure.'

'Then there were clearly shortcomings in your childhood.'

'Compared to yours, I don't doubt it.'

The light was still on in Awit and Angelika's bedroom, so Chyłka banged on the door.

'Are you asleep?' she asked, stepping inside.

Angelika was in bed. She looked up from her book and sighed.

'What do you want?'

'Have you been drinking?'

'What?'

'We need to fetch Zordon. Are you OK to drive?'

Seeing desperation in Joanna's eyes, Angelika nodded and threw back the duvet, gesturing for Chyłka to leave the room.

'Well?' said Kordian as she closed the door.

'We'll be leaving any minute.'

'Good. In that case we'll leave too. See you later.'

'See you, Zordon,' she said. She took a deep breath. She had been unnecessarily pessimistic: Oryński had managed easily without her help. She should never have doubted him.

She helped herself to another beer from the fridge and managed a sip or two before Angelika appeared. Wordlessly, she headed for the door. Chyłka picked up the keys to the X5 and went after her. The Szlezyngiers' car had been impounded by the police.

'Are you a decent driver at least?' asked Joanna, climbing into the passenger seat.

'I sometimes have trouble turning the wheel,' she said, 'especially when I'm driving a monster truck.'

'Careful what you say.'

It was the first semi-friendly exchange they'd had in some time. But as soon as they were settled, silence fell again. Angelika switched on the engine, then the radio, changing the station to RMF FM. Sting's voice floated from the speakers. Could be worse, Chyłka thought, it could have been Lisowska.

She entered the name of the village into the sat-nav and searched for a petrol station.

'Sixty kilometres?' exclaimed Angelika. 'I thought Kordian would have been closer.'

'They obviously took him somewhere further away.'

'They?'

'The smugglers.'

Angelika braked sharply and looked at her in fear.

'Watch it, this isn't a tractor. Now go.'

'What did you just say?'

'Calm down,' said Chyłka with a sigh. 'They smuggle tobacco, they don't traffic humans.'

Angelika kept looking at her, and it occurred to Joanna that since she and Tatarnikov had been together for a while, she should have known about his smuggling connections.

'How can you be sure, Chyłka?' she asked. 'Because, my God, if Nikola—'

'We know nothing about it yet,' Joanna interrupted, 'so we need to look on the bright side.'

'But you followed that lead, so you must think there's something in it.'

'No,' she said firmly. 'We're simply looking for Sakrat.'

Angelika drove on in silence. After a while she turned to Chyłka.

'I keep forgetting. You think Awit and I are guilty.'

'Got it in one.'

Angelika muttered something and began to go faster. Chyłka was never comfortable with someone else driving, and now she simply felt like getting out of the car. But she kept quiet, and managed to keep her silence up for nearly half an hour before she decided – probably spurred on by her dropping alcohol levels – that she had to say something.

'Slow down.'

'Not until you say I'm not guilty.'

'For God's sake, Angelika, how old are you?'

Angelika put her foot down, the turbo kicked in and the car lurched forwards. The not inconsiderable number of horses under the bonnet were making their presence felt.

'Have you gone mad?' shouted Chyłka, squirming in her seat.

'Look who's talking.'

'Give me strength. You're like a Sunday driver, you should—'

Angelika jerked so hard on the steering wheel as they rounded the bend that Joanna stopped what she was saying. She leaned against the window and looked furiously at her friend.

'You're going to kill us,' she said.

'I want you to say you think we're innocent.'

'I'm beginning to wonder which of us had more to dr—'

'You're not listening to me,' Angelika cut in. 'I want you, as my defence lawyer, to tell me you don't think we killed our daughter, for God's sake!' Coming out of the bend, Angelika put her foot to the floor. The turbo kicked in again, and again the car lurched forwards, this time skidding into the opposite lane.

'Watch out!' yelled Chyłka. They had scarcely rounded the bend when she saw the headlights of a lorry coming straight towards them. The driver didn't even have time to sound the horn. Angelika, panic-stricken, swerved in the other direction, too hard and too fast, and with a screech of tyres lost control of the car. She tried to veer to the other side, but it only made matters worse.

'Holy shit!' Chyłka managed to shout as the car hurtled into the ditch.

14

Angelika could hear a deafening noise, but she soon grasped it was only in her head. She opened her eyes. Everything was in a fog, and she could hear screaming in the distance. It didn't make any sense. None of this made any sense. A moment ago she'd been driving along, and now . . .

Straining her eyes, she tried to look ahead. One of the car's headlights lit up the slope of the roadside ditch, and the windscreen looked like a spider's web. Apart from that, it was hard to make anything out.

The car, she saw, had slammed forwards into the ground, and she was hanging from her seatbelt. The hazard lights were blinking on and off, and quiet music was floating from the radio. Angelika coughed. Her lungs hurt. She closed her eyes as she realised what must have happened.

'Hey!' she heard a man's voice call in the distance.

The lorry driver.

The first thing she had to do, she knew, was assess her own condition. The dashboard was shattered, and the airbag hung from the steering wheel, covered in blood.

My legs, she thought. She moved one, then the other, and sighed in relief. Then she checked her arms. She was all right, but the lower part of the steering column had come out of its casing and smashed into her chest. Next, she moved her torso, and felt excruciating pain. She groaned, and tried not to move anymore.

She could hear a man running down the street. He'd have phoned for help, surely. The ambulance wouldn't be long.

'Hey!' the lorry driver called again, coming closer to the shattered door. 'Thank God you're alive!'

Angelika opened her mouth, but nothing came out. The man quickly scanned her for injuries, then looked at the passenger seat. His eyes widened, and the blood drained from his face. Angelika hadn't thought of checking on Chyłka.

'Oh my God,' the driver whispered, racing round to the other side of the car.

Angelika turned her head slightly to see what had happened to Joanna. It was agony, but she had to check.

The first thing she saw was Chyłka's head hanging down. Then that her blouse was drenched with blood.

'I can't open it!' shouted the lorry driver, tugging on the twisted door handle.

And then Angelika saw the piece of metal protruding from Chyłka's abdomen. She felt faint.

'Can you hear me?' screamed the man. 'The door won't open!'

Angelika felt herself drifting away. The last thing she remembered was the anguished howl of the truck driver.

15

Kordian stood at the petrol station, smoking a cigarette. He felt guilty that he hadn't told Chyłka he'd gone back on their pledge, because then she could have bought herself a packet of cigarettes and joined him on the losing side. But instead, he'd got his own Marlboros, and was standing beside the building, smoking.

His new friends were getting ready to leave. They'd filled up their old Mercedes W124, and were preparing to say goodbye once and for all.

'Are you sure they won't kill me?' Kordian had asked, looking around.

'Don't worry,' Jordi had assured him.

'Besides, they saw who you came with,' added Wito. They shook hands, and Jordi got into the car. Wito held onto Kordian's hand a little longer.

'Do you think you'll get him?' he asked.

'Possibly. At least we have a chance now, thanks to what we found.'

'If you need me, text your old number. I'll get your phone from Kabior as a souvenir.'

'Good to know.'

'And if it turns out that Tatarnikov touched the child,' said Wito, 'well, you know how it goes. It's not the courts he should be worried about.'

Oryński nodded. He understood.

'Hand him over to us, then you won't have to prove anything.'

'I'll remember that.'

Wito clapped him on the back, then climbed into the driver's seat. The old diesel engine wheezed into life, and the Mercedes pulled out of the car park. Kordian took out another cigarette and watched the tail-lights disappear. His jaw still hurt when he breathed in, but it could have all been much worse.

He finished his cigarette, and decided there was no reason to stay outside in the cold. When Chyłka arrived, she'd know to look inside the building. Actually, 'building' was an overstatement. The petrol station was more like a shed.

He went inside. The pump attendant was half asleep behind his cash desk.

'How can I h ... Oh, it's you. You came with Wito and the others.'

Kordian nodded.

'Are you waiting for someone?'

'Yes.'

'Well, have a drink while you wait.' The man gestured to a smallish fridge, the kind in which, at a normal petrol station, you'd find ice-creams and soft drinks. Here there was only beer. Kordian decided he'd had enough for one day.

'No, but thanks anyway.'

'If you don't have the money, you can have it on tick. Wito will pay.' Oryński doubted that, but he'd never have to find out.

Although the dealers were greedy for money, they'd only taken his phone. He still had his wallet.

He looked around to see if there were hot-dogs in a warmer somewhere, but that concept clearly hadn't reached this establishment yet, so he chose an indifferent-looking pastry and sat down with it on a sticky chair by the window. Cars came and went, then an ambulance whizzed past, complete with blue lights and siren.

A disturbing thought occurred to him; but that often happened when you were waiting for someone and an ambulance drove past. Kordian looked at the attendant.

'Do you have CB here?' he asked, referring to Citizens' Band, a radio frequency used by long-distance lorry drivers to exchange messages.

'Of course. With an antenna on the roof to give us a good range.'

'Can you turn it on and find out what's happening?'

The man nodded and reached for the radio, turned the dial and picked up the microphone.

'Mobile, what can you tell me about the ambulance going towards Zagórze?'

When he heard only white noise, he repeated his request, this time changing the direction to Augustów.

'RTA, mate,' said a voice from the radio. 'I didn't see it myself, but others say it was an X5 and a freight shaker. X5's a write-off. They're waiting for the prosecutor, apparently there's a fatality. The smokeys have closed the road and there's a detour. Where are you coming from?'

'I'm at base station. Thanks though, and have a good evening.' The petrol station guy hung up the microphone, adjusting the dial to increase the set's effective range. He looked at Kordian. 'Did you hear him? Apparently there's been an accident.'

Oryński had heard all too well, and the words were still echoing in his head. He sat stock-still, staring into space.

'Hey, are you OK?'

Kordian stammered something, then slowly got up, clutching onto the back of the chair.

'Taxi,' was all he managed to say.

'You want me to get you one?' asked the pump attendant, frowning. 'The nearest ones are in Sokół, mate. It'll cost a fortune.'

Kordian felt himself grow hot.

'And even if they do come out all this way, they'll see you've been beaten up and they'll refuse to take you. They know how things work around here. Who's in charge.'

'Bus?'

'My mate Stefan drives a minibus. Shall I ring him?'

'P-please,' stammered Oryński, reaching for his cigarettes. With a shaking hand, he pulled one out of the pack and lit it. Hearing the click of the lighter, the attendant stopped texting and looked up.

'Hey! What do you think you're doing? Take your fags outside. And keep away from the pump!'

Kordian stumbled out. Instinctively he reached into his pocket for his phone, then swore quietly, and took such a deep drag of his cigarette it burned right down, leaving a column of ash. He glared at it, then flung it to the ground, turned on his heel and went back inside.

'I need to make a call.'

'I've already texted Stefan. He's on his way.'

'No, I have to make a call.'

'What are you looking for, a call box?'

Oryński pointed to the ancient Nokia on the counter.

'No way, mate. It's pay-as-you-go.'

'Then give me a twenty-zloty top-up, and let me borrow it a minute.'

Sensing this could work in his favour, the attendant gave Kordian the phone. Kordian entered Chyłka's number from memory. It was a relief just to hear the ringtone, although it didn't really mean anything. The phone automatically disconnected

227

after a few rings, so he tried again. After the third try, he gave up and handed the Nokia back.

'They'll call you on this number,' he said.

'Who?'

'Police, paramedics, I don't know.'

'The police? But just a minute, I—'

'Tell them to get in touch with Żelazny & McVay. It's a law firm in Warsaw. They'll find the number online. Did you get that?'

'Yes, but—'

'It's just a precaution,' Kordian cut in. 'Now tell me, how soon will your friend be here?'

'Ten minutes, tops. Where did you want to go?'

'Where's the nearest hospital with a surgical ward?'

The attendant thought for a moment.

'Probably Mońki. There's a big hospital there.'

'Mońki then,' said Oryński. He took one last look at the phone, thanked the attendant and went outside. He lit another cigarette, but was more careful with it this time. As he watched for the minibus, he could hear his heart hammering.

At last, two yellowish lights emerged from the gloom. As Stefan's minibus pulled into the car park, Kordian raised his hand, jumped into the passenger seat and said where he wanted to go, all before the driver had time to utter a word.

'Make it quick,' he added.

'Is this some sort of scam?'

'Just drive. I'll pay double if you get me there fast.'

'OK.'

The tyres didn't exactly squeal as he left, but Stefan didn't skimp on petrol either. They drove along deserted country lanes, the driver assuring his passenger they'd get to their destination within quarter of an hour. He wasn't lying. Exactly fifteen minutes later they pulled up in front of the hospital. Kordian took a hundred-zloty note from his wallet.

'Is that enough?'

'Well, it's . . .'

Without waiting for him to finish, Kordian got out of the car and raced into the emergency department. The nurse on duty came over at once, and it took him a minute or two to remember why he might have attracted her attention.

'How are you feeling?' she asked, stepping out from behind the reception desk.

'The accident. On Route 8,' said Kordian.

'Were you involved too?' she asked, surprised. 'They told us there were only two casualties.'

'Has the ambulance arrived yet?'

She looked at his injured face in confusion, but noted that the blood had dried hours ago.

'Yes, the ambulance is here.'

'Can you tell me if . . .' He looked away, pressing his lips together. He felt dizzy and had to lean against the desk. The nurse came to stand beside him.

'There were two casualties,' she said. 'Are you family?'

'I'm a . . . legal representative,' he managed to stammer. 'Please . . . Please can you tell me if they . . .'

The duty nurse looked around the room. Had they been in a large, city hospital, perhaps she wouldn't have been keen to give out information. But here, in the country, in the middle of the night, she had no qualms.

'One is in a critical condition and has extensive internal injuries,' she said. 'The other has bruised ribs and is in shock.'

'But on the CB they said . . .'

229

'They say all sorts of things on the CB,' she said. 'It's always fatalities, road closures and hours-long tailbacks. But at least they warn other road users to let ambulances past.'

Oryński scarcely heard her. He could see her lips moving, but he'd drifted away. He wondered if the beating might be taking its toll at last. Shock he could cope with, but what if this was concussion?

Not that it mattered right now.

'I need to see them right away.'

'I'm afraid that won't be possible,' said the duty nurse firmly. 'One is in the operating theatre anyway, as we speak.'

He closed his eyes and tried to calm his pounding heart.

'Driver or passenger?'

'Passenger.'

In that first moment he thought it would have been Chyłka behind the wheel. Then he remembered their phone conversation: she'd had too much to drink, and had asked Angelika to drive.

He felt faint, and fell heavily onto a bench by the wall.

'Will she be OK?' he asked weakly, hardly recognising the sound of his own voice.

'We'll know more once she's out of surgery. Try not to worry.'

He nodded absently.

'But right now, let's have a look at you.'

'No,' he said. 'You said she was in a critical condition. So that means . . .'

'It means she's still in danger,' said the nurse, sitting down beside him. 'That's all I know. That's all anyone knows.'

He leaned his head against the wall.

'How did you get these injuries?'

'Just a misunderstanding . . .'

'Did they beat you badly?' she asked, taking a closer look.

'It's not the worst I've had,' he said, recalling his encounter with Gorzym. On that occasion he'd ended up in intensive care. But even then, he'd been in a better state than Chyłka was now. He hadn't needed surgery, and was soon able to walk on his own. If Joanna got through this, it would still be some time before she was allowed home. She'd be furious that she wouldn't be able to see the case through.

16

The surgery took hours, and when it was over, all Kordian could get from the staff was that the patient's condition was still unstable, her life hung in the balance, and that she was in a medically induced coma. The doctor was significantly less talkative than the nurse, and told Oryński he would speak only to family members.

At his insistence, Kordian left the hospital. The staff had tried to contact the family, and their first port of call had been the number from which the most recent calls to Chyłka's phone had been made. The petrol pump attendant had directed them to Żelazny & McVay in Warsaw, so Old Rusty and the Old Man, as the partners were known, already knew about the incident and were probably on their way north.

Oryński stood outside the hospital and lit a cigarette. He hardly had the strength to smoke it, but it didn't matter. He watched the first visitors drive in and park their cars, and wondered whether to visit Angelika. He decided against it. He'd probably end up blaming her, and that was the last thing she needed. Also, Awit was due to be released from custody under police supervision today, and he'd probably come straight here anyway.

Kordian's time would be better spent looking for Tatarnikov. It's what Chyłka would have wanted.

'Excuse me,' he said, stopping a passing nurse.

'Yes?'

'How do I travel north from here?'

'Where is it you want to go?'

'Grajewo.'

'No problem. At the exit, you'll see signs for—'

'I don't have a car.'

'Then you could take the train. It takes just under half an hour, and there's a train around seven o'clock this morning and another at two o'clock this afternoon.'

Again, Oryński automatically reached for his phone, and again he swore under his breath. If only he'd handled the situation with the man in leather a bit better, he'd have been able to contact everyone. People would be going out of their minds worrying about Chyłka. And maybe he'd have a better idea of what to do next.

'It's seven fifteen now,' said the nurse, smiling kindly.

'Thank you.'

'So that leaves you two options: you can either hitch, or you can wait here for a few hours.'

Kordian looked down. The last thing he felt like was small talk. He was tired, and he'd had enough of the Szlezyngier case and all that went with it. But somewhere, in the middle of this mess, a little girl was missing – a little girl who might still be alive, waiting to be rescued.

He turned back to the hospital.

'Difficult situation?' ventured the woman.

Oryński looked at her properly for the first time. She had blonde hair pinned back in a bun, dark eyes and a sympathetic smile. He noticed she was also holding a lit cigarette.

'It's my . . .' he began, but stopped, not quite knowing how to describe her.

'Girlfriend?'

'No, my boss. My boss is in ICU.'

'Was she in the accident?'

'Yes.'

The woman finished her cigarette in silence, which wasn't a good sign. She smiled again as she walked away, but said nothing more. Oryński followed her into the building, and went to reception, where the same nurse was on duty. Her shift probably finished at eight.

'Someone's seen to your injuries, I see.'

Through a haze, he remembered that while Chyłka had been in surgery that night, he'd been taken to Accident and Emergency, where they'd cleaned him up and stitched his wounds. They'd also talked about his jaw, but Kordian couldn't remember anything they'd said.

'May I use the phone?' he asked.

'Of course,' the nurse answered, handing him a cordless handset.

He should have thought of this before. He smiled his thanks and took the phone.

'Sorry to be a pain, but I've lost all my numbers.'

'Along with your phone, I suppose.'

'Precisely.'

'So how can I help my mysterious night visitor?'

'I need the number for Żelazny & McVay, a law firm in Warsaw,' he said, gesturing towards the computer.

Moments later, he had what he needed. He dialled the number; Anka from reception answered. She sounded shaken, and wanted to know the details – clearly the hospital staff had already been in touch. It took Oryński a moment to calm her, but eventually he managed to get Artur Żelazny's mobile number. He rang it, and waited for him to answer.

'I'm on my way,' was Żelazny's greeting.

'How did you—'

'The area code. Eighty-five, same as the hospital. They already rang me,' said Artur. 'How is she?'

'No change.'

'I left as soon as I heard.'

'When do you think you'll get here?'

'According to my sat-nav, I'm a few minutes away.'

'A few minutes?'

'I left at five this morning. McVay is on his way from Poznań, he had some business to attend to there, and her sister left her daughter with her grandparents and is on her way too, along with her husband.'

Joanna, Oryński thought, would be none too pleased to see so many people gathered at her bedside. Like a funeral cortège, she'd say. He shook his head to dispel the thought.

'Go and stand outside, son.'

Whenever Old Rusty gave him an order, he felt he should reply with a 'Yes, sir.' Harry McVay was like a benevolent old uncle to the younger lawyers, while Artur Żelazny was the stern father who liked to have a drink then shout at his children. In his own way, Kordian was fond of both of them – one of only a few in the firm, as usually the dividing line between the followers of the British partner and the Polish one was very distinct.

It was only minutes before Żelazny arrived. He parked his black Mercedes a few metres away and got out, looking every inch the successful businessman in his well-cut suit. He glanced around, grimacing at the sight of the hospital building. Kordian raised his hand, and at last Żelazny noticed him.

Greeting the young man with a firm handshake, his eye fell on the stitches above Kordian's eyebrows.

'Were you in the car too?' he asked.

'No,' replied Oryński. 'It's a long story.'

'Right,' muttered Żelazny, heading towards the hospital entrance. He clearly wasn't particularly interested in the health of his trainees. 'We have to wait until McVay arrives before we can get more details.'

'Why?'

'Chyłka listed him as the only person outside the immediate family to be informed about her condition.'

That was no surprise. Joanna had started out in the Harry McVay camp, then they'd had an altercation and she'd changed sides. But recently they'd gone some way towards burying the hatchet, and were fast becoming friends again.

'So, have you got any further with your case?' Artur asked, scanning the room with its questionable interior design.

Kordian hadn't expected that would be the topic they'd start with, and he had no answer prepared.

'You know, the Szlezyngiers,' Artur prompted. 'What's going on?'

'You want to talk about that now?'

Żelazny grabbed his hand and spun him round until they were face to face. 'Did Chyłka teach you nothing? You should be living the case, shouldn't you?'

He nodded.

'You should be thinking about it the minute you wake, when you're eating, every time you're on the shitter ... isn't that right?'

'That's not quite how she put it, but ...'

'The point is that you have to keep at it,' continued Żelazny, 'and now that's more important than ever, because you need something to occupy your mind. So let's find a table, and you can tell me all about it.'

As they sat down in the hospital canteen, Kordian remembered he'd had no breakfast, so he ordered pierogi, probably the safest option. Everything else looked as if it came from communist times, transported in a time capsule.

Artur ordered them a coffee each, sat down opposite Kordian and, with a movement of his hand, urged him to start talking. Slowly, Oryński told him everything that had happened since the last hearing. He didn't leave anything out; Żelazny would have found out about it anyway, from the client.

Artur nodded with satisfaction.

'Good work,' he said. 'But tell me more about this new lead.'

Kordian took a deep breath and put aside his knife and fork.

'We found quite a bit of debris in that hovel in Lebiedzin, stuff Wito's boys swore hadn't been there before, including printouts.'

'Printouts?'

Oryński took a sip of coffee.

'Our current theory is that before meeting Sakrat, Ekiel had a meeting with someone he trusted enough to check something out for him and print the information out. The pages were torn up, but I salvaged some scraps.' Oryński patted his jacket pockets. 'I just need to glue them together and we might have something.'

'Show me.'

Reluctantly, Kordian pulled out a bagful of scraps of paper. Some were crumpled, others drenched in some sort of liquid. They came from only a few sheets of paper, ten at most, and it was difficult to see how they could learn anything from them.

'It doesn't look too good,' said Żelazny.

'All we need is a bit of patience.'

'Optimism, more like. These could be anything. And if the scraps were important, they wouldn't have left them.'

'Not necessarily. They wouldn't have expected anyone to trace them to Lebiedzin. As far as Tatarnikov was concerned, everyone he worked with could be trusted. And they'd have definitely kept stumm if I hadn't mentioned the little girl.'

'OK,' said Old Rusty, nodding. 'Let's say you manage to piece something together. What then?'

'I don't know.'

'Didn't you have a plan?'

'It's all good as far as the trial's concerned,' said Oryński. 'We just needed a credible alternative to the Szlezyngiers. Now we've got two. Their links to the smuggling ring speak volumes.'

'It won't be enough.'

Kordian shrugged. 'Chyłka had the rest of the plan in her head.'

'She didn't share it with you?'

'You ask that as if you didn't know her,' said Kordian, tracing the rim of his coffee cup with his finger. 'Anyway, what does it matter now? The Szlezyngiers will get someone else. Daniel, I expect, if he's free.'

There were few other options. Żelazny & McVay gave most of the high-profile cases to their two most senior lawyers, Chyłka and Daniel Kosmowski. They were polar opposites. Joanna wasn't hugely into pop culture, whereas Daniel could have been born with an iPhone in his hand. He was a typical corporate drone, all blue sky thinking and breaking down silos. Joanna had been known to say that if Kosmowski fell out of a window on the twenty-first floor of the Skylight building, she'd rush there to help him on his way.

'He's already got it in his diary,' said Żelazny, pulling out his BlackBerry, checking something and putting it back in his pocket. Then he hung his jacket on the back of his chair and looked expectantly at Kordian.

'I understand,' Oryński assured him.

'You're to hand over everything you've got so far, and if you don't manage to extract anything from those scraps of paper, put them in with the rest of the documentation.'

'Of course.'

When Chyłka woke up, Kordian thought, she'd be fuming, and the doctors would have to chain her to the bed to stop her unleashing her frustrations on whoever dared to take over her case. And Artur knew that. He looked at Kordian as if expecting him to leap to his supervisor's defence.

But Oryński just drank some more of his coffee.

'You understand why we have to do this?' Żelazny asked.

'Yes.'

'We can't wait until Chyłka gets better. It's not just the firm's reputation at stake, it's for the good of these people. We have to give them continuity.'

Of course it was about the firm's reputation. With Żelazny, everything was about the firm's reputation.

'I have no doubt you always put the client first.'

'Good.'

Artur finished his coffee, got up, and announced he needed the toilet. As soon as Old Rusty had disappeared into the corridor, Kordian leaped up and reached into his jacket pocket, pulling out the BlackBerry. He entered the number of the person he thought of as his last hope.

'I'll be two hours,' said a voice, in Polish, without a trace of a foreign accent.

'I need help,' said Oryński.

'Kordian?'

'The very same. I don't have much time.'

'But—'

'Artur wants to give the case to Kosmowski.'

'Are you surprised? Chyłka's not—'

'I'd like to take it,' Kordian cut in.

'That's not possible.'

'It is,' said Oryński, more petulantly than he'd intended. 'A trainee can take the place of the lawyer in court. They just need a signed authorisation.'

'Which you don't have.'

'I will though, as soon as Joanna wakes up.'

'If she wakes up.'

Kordian didn't hold it against him; it was simply McVay's good old British stoicism shining through.

'It's a risk worth taking,' Oryński went on, 'especially when you consider the alternative. Please, make a decision soon. And don't mention I called,' he added, then disconnected and quickly deleted the call from the phone's history. Then he replaced the phone and looked up.

A few minutes later Żelazny returned, and took his seat across the table from Kordian.

'How's Angelika?' he asked.

'Well enough to talk.'

'Have you been to see her?'

'No. I thought it might be better if you or Mr McVay visited first.'

'Good thinking. I need to talk to her about . . .' He stopped when his phone rang. He reached for it and sighed when he saw who was calling. 'Excuse me,' he said, and left the table.

Oryński picked up his plate and took it to the serving hatch. A woman in a stained apron smiled at him.

'You're a master manipulator,' she said, gesturing towards Żelazny, who stood by the door, clearly getting an earful.

'I do what I can, but women are the real experts. I'm just lucky I have a good teacher.'

She nodded her head in acknowledgement.

'Would you like anything else?'

'I'd love another helping of pierogi.'

'No problem,' she said with a wink.

When Kordian got back to the table with a fresh plate of pierogi, Żelazny was still deep in discussion with the other partner. Eventually he shook his head and ended the call, pushing down on the button as if he wished it were McVay's nose.

He sat down and stared at Kordian.

'OK,' he said. 'If Chyłka wakes up, you've got the case.'

'But . . .'

'Don't make me regret it, son.'

Kordian felt it best not to say anything and busied himself with his pierogi.

'And just be aware that today you've made an enemy. Of a man whose name may one day appear on the office door, alongside mine and McVay's.'

Oryński put a forkful of pierogi in his mouth and chewed, smiling. Now all that remained was for Chyłka to wake up.

17

Harry McVay stepped out of his Lexus and strode towards the hospital. He knew he was the last to arrive – he had meant to leave Poznań much earlier, but business had detained him. Chyłka's sister and brother-in-law were already there, which made things easier, as they'd be able to find something out at last.

In the hospital canteen, he almost didn't recognise Joanna's trainee, who had been with her for the last year. His face was cut and bruised, one cheek visibly swollen, and judging by the dark circles under his eyes, he hadn't slept much lately.

Harry greeted the assembled company, who were now sitting at the biggest table in the canteen. He pulled up a chair.

'Any news?' he asked, looking at Magdalena. He remembered that like her sister, she disliked being called by any diminutive or nickname. It was probably the only thing the sisters had in common.

'She's alive, and at the moment, that's all that matters,' she said, tears in her voice.

Her husband put his arm around her and kissed her temple. McVay couldn't remember his name, although they'd once been at one of the firm's parties together, at the Lucid Club on the top floor of Blue City. They'd even spoken, mainly about how two women brought up under the same roof could be so different.

'What's the prognosis?' he asked.

'The doctors don't want to comment,' Oryński answered. 'Not yet, anyway.'

McVay nodded.

'I've made some phone calls,' he said, 'and I've booked you all in at a guest house on Ełcka Street. Number fifty-seven. It's called Dworak. You just have to give your names, it's all paid for.'

'Thank you,' said Magdalena's husband.

Harry gave a perfunctory smile as befitted an Englishman, then got up and beckoned to Kordian, who quickly rose to follow him.

'I've given the matter some thought,' said McVay.

'That sounds ominous.'

'Maybe I haven't expressed myself properly. I think it's an excellent idea.'

'I'm so pleased,' said Kordian, relieved.

'Chyłka will be even more pleased, when she wakes up.' Harry stopped in the corridor and turned to Oryński.

'But?' said the younger man.

'But the timing gives us a bit of a problem.'

'I don't understand.'

'I think you've lost track of time a little, haven't you?'

McVay watched as understanding dawned. Kordian muttered something under his breath, and shook his head.

'It's nearly time for the second hearing,' he said.

'Precisely,' said McVay. 'And you don't have authorisation. So the doctors' prognosis is key.'

'We won't get anything more from them today.'

Harry hoped that wasn't true, but as the sun started to set, they still had no idea how Joanna was, or when they'd wake her from her coma. The doctors had muttered something about internal injuries, but seemed reluctant to give details. Magdalena was able to find out a bit more, but she'd understood little of the medical jargon.

McVay and Kordian drove to the guest house, mostly in silence.

'There's still one thing we could try.'

'Yes.'

'You don't even know what I was going to suggest.'

'I know perfectly well. Chyłka's desk is full of papers, already signed by her. We just need Kormak to work his magic.'

Kordian nodded.

'Mind you, it could be called a crime,' McVay added.

'Only if someone knows about it.'

'I know about it.'

'You do, but Mr Żelazny doesn't. We've never spoken about authorisation. Maybe he thinks Chyłka already signed a form for me, just in case.'

'Is that the sort of thing she'd do?'

'We're talking about someone who updates her will every six months, Mr McVay, and has it notarised. If anyone signed an authorisation "just in case", it would be her.'

Harry didn't reply, but deep down, he knew he'd already made his decision. He'd been thinking about it on the long drive over, and knew Joanna well enough to realise it was what she would have wanted.

'I know this isn't an easy decision for you, but . . .'

'You don't need to convince me,' said McVay. 'Make that call to Kormak. He can send the authorisation to our hotel.'

Until a few years ago, the issue wouldn't even have come up, but the law had been changed in 2013. Now a trainee could deputise for a lawyer after six months of traineeship, he just had to indicate on every document that he was under the authority of his supervisor.

'I'll help you, Kordian. We'll crush that prosecutor.'

'I hope so.'

'When Joanna wakes up, she'll be pleasantly surprised.'

'Fingers crossed.'

'You'll be fine,' said Harry McVay. And he really believed it.

18

The trial was scheduled to take place in two weeks' time. Chyłka was still in a coma, which even a layman could see was a bad sign. Angelika had been discharged from hospital, and had returned home with her husband. Kordian stayed in the guest house, and didn't once go and visit them.

Using McVay's laptop, he spent his time reading everything there was to read on the subject, but none of the studies and commentaries gave him any new insights into the case. Chyłka had raised everything that needed raising at the first hearing, and quite frankly, Kordian wasn't sure why there was a second hearing at all. With a little goodwill, the case could have been closed right away.

On the appointed day, he dressed in a black suit and white shirt, and added a black tie. His facial injuries were still visible, but he guessed that could work in his favour; in fact it would have been great if they had been even more noticeable.

McVay drove to court with him. Żelazny had gone back to Warsaw a week earlier, saying he had to keep things ticking over at the office. That, of course, was nonsense – the firm ran itself, requiring minimal input from the partners. The real issue might have been Daniel Kosmowski, whose ego needed stroking so he wouldn't be tempted to leave the firm and strike out on his own. When the case had been handed to Kordian instead of him, it had been not so much of a knockback for him as a knockout.

'Coping with the stress?' asked Harry, as they drove to the court in Suwałki in his Lexus.

'It depends what you mean by coping.'

'No vomiting or diarrhoea.'

'In that case yes, I'm coping.'

Kordian shuddered at the thought of what awaited him. One of the more practical pieces of advice he'd been given was to empty his bladder before leaving the house. A visit to the court toilets was an unusually traumatic experience: they always stank as if all the drains were blocked.

He tried not to think about it, focusing instead on what he was going to say. The cross-examinations didn't scare him, it was more his closing speech that filled him with dread. Everything depended on it.

They hadn't found either Ekiel or Tatarnikov, so if he played it right, Kordian should be able to paint them as incarnations of the devil himself. Meanwhile, the prosecutor would try to show that although they might be involved in smuggling tobacco, they had nothing to do with Nikola's disappearance. The closing speeches were their chance to tip the balance in favour of one side or the other.

The computer printouts had been pasted together, submitted as evidence and carefully analysed by experts. They had, of course, also been reviewed in advance by McVay and Kordian, but hadn't proved particularly helpful. They basically contained information about how to get a Belarusian visa, so at least the lawyers knew where the fugitives were headed. For more information, they'd have to visit Belarus, or at least speak to the secretary of state for the Ministry of Internal Affairs. Which would be awkward to say the least, as relations had been decidedly cool since the latest political shenanigans in that country.

'You'll be fine,' repeated McVay as he parked outside the court building. 'You've got it all under control.'

With each passing moment, Kordian was less certain this was true. Earlier on, it had seemed that simply by building on what Chyłka had started, they'd win the case with minimal input from him, and that all he needed to do was continue along the same path.

Now he was beginning to have his doubts. Zbigniew Aronowicz was a slippery customer, not always playing it straight: a prosecutor who loved springing surprises on his opponents. Not like Rejchert, the prosecutor they'd sparred with in the Langer case. He had been of a different calibre altogether.

Kordian stepped out of the Lexus and immediately reached for his cigarettes.

'When she wakes up, she'll be outraged that you've been smoking for the last fortnight while she has, to all intents and purposes, stuck to her resolution.'

'I know. I'll have to make it up to her.'

'Or quit again as soon as possible and make sure she never finds out.'

It was a thought – although not necessarily feasible, seeing as Kordian had not only started smoking again, he was smoking more than ever before. Two packs a day at least, almost without noticing.

'I've always thought smoking immediately before a hearing is a bad idea.'

'You're right. I'll chew some gum.'

'That's no better. Gum increases your saliva production, but it also makes it more concentrated. You'll see what I mean as soon as you sit down.'

Oryński threw away his cigarette butt, silently thanking McVay for being in his corner.

Moments later he was outside the courtroom, masking the smell of nicotine not with gum, but with orange juice. Awit and Angelika nodded to him diffidently.

'Is everything OK?' asked Szlezyngier. 'We haven't seen you for a long time.'

'I've been wading through piles of documents.'

'And what do you think? Are you optimistic?'

'Yes,' Oryński replied, but without too much enthusiasm. In his head he could hear Joanna telling him never to guarantee the client a win, but to maintain a polite indifference that suggested nothing.

'Will Angelika be cross-examined?' Awit asked.

'Yes, the prosecutor has more questions about Tatarnikov.'

'But she's already told them everything,' said Awit, 'in full, gory detail.'

He looked at his wife, but she turned away. She was clearly in a bad mood, which didn't please Kordian. The jurors would be looking closely at the defendants' behaviour. The judges too, for that matter.

'I don't know what they're going to ask,' he said. 'But whatever it is, we'll deal with it.'

Awit clapped Kordian on the shoulder. 'I think so too,' he said.

Oryński didn't know why, but his words sounded encouraging. There was something new in Szlezyngier's eyes. Confidence, perhaps, or hope. He appreciated it; it couldn't be easy to trust your fate to an inexperienced lawyer. In theory, there was nothing to stop the Szlezyngiers terminating their contract. In practice, though, they seemed to be relying on him.

He had no more time to think about it, as at that moment the case was called. This time the trial was to take place in the largest courtroom – a reasonable choice, given the number of cameras present. The presiding judge gave permission to record, and the camera operators spread out behind the onlookers.

Great, thought Kordian. My solo debut, not only in front of a judge, but on national television too. He took a deep breath, took his seat by the defendants and unfolded two sheets of paper on the bench in front of him. He scanned the most important points then looked up, only to see Aronowicz grinning. A rare sight, considering how sullen he usually was.

The prosecutor nodded to him, looking delighted. Kordian tried to look equally nonchalant, but failed miserably.

Aronowicz had every reason to be pleased. If this was the type of race where the final few metres decide the outcome, he was in with a chance. Kordian wasn't a complete rookie, but he wasn't familiar with every trick in the courtroom book.

A ringing tone announced the arrival of the judges, and everyone rose. Five people entered from the back of the room and took their seats.

The presiding judge adjusted his ceremonial eagle chain of office and looked at Oryński with disapproval. Kordian half-expected him to ask the defendants if they really wanted to put their fate into the hands of this young rookie lawyer, but of course he didn't. Instead, he declared the hearing open, and the cross-examinations began. At first, it all went smoothly, and Kordian felt the judges should be able to close the case at this session and deliver their verdict within the day.

After much persuasion, and with the lure of a seven-thousand-zloty sweetener, Oryński had persuaded Wito to appear as a witness. There would be no risk, he'd said, and explained he had the right to decline answering a question which might incriminate him. So he'd agreed – but demanded fifteen thousand. Kordian knew that, firstly, McVay would never agree to such a preposterous sum, and that, secondly, it was illegal, so it stayed at seven thousand, to be paid a few months after the trial.

'I call Witold T. to the stand as a witness,' announced the judge. 'Witold T. is thirty-six years of age, a car mechanic by trade, has no criminal record and does not know the accused.'

Kordian could scarcely believe the man had never been caught by the police for anything, not even driving under the influence.

'Do you know which case you are appearing in?'

'I do, Your Honour. The case of the missing child, Nikola Szlezyngier.'

The judge should then have handed over to the prosecutor, but Oryński noted with concern that he wasn't doing so.

'Do you have any new information about the case?' the judge asked.

'Not about her disappearance, no. I mean, at least I don't think so. But I've been called, haven't I?'

'True,' said the judge. 'Although I'm still wondering why.'

He waited for the information to percolate, then gave the floor to the prosecutor.

'Sir,' began Aronowicz, 'or would you rather I called you Wito?'

'Either will do.'

'But your smuggler friends call you Wito, don't they?'

'I don't have any smuggler friends.'

'Aren't those the sort of circles you socialise in?'

'I socialise with my friends.'

He glared at the prosecutor as if to warn him that one more stupid question and he'd come down from the rostrum and land him a well-aimed punch in the mouth. Oryński was gratified to see it, but it didn't help. But he was glad Wito wasn't letting himself be pushed around.

'Good. Well . . .' said the prosecutor, glancing down at his notes. He shuffled a few papers around, then looked up at the witness again. 'Did you assault the defence counsel?'

'Huh?'

'Did you cause physical harm to trainee lawyer Kordian Oryński?'

'What kind of bullshit is that?'

'May I remind the witness,' said the judge wearily, 'that violating the solemnity, peace and order of court proceedings may result in a penalty, and in being expelled from the court.'

'I understand,' answered a bewildered Wito.

'So please answer the question.'

Wito looked at Kordian as if he'd never seen him before in his life.

'I exercise my right not to answer the question, in accordance with Article Eighty-Something or other—'

'You don't need to worry about the article number,' the judge cut in, 'and neither do you need to give a reason for your refusal. A simple "No comment" will suffice.'

A few of the reporters gave a quiet groan.

'Yes, Your Honour.'

'Please continue. Mr Aronowicz?'

'Thank you, Your Honour,' said Aronowicz. 'And thank you to the witness for not perjuring himself.'

'Mr Aronowicz!' warned one of the other judges, frowning.

The prosecutor raised his hands and made a slight bow, then turned back to the witness.

'Have you ever committed a crime?' he asked.

'No comment.'

'Do you know any criminals?'

'No comment.'

Aronowicz pursed his lips. 'How am I supposed to cross-examine you?' he asked, shaking his head. But before any of the judges had time to intervene, he added, 'Are your parents still alive?'

'Yes.'

'And what do they think of your business activities?'

'What business activities?'

'I don't know. You tell me. Do you have a profession?'

'No com—'

'Your Honour,' said the prosecutor, spreading his hands. 'Surely questions about working in a particular profession don't come under Article 182, Paragraph 1?'

'You are correct, they don't. The witness should answer.'

'No, I don't have a profession.'

'So do your parents approve of your business activities?'

Kordian could see Wito wanted to protest, but realised it would be pointless. He and McVay had been preparing him for days, and he knew exactly what sort of questions he could and couldn't answer. Calling him as a witness had been a risk, but he had the information they needed to cast suspicion on Sakrat and Ekiel.

'I don't know what my parents think.'

'They've given you no grounds to think they disapprove?'

Wito shifted nervously. 'What is this, *Family Feud*?' he asked.

'The witness is reminded he is to respect the dignity of the court. This is the final warning.'

'Yes, Your Honour.'

'So, to return to my question,' the prosecutor continued. 'They've never given you a reason to think they disapprove?'

'They have.'

'So you believe they disapprove?'

'Yes, I think they do.'

Wito shuffled from foot to foot, staring long and hard at the prosecutor.

'And what makes you think that?'

'They disinherited me.'

'And that means?'

'They've cut me out of their will.'

'But you'll still have a reserved share of their estate?'

'No.'

Oryński looked over his shoulder at McVay, who was sitting a little way away. Neither of them had known this. The prosecutor must have dug deeper into Wito's past than they had.

'Let me remind the court of the situations where this may occur. If a son has persistently behaved in an antisocial manner, or committed a crime against the life, health, freedom or . . .'

The judge sighed heavily, so Aronowicz stopped there.

'Can you tell us why this situation arose?'

'Because it's what my parents decided.'

'Do you know why?'

'I do.'

'And could you please tell us?'

'No com—'

'Thank you,' said the prosecutor. 'Now let's go on to another question. Do you have any information about what happened to Nikola Szlezyngier?'

'No.'

'Have you seen any discarded items which may have belonged to her?'

'No.'

The prosecutor straightened up and looked at the ceiling. He remained in this pose for a moment, then leaned forwards again.

'What can you tell us about the case?'

'Only what I've seen. That at seven o'clock, the alarm . . .'

'Anything other than what's been in the media?'

'No, nothing else.'

'So how can you help us solve the case?'

Kordian wasn't happy with the way things were going. He'd known it might be problematic, but hadn't expected Wito's nerves to be his main worry. He was just about managing to keep them under control, but meanwhile the prosecutor was trying to discredit Wito as a witness. Declining to comment on a particular question didn't prove anything, but it raised suspicions. And now he'd made it look as if Wito didn't have anything pertinent to say.

'I was called by the defence. Ask them.'

'I'm asking you,' Aronowicz insisted. 'What do you know about this case?'

'The same as everyone here.'

'I mean, do you have any information beyond what's publicly available?'

'I don't know anything beyond that.'

'Thank you. No further questions.'

Oryński had expected that was how the cross-examination would end. He'd instructed Wito not to lead the prosecutor, and to answer only the questions he was asked. He'd deal with everything else when it was the defence's turn.

'Mr . . . er . . . Oryński?' called the presiding judge.

Kordian stood, alarmed to find his legs were shaking.

19

Feeling the eyes of the panel on him, Kordian cleared his throat and adjusted his robe. Then he straightened his back and took a deep breath. McVay had assured him that just by doing that he'd halve his stress levels, but right now, that seemed like a fantasy.

Either way, he had to get started, as every second that went by counted against him. He looked at Wito.

'As the prosecution has been unable to ascertain why the witness was called, perhaps I can explain.'

'That is not within your remit,' said the presiding judge with a hint of irritation. 'Please stick to your role and get on with asking questions.'

'Of course, Your Honour, I only wanted to—'

'Address your questions to the witness.'

'I will, and that will establish why he is here.'

Kordian was ready to confront the judge head-on, with McVay a hundred per cent behind him. He was clearly hostile, so any attempts to placate him would have been doomed, and while normally one would never attempt to antagonise a judge, this situation was far from normal. Kordian suspected that if he provoked the presiding judge in the right way, the rest of the judicial panel would begin to look on him more favourably. He'd have to write off one voice out of five, but the others might be more sympathetic when they saw him, a young trainee, being bullied.

Hearing Kordian's slightly haughty tone, the presiding judge sighed. 'I know you have little idea of court etiquette, but please keep a modicum of civility,' he said.

'Yes, Your Honour. May I proceed with my cross-examination?'

'Please do.' The judge gestured towards Wito. Oryński took another deep breath. Here we go, he thought.

'Do you know Sakrat Tatarnikov?' he asked.

'I do.'

'How did you meet? And what is your relationship to him? What can you tell the court about him?'

'No comment.'

Kordian looked at the panel. They frowned and for a moment looked confused, but they soon realised why the witness was evading the question. Kordian wanted to emphasise it further.

'Have you ever been involved in criminal activity?'

'No comment.'

Oryński nodded, appearing thoughtful.

'When did Sakrat Tatarnikov disappear?'

'I don't remember the precise date.'

'Did something happen to prompt him to go?'

'Yes. It was when that girl went missing.'

'Nikola Szlezyngier?'

'Yes, her,' said Wito, glancing fleetingly at the judges. 'He rang me as soon as it was light and said he had to disappear immediately.'

'Did he say why?'

'Not really. He just said the police would be out looking for him. He had a criminal conviction in Belarus, and he was afraid he'd be extradited or something. He asked me to help.'

'So as soon as the child was reported missing, he fled from Sajenko?'

'Exactly.'

'Do you know where he went?'

'Yes. I told him I needed a bit of time to arrange ... er ... suitable conditions for his escape. He was holed up somewhere in the woods, in a hunting lodge or something. He said some old man was bringing him food and so on. If I'd known he had anything to do with the girl, I'd have fu—'

'Stick to the facts,' warned the presiding judge.

'Sorry.'

Oryński adjusted the green jabot at his throat. It wasn't going too badly so far.

'This old man,' he said. 'Do you know who he meant?'

'He called him Ekiel. I don't know if that was his real name or a street name.'

'Antoni Ekiel, the only witness who allegedly saw a man with the child on the night of—'

'Mr Oryński,' said the judge. He took off his glasses, folded them up and placed them on the file in front of him. Then he glared at Kordian as if he'd like to throw him out of the court-room. 'What you're trying to do here is unacceptable.'

'I understand, Your Honour.'

'Do you really? Well in that case, may I ask you to stick to the rules, rules that have been in force since 1998 when the Criminal Code came into being. I would be hard-pushed to remember a time when someone flouted those rules as blatantly as you are doing now. This is your first and last warning.'

'Yes, Your Honour.'

Oryński returned his gaze to the witness, as if he had scarcely heard the judge's words.

'Where did Mr Tatarnikov go after that?'

'To Lebiedzin.'

'And is that where they found the printouts, which have now been submitted as evidence?'

'That's correct.'

Kordian was glad Aronowicz's cross-examination hadn't reached this point, because if it had, he might have been able to establish that there was no evidence the child had been anywhere near either the lodge or the hideout. It wouldn't have been sufficient proof *per se*, but it would have sown a seed of doubt in the minds of the panel. Luckily, the issue was never raised.

Suddenly, Oryński realised why this might be – maybe the prosecutor had something else. He pushed the thought away. There was no point agonising over it now. Besides, he'd checked and double-checked everything. If Aronowicz had come up with something unexpected, it was unlikely to be anything big.

'Mr Ekiel had a conviction for child abuse,' Oryński said quickly, before the judge had time to object. 'Did Sakrat Tatarnikov have a criminal record of any kind?'

'I'm pretty sure he had something.'

'But you don't know what.'

'Not really. But it was something major.'

Kordian grunted his disapproval and looked at the judges, then back to the witness.

'Could you give the court a character testimony?' he asked.

'A what?'

'Can you tell us what he was like?'

Wito shrugged, as if the question insulted his intelligence. 'He was a normal guy. Decent. Or at least that's what I thought then.'

'What does that mean? Was he calm, impulsive, secretive, snooty, what?'

Wito launched into a long monologue in which he made it clear that his one-time friend was a bastard of the highest order.

He went on to say that Tatarnikov never let himself be pushed around, and would object if he saw it happening to others – which was the only positive point in his entire diatribe – and then he outlined Sakrat's dire financial situation. Finally, he placed the cherry firmly on top of the cake by saying Tatarnikov was a bit of a womaniser, as long as the woman in question wasn't too old.

'Why might he have wanted to kidnap Mr and Mrs Szlezyngier's daughter?' asked Kordian, when he'd finished.

'How would I know? He's a psycho.'

'Would he have any reason to do it?'

'For the money, I guess.'

'But there hasn't been a ransom demand.'

'No, but that's not surprising,' said Wito, looking straight at the judges. 'If I was him, I'd have gone to ground too. I wouldn't contact the Szlezyngiers until I was safely in Belarus. They'd come over with the money, they'd get their brat back. Simple as that.'

'Thank you. No further questions.'

Kordian sat down, happy with the way things had gone. He could feel his shirt sticking to his back, but he'd achieved what he'd set out to do. Now all he had to do was field questions from the prosecution as other witnesses took the stand.

20

During a break in the trial, Kordian and McVay went downstairs and out of the building. Kordian pulled out a Marlboro and lit it, offering the pack to McVay, who declined.

'Only cigars and whisky for me.'

Somehow, Kordian wasn't surprised. What did puzzle him, though, was Harry McVay's broad smile. He knew he'd done fairly well in the courtroom, but it was rare to see such obvious delight on the stoic Englishman's face.

'What are you so happy about?'

'Chyłka woke up,' he said, beaming.

Oryński nearly dropped his cigarette. 'You're joking!'

'I'm not. Her sister rang me before the hearing started.'

Kordian shut his eyes for a moment, in gratitude to a higher power. He felt the tense muscles in his back relax, and suddenly there seemed to be more air in his lungs.

'Why didn't you say anything?' he asked, grinning.

'I didn't want to break your concentration.'

Oryński felt like berating his boss, but was too happy to do so.

'I've just had a message from Magdalena,' McVay added. 'Apparently they've been watching the trial.'

'Is it on TV?'

'NSI is streaming it live,' he said, as he dialled a number. He held out his phone. 'She's not strong enough to talk much, but she's got something to say to you.'

Kordian was dumbstruck. He stared at the phone as if it were a red-hot coal.

'Come on, take it. It's been a while since you talked.' Harry held out his BlackBerry again. This time, Kordian took it, held it to his ear and waited. There was silence on the other end. He supposed Chyłka's sister was holding the phone while Joanna summoned up the strength to speak. The effort was obviously too much, and the silence seemed to drag on forever.

'What on earth's wrong with you?' he said. 'You've only just woken up, and you're already trying to tell your precious Zordon what to do.'

He heard a quiet sigh.

'Good . . . work . . .' she said with difficulty.

If he hadn't known whose number McVay had called, he'd have had trouble recognising the voice. Joanna always spoke confidently, commandingly even, even when she was asking for something. Now she sounded like a wraith from the afterlife, trying to open the gates to this world.

'Thanks,' he said. 'I know you'd have screwed with the presiding judge's head far more effectively than I managed, but I did what I could.'

There was another sigh, presumably, Kordian thought, a substitute for laughter.

'Crush . . . him.'

'I will,' Kordian assured her. '*No pasarán*, Chyłka.'

Silence fell again, then he heard Magdalena's voice:

'I don't know what you just said to her, but it's brought the old deadhead to life.'

'That's the effect I usually have on her.'

'That's not what she said.'

'Did she talk about me then?'

'Only after a few stiff drinks.'

Kordian raised his eyebrows and smiled at McVay, as if he could hear the conversation too.

'Sounds good,' he said. 'We'll talk about it again when she's recovered.'

'Let's do that,' said Chyłka's sister. 'But for now, best of luck for the trial. You're doing well.'

'Thanks.'

They said their goodbyes, and Oryński finished his cigarette in peace. He thought Harry would have a bucketload of advice for him, but McVay didn't even mention the trial. He must have been happy with the way it was going. And if that was the case, Kordian might find himself on the fast track to changing the sign on his door from 'Junior Associate' to 'Associate'.

Back in the courtroom, he was sure he'd bring the case to a satisfactory conclusion that afternoon. And although it was likely the prosecution would try to delay the verdict, Oryński wouldn't let it come to that.

As more witnesses appeared, he kept his questions to a minimum, thinking this would send a clear message to the judges: the defence had proved everything it needed to prove, now let the prosecution sweat.

And sweat they did. Zbigniew Aronowicz was no longer as confident as he had been. He tried to show that the only logical explanation was that the parents had murdered their child and hidden the body, but the judges and jury seemed unconvinced: there was too much about Sakrat Tatarnikov they didn't know.

The key question for Oryński was who to call to the witness stand last. The final testimony was always the one that stood out in the jurors' minds, and he would be last to question them. Angelika seemed like the best choice. Although she'd been more reticent since the accident, she came across as likeable, and a mother weeping for her child never failed to make an impression.

The prosecutor was first to cross-examine her. Kordian took that time to rearrange his notes so he had only the last page in front of him. He was planning to ask Angelika just a couple of questions, purely as a formality. His problem would come later. The closing speech was always a great unknown. It was difficult to imagine what Aronowicz would come up with, and even more difficult to predict how he himself would perform. It was, in short, the most stressful part of the whole trial.

He took a deep breath and tried to focus on what the prosecutor was saying. Aronowicz was going over things they'd already established, simply trying to put them into different words. He was chasing his tail, and that gave Kordian a degree of confidence.

'The defence has argued that Sakrat Tatarnikov vanished because he had something to do with the disappearance of your daughter. Do you think that's likely?'

Angelika didn't reply. Kordian had been prepared for the question, just as he'd been prepared for Angelika's silence. When they'd last spoken, Angelika was still adamant that Sakrat had nothing to do with Nikola's abduction.

'Please answer the question,' said the presiding judge, sounding bored.

Angelika lowered her head. She no longer had the energy she'd had at the start of the trial; she was a shadow of her former self, seemingly resigned to her fate. The accident had only made her worse.

'No, Your Honour,' she said. 'I am certain that Sakrat Tatarnikov had nothing to do with my daughter's disappearance.'

'How can you be so sure?' asked Aronowicz.

'A woman always knows.'

The prosecutor pursed his lips, and folded his arms across his chest. He was beginning to lose control not only of the case, but of his body language, and it didn't look good.

'You wouldn't be the first woman to be deceived by a man.'

'No, probably not,' answered Angelika quietly.

'And as you know, everyone who has ever been betrayed says they never expected it from their partner.'

'I'm sure that's true too, in the majority of cases.'

Aronowicz unfolded his arms and frowned. 'You're a sensible person,' he said. 'Why are you so sure Sakrat didn't do this? After all, if he's the prime suspect, that can only work in your favour.'

Angelika was silent.

'Do you love him?'

Kordian looked pleadingly at the presiding judge, silently begging him to stop. This was embarrassing. But the judge didn't flinch.

'I don't know why that should be important,' answered Angelika faintly, her voice breaking and her eyes filling with tears. Oryński realised he'd misread the situation. Actually, the longer this farce went on, the better it would be for him.

'Believe me, it's very important.'

'Mr Aronowicz,' said one of the other judges. 'Is there a point to this?'

'There certainly is, and without a reply I can't—'

'Yes, I love him,' Angelika interrupted, looking at her husband. Something inside her snapped. She hid her face in her hands and began to weep silently, which, Oryński thought, was the perfect prelude to what he was about to do. He planned to get up, tell Angelika he had no questions for her, and then help her to her seat.

Chyłka had taught him well.

The prosecutor leaned against the bench as he waited for Angelika to stop crying. He looked as if he'd like nothing better than to bolt from the room before the closing speeches. Kordian sent him a wry smile.

The court sat in silence, the presiding judge shifting uncomfortably in his chair.

'Mrs Szlezyngier,' he began.

Angelika lowered her hands so everyone could see her tear-stained face. Her emotions were beginning to get the better of her, and she looked like she might shatter. Her face was contorted with pain, as if someone was stabbing a knife into her flesh. She gave a howling sob and lowered her head.

'I'm sorry, my God, I'm so sorry,' she began to wail. Kordian felt uneasy.

'May God forgive me. I beg of you . . .'

Oryński turned and looked anxiously at McVay, who was clearly also uncomfortable.

'I'm sorry . . .'

The prosecutor straightened up. This time it was his turn to smile at Kordian. It was like being stabbed in the back with a dagger.

'Sakrat didn't do it,' she said through a storm of tears. 'I'm so sorry. Nikola is his daughter.'

She hid her face in her hands again, while Kordian looked at Awit in horror. Awit was as shocked as his lawyer was, and looked as though he'd like to get up and rush over to his wife.

'He . . . I . . .'

'Take your time,' said the prosecutor.

Oryński glared at him, and realised it had all been play-acting. Everything he'd looked on earlier as a sign of defeat had been a smokescreen.

'She's his daughter. His daughter . . .' Angelika repeated over and over. Aronowicz waited a moment.

'Are you sure?' he asked.

'Yes, I took a DNA test, to rule out . . . to rule out Awit.'

Awit opened his mouth to say something, but froze. It was all collapsing like a house of cards. Kordian looked to his client, surprised to find all he could summon up was rage.

'Awit . . . found out.'

Oryński felt a shiver run down his spine.

'He found out that night, the night of the argument. I told him everything.'

The prosecutor looked at Szlezyngier as only a prosecutor can.

'And what did your husband do?'

'He killed my child,' stammered Angelika through her tears.

Kordian thought he was going to faint.

Part 3

1

The judge responded instantly to Angelika's confession. He informed her of her right not to incriminate family members, instructed her that either she or Awit should terminate their agreement with their defence team, and promptly adjourned the hearing.

Chyłka saw it all on NSI, and couldn't believe her eyes. When Kordian came to the hospital the next day, she forced a slight smile. He had dark shadows under his eyes and tiredness written all over his face. She doubted he had slept at all. Although she probably looked a lot worse herself.

He pulled up a chair and sat beside the bed.

'What a piece of shit,' she said quietly.

'And I had such a brilliant closing speech lined up,' he countered.

'I bet it was rubbish.'

He tilted his head to the side. 'I see that despite your close call with death, you're as insightful as ever.'

'Of course,' she rasped.

She was trying to put on a game face, but the truth was, she could hardly utter another word. Kordian looked at her with concern, and she realised she hadn't managed to camouflage her condition.

'Magda said that—'

'Magdalena.'

'Sorry, I mean Magdalena,' Oryński corrected himself. 'She said you drifted off right after Angelika made her tearful confession.'

'She was right.'

'So you don't know which of our clients has renounced our services?'

'No.'

'Guess.'

'Sod off, Zordon.'

He raised his hands in a helpless gesture and smiled.

'Angelika,' he said. 'She told me as soon as the trial was adjourned that she no longer wished to use the services of Żelazny & McVay.'

'What a bi—'

'Quite.'

For a moment Chyłka struggled to swallow, but eventually she managed, although she must have moved in the process and now had a sharp pain in her chest.

'So who did she hire?'

'Kosmowski.'

'That dickhead? But . . .'

'When you ended up in hospital, he was supposed to take over the case,' Kordian began to explain.

Joanna nodded, but quickly regretted it, as she did any movement.

'As you know, he didn't get it, thanks to the signed authorisation you'd prepared just in case and kept in your desk drawer.'

'The what?' she began. And then it dawned on her. 'I see.'

'Your prescience is to be marvelled at.'

'It's the way I was born.'

'So Daniel Kosmowski had to kiss the case goodbye,' continued Oryński, 'and, according to Kormak, he was really cross it had all happened because of a trainee. He threatened to leave the firm and so on.'

'He must have done more than threaten.'

'Well, yes. He left.'

For Joanna, it was a matter of logic. Kosmowski would never have been permitted to defend someone who had incriminated another of the firm's clients. There would be a conflict of interest – and in this case, it was hardly a euphemism.

'But I'll advise Awit,' said Kordian.

'Quite right.'

'And I'll keep in constant contact with base,' he added, patting his ear. 'I'll give you an earpiece too, and you can keep me going with words of encouragement and support.'

'Over my dead body.'

'OK then, with knowledge and experience.'

'Much more likely.'

'But only if you're strong enough to talk,' he warned. 'Because at the moment you look like death warmed up.'

She raised her hand to wave the subject away, but could scarcely lift it off the covers, and it fell straight down again – right on top of Oryński's own hand. He looked at her, but didn't pull away. Neither did she, telling herself she didn't have the strength.

'So what do we know?' she forced herself to say.

'Not much. The judge adjourned the hearing before Angelika got going properly. She says she's got a paternity test that proves Awit's not the father, but the experts are doing their own tests. Then we have to bear in mind that Angelika's got some neat little story about how Szlezyngier killed the girl and removed the body without triggering the alarm.'

'A story.'

Kordian looked at her reproachfully. A discussion about whether or not Angelika was telling the truth was probably the last thing he wanted. Joanna was inclined to think she was. It would explain a lot, not least the furious row when she told Awit about her affair. The fact that Nikola wasn't his child might have been the last straw, and Szlezyngier might well have snapped. Then maybe he hadn't removed the body straight away, but waited until morning, and done so after turning off the alarm but before calling the police.

The only sticking point was why Angelika had said nothing about it before. Had the car accident and her own brush with death changed something? Or was the wound now so deep she couldn't stem the bleeding anymore? Either way, it looked as if Chyłka and Kordian would be defending the guilty party.

There was just one thing Chyłka couldn't fathom: where had Szlezyngier hidden the body?

'What does Awit say?' she asked.

'Not much.'

'Is he doing a Langer?'

'No, not that bad,' smiled Oryński. 'But he told me straight off that if I even entertain the fact that he might have killed Nikola, he'll fire me.'

'OK . . .'

'He sounded convincing,' Kordian added, 'but right now I don't know what to think.'

'Nothing.'

The young man raised his eyebrows. 'The less you say, the more eloquent you seem.'

'I'd say try it yourself, but I think you're beyond help . . .'

'Save your strength now,' he said, frowning, and withdrew his hand. They both pretended there had been no physical contact.

What Joanna needed was peace and quiet. Suddenly, she sniffed.

'Zordon.'

'Yes?'

She glared at him. 'You miserable, low-down, ugly—'

Oryński leaped up, but it was too late. Chyłka had smelled his cigarettes. 'Calm down,' he said, 'you don't have to go off the deep end.'

'You've been smoking.' She said it quietly, but it sounded like thunder.

'It was just the one.'

'A likely bloody story.'

'OK then, maybe a few more.'

'How many?'

'Since you've been in here? Oh, I don't know. Maybe a dozen packs or so?' She kept staring. 'OK, maybe a few dozen. I started when I was with the smugglers, and then somehow, I couldn't stop.'

'You've earned my purest form of . . . hatred.'

'No change there then.'

She scowled at him.

'So what do you want me to do next, boss?' he asked.

'Question him. In minute detail.'

'He's not that keen to talk about it, I already told you.'

'Make a deal.'

'A deal? You mean like win him over?'

She murmured her approval. 'Now get out of here,' she said. Kordian raised his hand briefly, bidding her goodbye, and did as he was asked. After so many weeks on her back, Chyłka would have loved to turn onto her side, but there was no way. The arm-raising fiasco made all further attempts at movement inadvisable. Besides, she'd probably burst her stitches.

A piece of twisted metal had penetrated her body, missing her vital organs by centimetres. Mind you, the same distance separated the piece of metal from slamming into the car seat and missing her torso altogether.

She dismissed the thought and tried to focus on the positives. She was still alive when she could easily have been looking at everything from above, a passive participant in life. If that had happened, Zordon would have been finished. The case had become so complicated that it would take Żelazny & McVay's finest legal minds to keep their client from ending up behind bars.

And there was still no sign of the girl.

Maybe this should be considered one of the positives, because if it were otherwise, the prosecution would have material evidence of Szlezyngier's guilt in the form of a child's body, a child Awit had for years believed to be his own.

2

Kordian returned to the guest house, where the owners were ready to give him a record-breaking discount. They'd already earned a fortune from Żelazny & McVay, but it was a kind gesture. And now Awit was also staying there. He'd moved in straight after the hearing, refusing to spend a moment longer under the same roof as 'that lying bitch'. Oryński found him downstairs in the bar. It was only late afternoon, but Awit had already drunk so much he'd lost track. He looked belligerently at the barman.

'Another,' he said, pointing to the bottle of vodka behind the counter.

'You've had enough.'

'I said, give me another.'

The barman looked pleadingly at Kordian, who sat down beside his client and nodded discreetly.

'Just one more shot,' he said to the barman.

'OK. But this is the last one.'

'And I'll have a beer,' Kordian added.

They took their drinks, and Kordian observed Szlezyngier for a while, waiting for him to acknowledge his presence in some way. It didn't happen, so he had to make the first move himself. He needed to be extremely cautious – in Awit's place he would have unceremoniously sacked any lawyer who'd let it come to this, even though it wasn't their fault. Someone always had to be the scapegoat, and in this instance, Oryński was the perfect candidate.

'Awit,' he began.

'I'm not going to go over and over the same thing,' he said, scarcely slurring, as if his marathon alcohol session had only just started. The only thing giving him away was his glassy stare. Mind you, that might not have been the vodka.

'I realise that,' said the lawyer. 'And that's not what I want either. I just need a bit of information.'

Szlezyngier snorted.

'You're joking,' he said. 'You've had nothing but the truth from me. I've got nothing more to add.' He downed his shot in one, then instead of setting the glass down on the counter, he started turning it over and over in his hand. 'What more can I tell you? I don't know any more. My daughter's missing, my wife's setting me up . . . What the fuck do you want me to do?'

He slammed the glass against the counter, making the barman jump.

'I've got to get my head around this somehow,' said Oryński.

'So do I, even more so.'

'Why did Angelika change her story?'

Awit glanced at the waiters, but Kordian waved his hand. Any rumours started as a result of their conversation would work in their favour.

'She must have made some deal with the prosecution, mustn't she?' said Szlezyngier, looking down.

'Did she say or do anything to make you think that?'

'No . . . no, I don't think so. She's been a bit sharp since the accident, maybe she was before as well, but damn it, our child's missing.'

'Do you think she could have abducted her?'

Awit snorted and leaned back.

'No,' he said. 'Although right now I'd be glad if she had.'

'How can you be so sure?'

'Because we spent the night together in the same room.'

'She could have crept out while you were asleep.'

'You think? And disarmed the alarm without the system noticing?'

He was right. He and Angelika had the same alibi. For her, it was worth its weight in gold. For him, it was of little use. With all the allegations against him, the alarm was almost irrelevant.

'We'll have to go through it again, step by step.'

Awit looked longingly at the barman, who pretended not to notice, instead busying himself with drying a tankard.

'Did you hear me?'

'I know, I know.' Awit was already slightly calmer. 'But you know as much as I do.'

'You might have missed something. Let's go through everything you did that day, every little detail. We might discover something.'

Szlezyngier reached for Kordian's beer and took a sip before Oryński could stop him. He gave the glass back.

'Keep it,' said Kordian.

Awit smiled his thanks. 'What about the Belarusian connection?' he asked after another sip.

The Belarusian connection would have been good – very good even – if Kordian could assume his client wasn't guilty and Sakrat Tatarnikov had taken the child. But now he wasn't so sure. Finding Sakrat could turn out to be the final nail in Szlezyngier's coffin. Awit probably realised that finding him would be bordering on the miraculous; perhaps that was why he was so keen to suggest it.

'I'll carry on looking,' Kordian assured him.

'Is there any chance at all?'

'Not much of one, I'm afraid. The way it works in Poland is that Żelazny & McVay have contacts, and sometimes a friendly investigator will help us. It's a different matter in Belarus, where only money talks.'

'I've got money.'

'I know.'

Szlezyngier turned to Kordian. 'I'm happy to put all my money on the line if it'll help find Nikola.'

Kordian nodded. He wasn't surprised. And if Awit was prepared to spend a small fortune to find the man he believed had kidnapped his child, it would be a strong argument in his favour when it came to court. The more he spent, the better it could be for him. It probably wouldn't influence the judges much, but the jury would be impressed.

Oryński left his client in the bar, telling the barman not to skimp on alcohol for his client.

Awit could do with a hard reset.

He went back to his room, picked up a book and tried not to think about what he was mixed up in. Twenty-four hours ago it had all seemed quite promising. Now it was collapsing about his ears.

He read a few dozen pages of Follett's latest blockbuster without taking any of it in, then put the book down and reached for his phone. He rang McVay, who had packed his things shortly after the hearing and gone to Kraków.

'Not a good idea,' said McVay in place of a greeting.

'I'm sorry?' said the young man.

'You're ringing to say you want to talk to the prosecutor.'

Oryński said nothing, but it spoke volumes.

'Don't do it now,' McVay continued. 'Wait until emotions have subsided. At the moment Aronowicz thinks he's lord and master.'

'True.'

It was telling that McVay hadn't dismissed the idea out of hand – he must have realised how difficult it would be to wring something out of this new line of defence.

'As far as the public are concerned, Awit's toast,' the Englishman continued. 'He was the one behind bars while Angelika remained free, and now things look even worse for him. It'll be hard to get past that.'

Kordian was grateful that his boss understood, and was even helping him justify what could be seen as giving up.

'How much do you think I'd get with a deal?' he asked.

'Not much.'

'Ten years?'

'More like fifteen, if everything keeps going the way it is now. Is Awit any help?'

'Not really. He says he's told us all he knows.'

'What about that Belarusian?'

'We're going to keep looking for him.'

'Across the border?' McVay was surprised. 'That's probably an even worse idea than making a deal with the prosecution.'

'I'll get the right people on it.'

Harry was silent, possibly remembering a witness who, at one particular trial, had amassed an unprecedented number of penalties for obstruction and contempt of court.

'You do realise this has to be handled . . . skilfully?'

'I do.'

'Then all that remains is for me to wish you luck.'

'Thank you.'

'And let's hope Chyłka gets out of hospital as soon as possible.'

They said their goodbyes, and Oryński stretched out in the tiny armchair. He knew exactly what McVay meant when he said it had to be handled 'skilfully' – that if Wito agreed to look for Tatarnikov, he'd also have to agree to keep quiet if it turned out he hadn't abducted the girl. It was risky, but Kordian was out of other ideas.

He rang Wito, and they arranged to meet the following day. Oryński assured him this would be his chance to make some proper money, and if all went well, to kick the prosecution where it hurt. Wito agreed readily.

He was just surprised that Kordian wanted to meet at the hospital.

3

Other than Kordian and his new sidekick, Chyłka wasn't expecting any visitors that day. Magdalena and her husband had gone back to Warsaw and McVay to Kraków, and she anticipated a peaceful day. How wrong she was. As soon as visiting hours started, there was a rap at the door. Not many people Joanna knew would bother to knock before coming in, so she prepared herself for the worst.

At the door stood a slender man in a tight-fitting jacket and narrow trousers, sporting hair shaved on both sides and a long fringe, which he constantly flicked to the side.

'The Cristiano Ronaldo of the Polish legal system,' she said in greeting.

She felt a little stronger than yesterday. She still couldn't get up on her own, but felt able to have a longer conversation. And today, she'd definitely find the strength to pull her hand away if it fell onto Oryński's.

'Nice to see you're in good spirits,' said Daniel Kosmowski, looking around for a chair.

'Get out.'

'Don't you want to hear what I have to say?' he asked.

'I don't talk to corporate lackeys. Or to traitors.'

'Traitors?' He laughed. 'It was Żelazny who stabbed me in the back, Chyłka. He turned his back on me at what could have been the pinnacle of my career. This case could have made me. My name would have been known nationwide. Or we could have played as a team, I'm sure we'd have had plenty to bring to the table.'

She knew he was doing it on purpose. To her, corporate speak was like a red rag to a bull.

He pulled up a chair, sat down, stretched out his legs and crossed them at the ankle. Chyłka glared.

'Look at you sitting there like butter wouldn't melt.'

He shrugged.

'Well you're lying there like a vegetable, so I guess of the two evils . . .'

'Why don't you just fuck off,' she said.

He hadn't been prepared for her bluntness, and it silenced him for a moment. But then he shifted in his chair and cleared his throat.

'I'm here to save you from being humiliated,' he announced. 'Try to focus on—'

'Fuck off.'

He rubbed his temples and tried to ignore her words, but in the end it was Joanna's glare that finished him. He got up, adjusted his lapels and sauntered towards the door.

'My client described to me in detail what happened,' he said on his way out. 'It was an accident.'

Daniel stopped at the door, but Chyłka said nothing.

'Did you hear me?' he asked. 'Your boyfriend fucked up big time.'

'Bullshit.'

'It's not,' he said with a smile and turned around. 'Angelika told her husband everything that night. Apparently he got really angry, and started yelling and waving his arms around. And then he threatened her. She picked the girl up, fearing for her child as well as herself. The argument escalated into a fight, Awit shoved his wife, and she dropped the child.'

Joanna listened with growing interest. Not because she wanted to know what had happened, but because she wanted to know why Kosmowski was telling her.

'The girl fell on her head,' he went on, his tone completely dispassionate, although it was clear he wanted to trigger some sort of emotion in her. 'I don't expect it takes much for a three-year-old to suffer a fatal injury. They both tried to revive her, but to no avail.'

'And?'

'There was no silver bullet. They needed to get all their ducks in a row,' said Daniel, returning to his chair. 'Angelika wanted to call the ambulance ASAP, but Awit kept his cool. He knew the child was dead, and that he'd be charged with her murder. He snatched away Angelika's phone, and tried to talk some sense into her. She was in shock, and was easily manipulated.'

Joanna shifted nervously on the bed, and felt a searing pain in her ribcage.

'Szlezyngier told her if she went to the police, they'd both end up in prison – she'd been the one to drop the child, after all. And he managed to convince her. He removed the body from the house and told her to clean up. When he got back some time later, he set the alarm so they'd both have an alibi.'

Kosmowski looked at Chyłka expectantly, but she remained silent.

'Haven't you got anything to say?' he asked.

'No, I'm waiting for you to finish.'

'That's it. I'm done.'

'What about the rod they found by the lake?'

'She planted it there, and she's prepared to admit that,' he explained. 'She knew Nikola had hurt herself in the workshop, and she hoped that this way, she'd focus the police's attention on her husband.'

'She could have told them the truth.'

'No,' he replied, shaking his head. 'She didn't know what to do. And when she finally came to her senses and realised she had to face the truth, she had no idea how to go about it. Then you had the accident, and everything changed.'

'And you came along.'

'What?'

'You didn't suddenly pop up out of nowhere.'

'Maybe not,' he said with a smile.

Clearly, to Chyłka at least, when Daniel Kosmowski had left Żelazny & McVay, he'd tried to poach the clients who'd been whisked away from under his nose. He'd realised they probably wouldn't agree to change their defence team at this stage, so the best way forward was for him to set them against each other.

'I reached out to Angelika,' he said. 'If she hadn't taken me on, I'd have contacted Szlezyngier. 'You know how it is. Co-defendants always start slinging mud at one another in the end.'

'True.'

Kosmowski hooked his hands over the back of his chair. Joanna thought his ribs would pop out through his jacket.

'She was lucky I got in touch,' he said. 'If I hadn't, she'd still be living a toxic lie.'

Chyłka waited for Kosmowski to tell her more. When he didn't speak, she knew she'd learn nothing else from him. It was time for her to regain the initiative. Normally it wouldn't faze her, but here, confined to bed, she felt weak both physically and mentally.

'What is it you want?' she asked. 'Because I'm going to assert manslaughter. With your client as an accessory.'

'Really? Why would she drop her child deliberately?'

'To get rid of the problem.'

'What problem?' he smiled. 'When it all came to light, she'd have perfect grounds for divorce.'

'They have separation of assets.'

'So?'

'So it's not even his child. She wouldn't stand to gain much.'

Kosmowski laughed. It wasn't a particularly strong argument, Joanna knew that. She swallowed, and glanced towards the door. For the first time, she hoped another lawyer would show up to support her. Kordian said he'd be here early, but they hadn't agreed a time.

'There's no way you can prove she was complicit,' said Kosmowski. 'Awit killed that child.'

'Unintentionally.'

Suddenly, Kosmowski grew serious. His face hardened.

'I'm prepared to tell my client to say all of this in court.'

'What?'

'Angelika will repeat everything I've told you in court, if you just . . .'

'You bastard.'

'. . . If you just get on board with certain conditions,' he finished. 'Because if you don't, I'll tell her to say that her husband was furious, and how he threatened to kill that "fucking bastard-child". I'm quoting Mr Szlezyngier, of course.'

Chyłka shook her head, and quickly regretted it.

'Angelika's not going to lie on the stand.'

'Of course she's not. She's going to tell the truth.'

There was no point getting into a moral tussle with Kosmowski, thought Chyłka. The truth was, in his shoes she'd have looked to crush her opponent too.

'You're pretty confident for a poof,' she said.

'Spare me the insults.'

'It's not an insult, more of a compliment.'

He got up, and put the chair back where it came from.

'But, Mr Corporate Flunky, there's one thing you're not aware of.'

'Really? And what's that?'

'That I can destroy Angelika as easily as you can destroy Awit. You mess with him, I'll mess with her.'

'Ooh, are you throwing down a gauntlet?'

Joanna rolled her eyes. 'I can charge her under Article 239.'

'Obstructing or impeding criminal proceedings?' said Daniel. 'Sure, I'd go for that too – if I was desperate. What would she get? Three months to five years? It would probably be suspended anyway.'

'Let's wait and see, shall we?'

Kosmowski smiled and turned towards the door. 'We both know that's what would happen. After all, she's a poor, wronged woman, whose child died before her very eyes, who'd been intimidated, and was terrified of what her deranged, powerful husband might do to her. It won't help you much.'

He was already in the corridor when she spoke:

'So what do you suggest?'

'Let's wait and see, shall we?' And with that, he disappeared.

4

Chyłka let loose at Kordian as soon as he was in the room, as if the other man wasn't there at all.

'Where the hell have you been?'

'I see you're feeling bet—'

'I feel as if I've been dumped on from a great height,' she hissed, 'and that all the shit should be on your shoulders.'

Kordian and Wito exchanged bemused glances.

'Not bad,' said Wito. 'You were right.'

'Right about what?' asked Joanna sharply.

'He said you were unusually . . .' began Wito, then stopped.

'What did you tell him?'

'That you were unusually endearing.'

'Sit down, Zordon,' ordered Chyłka. 'And you, go and find something to do in the cafeteria.'

'Like what?' snorted Wito.

'Like getting something to eat. Oryński's treat.'

Wito looked at Kordian, who nodded. Alone with Joanna, Kordian sat down on the bed, noting she'd already withdrawn her hand.

She began to recount her conversation with Kosmowski, agitated at first, but growing gradually calmer, until she got to the moment he was leaving the room. Then she flared up. Oryński cursed himself for not arriving earlier. He should have been here at the crack of dawn.

'I'll tell them not to let him in again.'

'Don't do that,' she said. 'It taught us a lot.'

'Including that we're even more screwed than we thought?'

'Not really.'

Kordian shook his head – he wasn't in the mood for false optimism. He was fully aware of what drove the majority of court verdicts, and not just in criminal cases. Sentencing a defendant mainly on the basis of witness testimony was repeatedly condemned both by judges and legal theorists, but in practice it remained the most significant form of evidence: the bulk of cases still came down to the fact that someone had said something to someone else. It was one of the greatest flaws in the criminal justice system, and had existed since Ancient Rome. So far, no ideal solution had been found.

'She's going to drop him in it,' said Kordian.

'Only for manslaughter.'

'It doesn't matter, Awit will still go to prison.'

'But not for twenty-five years.'

For the first time, Kordian saw Joanna ready to give up. She'd always been prepared to tackle tricky situations head-on; she set out to win every case, no matter how hopeless. But now she was looking at meeting the prosecution in the middle – which for her, would normally spell defeat.

He looked at her carefully. She seemed beaten. The accident, then the coma, had changed things, and work was probably no longer the most important part of her life.

Then it occurred to him that while Chyłka had changed, Kosmowski shouldn't have, and for him too, compromise was usually synonymous with personal failure.

'Why did he come here?' asked Kordian, frowning.

'He wanted to see with his own eyes how the mighty have fallen.'

'I'm serious.'

'So am I. It's not often a colossus topples.'

Kordian got up, walked across to the other side of the bed and gazed out of the window. Then, leaning on the windowsill, he turned around.

'He's got us by the short and curlies,' he said. 'So why come up with a deal at all?'

'Maybe he's worried that if we go too hard on Angelika, the old cow will let something slip.'

'Like what?'

'No idea. And from our point of view, it doesn't matter.'

'Suppose Szlezyngier didn't do it?'

Joanna laughed. Within a fraction of a second, her cheerfulness gave way to pain. She hunched up and glared at him.

'Just stop it,' she said.

'I'm not saying I believe him . . .'

'You always believe them, Zordon. And until you realise that it's your biggest mistake, you'll never make the defence lawyer super league.'

He perched on the windowsill. 'Really, why do you think Kosmowski came here?'

Chyłka took a deep breath. 'Awit will be called as a witness in the trial against Angelika,' she said. 'If we don't reach some sort of agreement, he'll do whatever he can to get revenge on his wife. Isn't it obvious?'

'Possibly. But it's still not enough for Daniel to come looking for a compromise.'

'That's just you being naïve,' she said. 'You're still deluded enough to think you're defending an innocent man.'

The look she gave him brooked no argument. If she'd looked that confident when Kosmowski was here, things might have turned out differently. They couldn't count on miracles, but

Chyłka had shown in the past that she could achieve the impossible.

'I'm glad we've got that settled,' she said.

'We haven't.'

'And now tell me why you brought that lowlife to see me,' she said, ignoring him.

'He's prepared to go to Belarus for us.'

'For us?'

'Well, for a few thousand.'

'That's coming out of your pay.'

'If it does, I'll have to stay at your place for a good six months. And live at your expense.'

'In that case, I'll pay him.'

He gave a wry smile.

'Has he got a visa?' asked Joanna.

'I doubt it, but he wouldn't need one anyway. He'll cross at a place where there aren't any border guards.'

'Will he find him?'

'I don't know,' said Kordian, looking over his shoulder. 'If you hadn't booted him out, he'd have been able to tell you himself what the chances are.'

'I didn't boot him out, I invited him to leave. You've clearly never seen me boot anyone out.'

'Oh, but I have,' he assured her. 'I remember as if it were yesterday. My first day at Żelazny & McVay, and you, my new supervisor, told me to f—'

'Stop, I'm not in the mood.'

Oryński walked from the window to the bed.

'So give me my orders,' he said.

'Send that guy to look for Sakrat, if he really thinks he can find him.'

'Don't you want to ask him yourself?'

'We're not in court, we're in a sodding hospital,' she reminded him. 'I'm not about to question anyone.'

'OK,' he said, looking towards the door. 'And then what?'

'Then find out if Kosmowski has already made a deal with Aronowicz.'

'How?'

'Go to Aronowicz yourself.'

Despite McVay's advice not to speak to the prosecutor for the moment, Kordian realised he wouldn't get away without it. That would be his half of the job, he thought, while Chyłka dealt with Daniel Kosmowski.

He was wrong.

'You can also represent us in our dealings with . . . whichever law firm Cristiano Ronaldo works for.'

'What?'

'I haven't got the strength to deal with the howling mob, Zordon. I need a bit of peace.'

He thought she might be winding him up, but she was deadly serious. It probably wasn't her wisest move: he might have been a full-blown hot-shot in court, but outside the courtroom he was like a chicken let loose among foxes. People like Kosmowski knew plenty of ways to tear their opponents apart, not all of them legal, and that wasn't something Kordian had learned in law school.

'You'll be fine,' she said, as if she sensed his concern. But he wasn't going to protest. If that was what she wanted, she must have her reasons.

'We'll be in touch. Just buy those Bluetooth earbuds, OK?'

'Will do.'

Joanna sighed. 'I'm not getting out of here any time soon, Zordon,' she said. 'You'll have to manage somehow.'

He gave her a smile she didn't see, then said goodbye and walked out. He didn't do too badly in court last time, he thought, except that that had been like a sprinter running the four hundred metres. This would be like taking on an ultramarathon without knowing the route, and with no preparation.

He left the hospital, lit a cigarette and texted Wito: *I'm downstairs*. Wito came to join him. He stretched out his hand and Kordian passed him the Marlboros.

'That was her? Your wannabe fuck-buddy?' said Wito. Oryński looked at him as if he were a lunatic.

'Don't you dare speak like that about Chyłka!'

'What the fuck are you talking about?'

'If she heard you, she'd kill you. A slow, painful death.'

Wito took a pull on his cigarette, somewhat nonplussed. 'Not a bad piece of ass, I'll give her that. Even without make-up. But it's true what they say. The pretty ones are mean, the smart ones are—'

'Shut up. Just shut up.'

'Why are you being such a dick?'

Oryński rubbed his temples, holding his cigarette between his fingers. He wasn't getting involved in any inane discussions. All he wanted was to sort things with Wito, then set off for Suwałki and get his meeting with Aronowicz over with as soon as possible.

'Right, here's the deal,' he began. 'Nine thousand for information leading to her—'

'Fifteen.'

'Eleven.'

'Thirteen.'

'Done,' said Oryński. 'Thirteen thousand for the name of the place where Sakrat's hiding. Including photographs. And bringing him back to Poland, if need be.'

'Are you joking?'

'Well what do you want me to do, send out a European arrest warrant?'

'A what?'

'They're only valid in the EU anyway.'

'I've got no idea what you're talking about, but I won't be able to get some guy out of Belarus just like that. We talked about finding him, that's all.'

'Well that's you thirteen thousand down then,' said Oryński, flinging his cigarette to the ground. And without even stubbing it out, he strode off to the bus stop. It would have been infinitely more impressive if he'd had a car in which he could nonchalantly drive away – somehow waiting for a bus didn't have the same dramatic impact.

'OK!' came a voice from behind him.

He grinned triumphantly, then checked when the bus was leaving: 1.20 p.m. Excellent, just a few minutes to wait.

He changed buses in Grajewo, and arrived in Suwałki two hours later, deciding it was high time he invested in a car.

Some time earlier, he'd been to the police compound to see Chyłka's beloved X5. The front had been crushed in the accident, and the officer on duty told him it was a write-off. Nobody had told Chyłka the bad news yet, and Kordian rather hoped she'd figure it out for herself.

As he climbed out of the ageing bus, aptly named Rameses, he felt as if he'd been born again. He stretched out his back and set off towards the dual carriageway behind the station building, stopping to ask a passer-by the way to the prosecutor's office. The man looked bewildered and hurried away, so Kordian threw himself on the mercy of Google Maps. Apparently it was only a twenty-minute walk, so that's what he decided to do.

On arrival, he asked for Aronowicz, and was met with at best reserve, at worst rudeness.

The prosecutor received him in his office.

'Welcome, welcome,' he greeted him. 'I see Mohammed has come to the mountain without even checking to see whether the mountain would be willing to come to him.' He gestured to the chair. 'Please, take the weight off.'

Kordian didn't like his overfriendly tone – like a tiger wearing a tutu.

'I was passing,' said Oryński, settling himself by the desk.

The office was neat and tidy, but the décor wasn't something you'd want to see every day. It was all a bit austere, and made him think of an army barracks.

'Don't you like it?' asked Zbigniew, noticing the young man looking around. 'It's a bit gloomy, I grant you, but that's deliberate, to put prosecutors in the right frame of mind. Personally, I prefer it to the bland minimalism you find in lawyers' offices.'

'You could be right.'

Aronowicz slid the desk drawer shut, as if closing the case he'd been working on. Then he looked up, folded his arms and smiled.

'So you were passing?'

'Uh-huh.'

'Well that's strange, because I was sure you'd been to see Chyłka this morning. I hear she's feeling better, although she's lost some of her sparkle.'

Kordian laughed at this none-too-subtle way of telling him he was in close touch with Angelika's lawyer. Although he'd never admit it, so there was no point trying to make him.

'Something amusing you?'

'You. You're so cloak-and-dagger.' He waved his hand. 'But not to worry. I've come for one reason and one reason only, and I won't be spending any longer here than absolutely necessary.'

'I see.'

Aronowicz clearly wasn't going to make it easy for him. Good, at least the ball was squarely in his court, and as any negotiation guru would tell you, the initial proposal was the most important. It was like casting an anchor which would be tricky to move later. And as long as the offer was reasonable, the other side would feel psychologically reluctant to overturn it.

Kordian could have been bombastic, claiming only a full acquittal would do, but they both knew it would never happen.

'So?' said Zbigniew Aronowicz. 'What have you got for me?'

'One year. Suspended for three.'

'One hundred and fifty-five?'

Oryński nodded. For an out-of-court settlement, manslaughter was their best bet. Szlezyngier's reputation would be in tatters, but at least he wouldn't go to prison – and that was something they couldn't guarantee if the case went to court.

'You're kidding,' said Aronowicz, unfolding his arms and drumming his fingers on the table. 'You can do better than that.'

'It's a perfectly reasonable proposal.'

'Not from my point of view.'

'What's the alternative?' asked Oryński. 'It'll be his word against hers, and we'll be able to show our client had nothing to do with dropping the child.'

'It won't work, and you know it,' said the prosecutor, taking a deep breath. 'Now, let's drop the formalities. My name is Zbigniew, and may I call you Kordian? That way it'll be easier for you to deal with when you lose.'

Oryński snorted. 'OK,' he said, not best pleased. Zbigniew had failed to present a counter-offer, which put him in a difficult position. Now he'd be the one to reset the threshold. The anchor was shifting. 'Two years suspended for five. That's my final offer.'

Aronowicz sighed.

'You do know, don't you, if it's manslaughter I can call for up to five years in jail?'

'I do.'

'Then you must also know that if the sentence exceeds two years, there's no such thing as conditional suspension.'

'I didn't come here for a lecture.'

'Looks like you need one,' said the prosecutor, more sharply this time. 'Your proposal is an insult, firstly because you assume that I accept the manslaughter charge, and secondly, because you think I'd choose the lowest possible penalty.'

Kordian swore to himself.

'Also, I think it wouldn't be fair,' Aronowicz continued. 'Your client saw his opportunity and knowingly knocked the child from her mother's arms.'

'If this is some sort of joke . . .'

'He murdered her, Kordian. And the mother's testimony will prove it. Besides, your client plainly said that if she wasn't his child, he would kill her.'

'That's rubbish.'

'I'll be accusing him of murder. Aggravated murder at that.'

'What?'

'Paragraph 2.3.'

Kordian knew very few of the provisions by heart, but everyone knew Article 148 – and not just experts in criminal law. It applied when the motivation behind the crime made it more severe than 'standard' murder, and incurred a harsher penalty. The minimum was twelve years in prison, the maximum, life.

'But that's complete nonsense,' said Kordian. 'You'll never get it through.'

'Let's see, shall we?'

They sat for a moment in silence. Eventually Oryński decided there was nothing more he could do here; it had been a fool's errand. He rose, and without another word, headed for the door.

'Don't you want to know what I'm willing to offer you?'

'No.'

'If he pleads guilty, I'll downgrade it to simple murder.'

Kordian didn't want to listen to any more. He left the office and hurried along the corridor, convinced all the prosecution staff were looking and pointing. Once outside, he pulled out a cigarette. He smoked mindlessly, not even realising when he was down to the filter. He didn't want to think about anything, least of all his own failure.

The prosecution had a strong hand and they knew it, while the defence had nothing that could shift the balance of power. Oryński lit another cigarette from the stub of the previous one, wondering where to go next. And then it came to him.

He went back to the bus stop the same way he had come, and checked the timetable for the next bus to Augustów.

5

Kordian stood outside police HQ. It was late and there was no guarantee Satanowski would still be in his office, but he decided to go in nevertheless. He stopped at the duty officer's window.

'Is Sergeant Satanowski from Search and Identification still in the building?'

'No.'

The duty officer went back to his newspaper.

'When did he leave? Maybe I could still catch him.'

'A long time ago.'

'Well, perhaps you could—'

'What do you want him for?' the officer interrupted.

'It's about a little girl, and it's a matter of life and death. Is that good enough for you?'

'Thank you, it is,' said the officer, finally tearing himself away from his tabloid. 'There's no one here from his unit at the moment. I can call someone in, but first you need to report the child missing.'

'That was done some time ago.'

'So what is it then?'

'I have new information,' said Oryński, his head almost through the window. 'I have to speak to the sergeant. Can you call him? It's not that late.'

The officer thought for a moment, but decided that the situation was serious, and that no one would laugh at him if he got it wrong. He rang Satanowski, informing him there was a mysterious visitor at the station for him. He hadn't asked for a name, but that didn't surprise Kordian. He must have worked out who he was.

The sergeant turned up twenty minutes later, time Kordian had spent smoking outside the building. Seeing the old Peugeot and the familiar face behind the steering wheel, he raised his hand in greeting.

Satanowski parked in the employees' car park and got out of the car.

'This had better be good,' he said.

'Depends what you mean by good. Where can we talk?'

Satanowski pointed to a dilapidated bus shelter a few metres away. They walked there in silence, and only when they were both sitting on the sagging bench and Kordian had taken out his Marlboros did the sergeant speak.

'You realise this little treat is going to cost you five hundred zlotys,' he said.

'You're joking!'

'No, that's the penalty for smoking at a bus stop.'

Oryński put his cigarettes away.

'Now, what have you got for me?' Satanowski asked.

'Are you following the case?'

Satanowski shook his head, annoyed. Kordian decided to skip any preliminaries and get on with passing over information.

'We've tracked down Sakrat Tatarnikov,' he fibbed, watching the sergeant's reaction. Satanowski twitched visibly, which made Kordian think the police had been searching for him too.

'Where is he?'

'Belarus.'

'I know that much from the hearing. Where exactly?' Oryński shrugged.

'You mean you've dragged me away from dinner with my wife to tell me you know but you won't say?' spat Satanowski. 'Don't play silly games with me, son.'

'I'm not. I'll tell you where he is if you'll help me.'

Satanowski paused for a moment. 'How?' he asked finally.

'It's simple, sergeant,' said Kordian, staring fixedly at the flats opposite. 'You'll get the information you want if you promise to turn it into a media circus.'

'What are you talking about?' said the sergeant, turning to face him.

'I want it made public. All of it.'

'What do you mean, "all of it"?'

'The whole operation,' said Kordian, looking away from the building. 'From the moment you leave here to the moment you catch him. The only condition is that you leak it to the media, so that—'

'So that it'll turn into a witch-hunt, and get a bunch of reasons to show your client's not guilty. No way,' said Satanowski.

'He's not guilty, so—'

'That's not for me to judge. And I won't be seen supporting either party in a criminal trial. Are you completely mad?'

'This wouldn't show support,' said Kordian firmly. 'And if you're still looking for Sakrat, it means you must think that child is out there somewhere.'

'She's still out there all right, no matter who took her or . . . hid her. I have to find her, and that's all I'm interested in. Do you understand?'

'Perfectly,' said Oryński, turning to him. 'But if that's true, there's nothing to stop you grabbing this offer with both hands. I'm not asking for much. And then when you arrest Tatarnikov, it'll clear the whole case up, won't it? You'll help put a dangerous criminal behind bars, and everyone will see my client is innocent.'

The men lapsed into silence. A bus stopped at the stop and the doors opened. No one got off, and it drove away again.

'Give me your number,' said Kordian. 'I'll ring you tomorrow and find out what you've decided.'

'I could charge you with obstruction.'

'I'm not obstructing anything,' said Oryński. 'If there's something I'm not telling you, it's because it comes under client confidentiality.'

'Bullshit.'

'Perhaps, perhaps not. But if you want to know for certain, you'll have to go down the official route.'

After another moment's silence, Satanowski pulled out his phone and they exchanged numbers. Then the officer left, and Kordian stepped away from the bus stop to light his cigarette.

He hadn't achieved much, but at least when he put the police onto Sakrat's trail – maybe falsely, maybe not – he could be sure of media coverage, and that would shape public opinion against Sakrat. Whether it was justified or not was of secondary importance.

Kordian took a deep breath and checked the bus timetable. It was too late to rely on public transport, so he set off towards a nearby roundabout, hoping to at least find out which direction he needed to go in. Suwałki and Ogrodniki were straight on, Lipsk to the right, while turning left would take him to the town centre. He looked for a taxi. There were usually plenty around in high season, taking a constant stream of tourists from Augustów to Sajenko and back. Now they were in short supply.

He considered hitching, but after half an hour nobody had stopped, so he gave up that idea and decided to walk. He even ignored a passing cab, despite the driver sounding his horn. It took him less than an hour and a half to get back to Sajenko, and the exercise did him good.

Back in the village, it was time to put the next part of his plan into action, so he went to visit Stanisław, who had opened Ekiel's house up for them before. Just as before, the dog barked as if someone was skinning it, and the old man shuffled out of the cottage.

'Good evening, Stanisław.'

'Who are you?'

'Kordian Oryński. You know me, this is my third visit.'

'The young lawyer?'

'That's right. I need another favour.' The man squinted and looked around.

'Where's your wife, son?'

'She's not well.'

'Oh dear . . .' Stanisław lowered his head and thought hard for a moment. 'There was something I was going to—'

'I wanted to ask if I could borrow the keys to Antoni Ekiel's house again.'

'Did you now?'

Oryński spread his hands. 'Yes. You owe us a debt of gratitude after all.'

'I don't know what you mean, young man.'

'I can't see any customs officers here, or police, can you?'

The old man frowned and pursed his lips. No one would have been remotely interested in the modest number of contraband cigarettes he had, even if the lawyers had reported him. But the old man stepped inside, rummaged in the cupboard and came back with a key. Kordian climbed the steps to take it from him.

'Thank you,' he said. 'I'll bring it back in a moment.'

And he did. He intended to spend the night at Ekiel's, but didn't want to alarm the old man, so he opened the door, brought the key back and simply returned to the house.

The inside smelled musty and needed airing. Kordian opened windows on opposite sides of the house to create a draught; only then could he breathe properly. The milk in the fridge had gone sour, and other items lay rotting. He shut the fridge door as quickly as possible. He wasn't about to start cleaning; let the new owners do that. Because there was little chance Ekiel would be returning.

Oryński settled into the armchair and turned on the television. He'd meant to search the house as soon as he arrived, but he was too tired. The day's events had left their mark, and he needed a few moments' peace. Plus, the walk back from the centre of Augustów had been exhausting. He'd conduct his search in the morning, by the light of day.

He didn't even notice when he fell asleep, but he woke in the night, and, too tired to move to the sofa, simply changed position.

When dawn broke, Kordian woke properly. He ached all over and cursed his laziness, then dragged himself out of the armchair and went to the kitchen. The juice in the carton had already fermented or whatever juice did, so he put water on to boil to make himself a tea or coffee. Probably his safest bet, given the hostile environment.

He heard his ringtone coming from the living room – Will Smith exhorting everyone to get up and clap their hands – and padded off to get the phone. From the display, he saw it could only be good news.

'What have you got for me?' he asked.

'I'm in Belarus,' said Wito in an Eastern accent.

'And have you found anything interesting?'

'Lukaszenko still has a thick but well-groomed moustache.'

Kordian laughed. 'Right. Besides that? Any sign of Sakrat?'

'That Tatarnikov is a slippery son of a bitch.'

'Right . . .'

'He covers his tracks like a vole underground.'

'Actually, voles don't . . .' began Kordian, then thought better of it. 'Never mind, it doesn't matter. What have you learned?'

'That he's a f—'

'OK,' Kordian cut him off. 'Let's leave out the character assassination for now. Where is he?'

'No idea.'

'Any leads?'

'I did have, and quite a good one. It seems he made friends with a few of our mates at the border, and they helped him and Ekiel cross. He had the nerve to use my name too. He said this would pay better than the cigarettes.'

'And?'

'And he got everything sorted and crossed the border. I tried to follow his tracks.'

Kordian heard shouting in Belarusian in the background. Wito must have moved away from his phone for a moment, because his voice sounded distant.

'Sorry,' he said. 'Some goons mouthing off here.'

'So I heard.'

'We spent the afternoon and the whole night looking for the old dog. And zilch. Nada. Nothing. No trace of him. Until today, that is.'

Kordian was suddenly fully alert. He pressed the phone more firmly to his ear, and even noticed the water had boiled.

'Today I figured out there was no trail because they hadn't crossed the border at all.'

'How come?'

'They just made it look as if they had,' said Wito with a note of triumph in his voice. 'It makes sense, doesn't it? They knew the full force of the law would be after them. Maybe they even thought the pigs would fall for it. Are you keeping up?'

Not only was Oryński keeping up, he was already miles ahead.

'Of course, Sakrat wasn't stupid. Do you get what I'm saying?'

'Uh-huh.'

'Tatarnikov had no reason to go back to Belarus. He's got an unspent conviction, and if he was caught, he'd be better off doing time in Poland.'

'True,' said Kordian.

'So me and the boys turned back to check the trail. And we didn't find shit. There's no way they crossed that border.'

Again Kordian heard shouting, first in Belarusian, then in a language he didn't recognise.

'I have to go,' said Wito. 'But in any case, we've got to look for that bastard in Poland.'

'But where?'

'How am I supposed to know? Maybe he'll go home.' Kordian looked around nervously. Then he looked up. Maybe Ekiel's house had an attic? He dismissed the thought with a shake of his head. Why would the two fugitives come back here?

'Shut the fuck up!' he heard Wito yell.

'Find out what you can.'

'What?'

'Once you've dealt with the . . . er, goons, try and . . .'

'Yes, we'll go back to sniffing around on our side of the border. Right, I'm off.'

He hung up, and Kordian went back to the kitchen. He made both tea and coffee, then stood by the window, contemplating the denseness of the forest. What Wito had told him complicated everything. He'd wanted to give the police something vague, something that would take them off in the wrong direction. Satanowski wouldn't achieve much in Belarus, but the media response would be tremendous, and could help slant the next trial in such a way that Żelazny & McVay had a chance of winning.

Swearing silently, he took his coffee, sat down in front of the TV and switched on NSI. To his horror, he saw he'd picked the worst possible moment. Daniel Kosmowski was outside the Szlezyngiers' summer home, together with Angelika and a host of cameras. And it was a live broadcast.

'My client has been treated in the most appalling way imaginable,' he was saying. 'And when I think about why this might be, I can only see three possibilities.' He held up three fingers. 'Either her defence team were incompetent, or they focused on defending the person paying their bill. And the third reason? Their actions were premeditated, aimed at clearing Szlezyngier at the expense of my client.'

Awit was no longer a husband, or the accused, or even Mr Szlezyngier, and that put a whole new slant on the trial. But it could have been a lot worse, all things considered. Kordian remembered Marek Dochnal, who had been dubbed a lobbyist at one of the most decisive moments in his trial. The description was associated with him to that day. Said in a particular tone of voice and at a particular point in time, it could be considered offensive.

'In a wild rage, Szlezyngier attacked a defenceless woman,' Kosmowski went on, 'but that wasn't his only crime.' He gave Angelika a look so full of sympathy, he could have been about to hug her. 'Because not only did he murder the poor child, he forced my client to keep quiet. And no, he didn't handcuff her, beat her or tie her up: he crushed her, destroying her mentally and taking away what remained of her dignity.'

Angelika looked down.

'We've called this press conference because, despite our best efforts, the accused is refusing to contact us.'

Kordian gritted his teeth in anger. Kosmowski had omitted to mention that Angelika was also accused.

'We'd like to make a public appeal to Szlezyngier,' he added, gazing straight into NSI's camera lens, then shifting to look at each of the other cameras in turn. 'Tell us where you've hidden the girl's body.'

Oryński put his coffee mug on the table and picked up his cigarettes, surprised to find there were any left. At the rate he'd been smoking, they should have run out a long time ago.

'Please end this cruel charade,' Daniel was saying now. 'It's time this family found some peace. Tell us. Tell us what you've done with the body.'

Beside him, Angelika wept quietly.

'Do it for the sake of Nikola's memory. Because remember, you're on your own now. Nobody supports you in your lie. So now that all charges against my client have been dropped, it's time for you to face the truth.'

'What?' breathed Kordian.

6

Chyłka didn't watch Kosmowski's brazen performance live, she only saw the highlights on the evening news. Her daily routine was in total chaos. She'd wake up every so often, then fall back into a deep sleep, only to wake again in the middle of the night. She'd switched on TVN24 hoping the talking heads would bore her to sleep, but instead they gave her a shot of energy more effective than ten coffees.

Kordian appeared first thing in the morning, and she doubted he was getting much sleep either.

'Why didn't you call?' she asked.

'I didn't want to bother you for no reason.'

'For no reason?'

He sat on the bed looking dejected. Joanna tried not to lose her temper, knowing there was little he could have done. The prosecutor, together with Kosmowski, had completely screwed them over. They'd clearly made a deal on the side, now they were doing what they pleased.

'We don't stand a chance at this hearing,' Kordian declared.

'The way things are going, not at the next one either.'

'But . . .'

'Have I ever told you that conducting a trial and counting on it going to appeal is like murdering someone by hoping they'll die of natural causes?'

'No, you've never said that.'

'Well, I'm saying it now,' she said, changing position. She could move more easily now, but a wash, or a visit to the bathroom unaided, was still impossible. It was mortifying, but she kept telling herself it was better than the alternative.

'So what do we do?' asked Kordian.

'I don't know yet. Has your tobacco-smuggler friend found anything yet?'

'Just a dead end. Ekiel and Sakrat never even crossed the border. God only knows what's happened to them. In fact maybe even He doesn't, that's how carefully they've covered their tracks.'

'How long until the next trial?'

'A few days.'

'I need a date, Zordon. I'm losing track of time here. It's as if I'm reading that book.'

'Which book?'

'You know, *Rah'ma'dul* and all that.'

He rubbed his forehead. 'No, I don't know,' he said. 'But the trial's in three days, and although it's a complete suicide mission, I doubt we can put it off.'

'You're right, we can't. And the verdict should be delivered at this one.'

'So what do we do?'

She shrugged, and for the first time since the accident, it was almost painless. She'd always believed she was quick to heal, but this experience made her question that belief. She felt as if she'd been chained to her bed for weeks.

'So what do we do?' Kordian repeated, a note of hope in his voice.

'Only Sakrat can save us now.'

'What about Angelika's testimony?'

'We've got to discredit it somehow.'

'How?'

'I don't know, damn it. You think of something!'

She knew he'd spent the last few days trying to do exactly that. So had she, to be fair. The problem was that anything they came up with involved some sort of conspiracy theory. If they claimed Angelika was lying, they'd be saying it was all a set-up and that Awit had been framed. No court would buy that, not without evidence. And evidence was what they didn't have.

'Have the police followed the lead you gave them?' she asked.

'No.'

'Weren't you supposed to give them a sniff of Tatarnikov and set them off in the right direction?'

'Yes, but that was when we were sure he was in Belarus,' Kordian said. 'It wouldn't make sense now. What am I supposed to say? Hello, it's me again, I want to report that Sakrat's now somewhere in Poland?'

'Let's stick to Belarus.'

He raised his eyebrows. 'You want to deliberately mislead the police?' he asked.

'You flatter me by asking.'

'Think carefully about that.'

She had thought about it. Sending the police chasing after Tatarnikov would have created the perfect media buzz, but now, with Kosmowski's revelations, the story would disappear under a landslide of other news. Despite her outward show of confidence, Chyłka was ready to admit they no longer had the upper hand.

Silence descended. Neither wanted to talk about it anymore. There was no point leading the police by the nose – they'd be risking everything.

'Let's assume she's lying,' said Oryński finally.

'I try to assume that all the time, but although I dislike her in general, I find it difficult to believe.'

'But if we assume . . .'

'Zordon, please,' she said. 'I know you want to think our client's innocent, but at this stage, you really need to face facts.'

'No, I know he did it.'

Joanna was surprised.

'I think we should work on a conspiracy theory, a plausible one.'

'Believe me, I've tried. Those judges aren't stupid, they'd demand evidence to support it.'

They kept up a lively discussion for a while longer, then Kordian got up and walked over to the window. He swore as he gazed out at the car park. Chyłka wondered whether she should try and lift his mood, but decided it would be awkward at best.

'You can stop snivelling,' she said instead. 'This isn't the first time we've taken a drubbing, and it won't be the last.'

'I know. But for it to happen like this?'

'No crappier than any other way.'

'We've been royally screwed.'

'Technically speaking, you have,' she said with a faint smile. 'I was waking from a coma at the time.'

He sat on the other side of the bed and smiled too. They both knew even the most competent lawyer wouldn't have any advice on how to deal with what Angelika's revelations dumped on them.

They gazed at each other, as if seeing one another anew after a long separation. Joanna felt uncomfortable, but didn't turn away, which she blamed on the ridiculous amounts of medication the doctors were pumping into her. Her brain was foggy at times, and it took her an hour or more to wake up properly.

Kordian moved slightly, and she noticed he was moving his hand towards hers.

'What the hell are you doing?' she asked.

'What?' He withdrew his hand, embarrassed.

'I think what happened last time has given you the wrong idea.'

It would have been difficult to find a more convoluted way to say it, and Chyłka was very pleased with herself.

'What happened?'

'When our hands touched.'

Oryński's eyes widened. She could see he'd have happily leaped up from the bed and left the room; but he stayed, growing increasingly flustered – which gave her immense satisfaction.

'It was . . .' he began.

'Unintended, accidental and meaningless,' she chimed in. 'Yes?'

'Correct.'

'So why are you trying it again?'

'I was only . . .'

'Plus, you stink of cigarettes. Which makes me doubly nervous, because I never thought I'd say that to anyone. Haven't you ever heard of chewing gum?'

'I have. It was invented by the ancient Aztecs. They say—'

'Then stick some in your mouth occasionally. Especially before coming here,' she said. 'It's all very well giving me the come-on, but what would it be like for me? You couldn't hope for much, not with that nicotine breath.'

He smiled and shook his head.

'I can't hope for anything anyway.'

'Those are sacred words,' she agreed. 'Remember them. And now get out of here, I have to think.'

'About romance?'

'About the case, idiot. Now leave.' She watched him walk away. He stopped in the doorway and looked over his shoulder.

'You should be more like Angelika,' he said with a smile. 'She re-evaluated everything after the accident. So should you.'

'Really?'

'Of course,' he said, leaning against the doorframe. 'You could decide, for example, that it's not worth losing what we have together just because we're bound by an official relationship as defined by the Prosecution Service Act and the Supreme Bar Council.'

'Are you still here?'

'I've got more I want to add, but seeing—'

'Come back when you're older and wiser, Zordon,' she said. Then she turned on her side and smiled. She had to admit the silly idiot had definitely lifted her spirits. But she had a job to do, and it wasn't going to be easy: she had to find a way to dig them out of the quagmire they were in.

After half a day of thinking, she hadn't come up with anything that could give them the remotest chance of victory. When the doctor appeared, she plastered on her professional face.

'And how are you feeling today?' he asked.

'Terrible.'

'So no change, then.'

Joanna stared at the man in the white coat as he went about his business, checking the readings on the machines around her bed. She wondered how it was that his outfit alone made patients so willing to trust him – and it suddenly occurred to her that she and Zordon might win their case by relying on appearances. But as all the actual evidence was pointing against them, they'd have to handle things very carefully indeed.

That wouldn't normally be a problem for Chyłka, but now she was holed up in bed, all the efforts at sophistry would fall to Kordian. And that made her uneasy.

'If you need anything, feel free to call a nurse,' the doctor muttered.

Chyłka knew his 'anything' was a euphemism for certain bodily functions. Ignoring this valuable advice, she looked him straight in the eye.

'What's your name?' she asked.

'I'm sorry?'

She rolled her eyes. It was a simple question.

'I'm Doctor Kiedrzycki,' he said.

'Well, Dr Kiedrzycki, listen to me. I've got a case coming up in court in three days.'

He nodded. 'I'm sure they'll be streaming it again,' he assured her.

'No, you misunderstand.'

Seeing the look of determination on her face, he understood in a flash. 'Absolutely not,' he said before she had a chance to explain. 'It'll be at least two weeks before you're ready to leave.'

'Nonsense. I'm leaving the day before the court hearing.'

'Not possible.'

'Of course it is,' she said. 'I'll just need a wheelchair. Can I get one and get it refunded?'

'You won't be going anywhere.'

'That's where you're wrong, Dr Kiedrzycki. And answer my questions please. Because I'm not just your patient, I'm a lawyer.'

He shook his head and headed for the corridor.

'Hey!' roared Joanna, and immediately felt as if her ribcage would split in two. 'What about my wheelchair?'

No reply. But it didn't matter; Chyłka had made her decision. And she wasn't going to wait until the day before the trial.

When Kordian arrived the next day, she ordered him to prepare the papers she needed to discharge herself. He protested at first, checking at least ten times that she was sure she knew what she was doing, then finally did as he'd been told. She'd expected nothing less.

He helped her into a wheelchair they'd borrowed from the hospital, then into the easy-access SUV which was to be her mode of transport for the foreseeable future.

'You look like death,' he said as they drove off to the guest house.

'That's the whole point, Zordon.'

'What?'

'From now on, it's all about appearances.'

'I don't understand.'

'And I guarantee you, those two sons of bitches better known as Aronowicz and Kosmowski won't understand either,' she said emphatically. 'No more trampling all over Żelazny and McVay. Today we launch our counter-attack.'

'And how are we planning to do that?'

'By upholding the noblest traditions of our illustrious firm.'

'So we're going to lie, distort the facts, bend the truth and manipulate and intimidate people?'

'I couldn't have put it better myself.'

The driver looked over his shoulder and smiled. He could tell that the next few days would be interesting, to say the least.

7

The owner of the guest house had allocated Chyłka an apartment on the ground floor. Having struggled to push the wheelchair into the corridor, Kordian then faced another problem – there was no way the chair would fit through the apartment door.

'I'm going to have to carry you myself,' he said.

'My dear Zordon, you're going to have to do a lot more than that.'

'What do you mean?'

'For now, just concentrate on lifting your lord and master over the threshold.'

He looked around, cleared his throat and locked the wheels of the chair, then standing to one side of it, slid his hands under Chyłka's thighs. She felt pleasantly soft, and when he lifted her he could feel her muscles. Even though they'd known each other for quite a while, he wasn't sure what she did for exercise, but it was clear she did something.

She kept her life outside the walls of Żelazny & McVay very much to herself. One day as he'd sat at her bedside, he'd ticked off all he really knew about her. She listened to Iron Maiden, didn't really like J.K. Rowling other than Harry Potter, and ate meat as if it was going out of fashion. And that was about all.

When she put her arms around his neck, he stopped thinking altogether.

'I don't know if I'll be able to hold on,' she said, 'so I'm going to have to trust you.'

She was as weak as a kitten, so he hadn't expected any help from her anyway. When he picked her up, she clung to him as if she were on the edge of a cliff, and he felt himself becoming aroused. He winced, and tried to stay calm as he brought her into the apartment.

'Make one comment about what's happening here and I'll rip your tongue out.'

'Got it.'

He put her down on the bed and withdrew his hands, inadvertently touching her buttock. He cursed inwardly, hoping she hadn't noticed. Some chance.

She pointed to his crotch.

'Zordon.'

'Yes?'

'You're aroused.'

He swallowed, and hurried out to get the wheelchair.

'Sometimes I hate you so much I could burst,' he muttered from the corridor.

'Oh yes, I can see that from here.'

'Occupational hazard.'

'I see.'

He stepped back into the apartment, shut the door behind him and went to the kitchenette. It was only a studio, but quite spacious. The bathroom could have graced a top Warsaw hotel, and the terrace was perfect for parties.

'I could use a drink,' Chyłka said. 'Would you get me something from the fridge?'

'You're loving this, aren't you?'

'Yes, it's all I ever dreamed of, Zordon. I've always wanted to see what it's like to be disabled.'

'You're not disabled though.'

319

'No, but the effect's the same. Either way, pass me a beer.'

'No alcohol, remember?'

'A non-alcoholic one then.'

'There aren't any.'

'There are in the shop.'

'Chyłka, you must be joking.'

'Listen,' she said. 'If you really want to look after me, you need to provide a steady supply of strong drink, or I won't be able to function. I need to lubricate my brain cells, and only a hop-based beverage can do that.'

He stood by the bed, arms folded across his chest, waiting for her to change her mind. But he knew she wouldn't give in, even if she stopped craving beer. It was a matter of pride now.

'I didn't want to mention this, considering our professional relationship, but a beer is going to make you pee like crazy.'

'You're right, that remark doesn't befit your professional position as a trainee.'

'Given the situation, I felt compelled to say something.'

'What you didn't take into account is that it's not my problem.'

'Isn't it?'

'No,' she said with a grin. 'We both know I'm going to need help with . . . certain things.'

He unfolded his arms and let them hang by his sides, shaking his head as if trying to avoid the truth.

'Absolutely no way.'

'So am I supposed to get a carer?'

'Yes.'

'We don't have time for that. And besides, who knows where the nearest nurses' home is.'

'But you—'

'You take me to the bathroom, Zordon, the rest I can manage perfectly well myself,' she said, still beaming. 'Don't be such a baby.'

'I'm not.'

'Or you can take your things and move out.'

'Me?'

'Who else?' she asked, lying down on the bed and making herself comfortable. 'Don't tell me the practicalities hadn't crossed your mind. Did you think I just wanted you here in case I kicked the bucket?'

'No, that's—'

'Enough,' she said. 'And before you go out for my beer, bring me the case file.'

Actually, he should have expected this. He brought the files from upstairs and laid them out on the bed. Then, with Joanna's eyes urging him on, he left the apartment in search of a non-alcoholic beer.

When Kordian returned, Chyłka was in her element. The colour was back in her cheeks, and she hardly noticed him coming in with the drink she'd coveted. He opened the small bottle of Lech, handed it to her and sat down on the bed.

'You'll burst your stitches if you keep struggling with all this.'

'Right.'

'Have you found anything?' he asked, hopefully.

'No, it's just one big pile of shit,' she said, moving a sheet of paper aside.

Oryński got up and fetched himself a normal beer. He put the rest in the fridge and went back to the makeshift centre of operations. Despite what she'd said, it looked like Joanna had an idea. Or maybe she simply wore her helplessness differently. He wilted; she took destiny into her own hands.

Eventually she sat up, leaning against the headboard. She looked around, located the bottle of Lech Free, took a sip and groaned with pleasure.

'Nectar.'

'I know a lot of words to describe alcohol-free beer, but that's not one of them.'

'Give up drinking for a while and you'll see what I mean.'

'I'd rather you told me what you've found in this lot,' he said, gesturing to the papers.

Joanna sighed, and picked up the printout from the security company.

'This is still our biggest problem. Angelika managed to get round it somehow, but we can't,' she said. 'For Szlezyngier, it's like being found with a smoking gun.'

Oryński looked at the printout, lost in thought.

'If we want the court to buy the idea that he's not guilty, we have to prove that the child was at home after seven o'clock in the evening,' she continued.

'What?'

Joanna turned to him. 'Pretend you know nothing, Zordon.'

'Thanks.'

'Imagine you're the naïvest of all naïve trainees. Pretend you still believe there's an element of goodness in all of us.'

'I'm not sure if that's an insult or a compliment.'

'Shush, just listen,' she said. 'Get into character.'

'OK, I'm starting to feel it,' he said, taking a sip of beer. He wanted to reach for his Marlboros, but realised that if he lit up, Chyłka would be passively inhaling his nicotine, and she was half-dead as it was.

'In your role as company mug, you're convinced that your client is innocent, OK?'

'Sure. I'm not too keen on your description of me though.'

Joanna ignored him. 'You believe that Awit had nothing to do with his daughter's disappearance. So that means you must have a different suspect in mind. And since his wife's lying about it, she's the obvious choice.'

'True.'

'For the court, this is a complex situation. His word against hers. Unless we add an alibi that works for both of them. The alarm, switched on at seven p.m.'

'Right.'

'The wife then trashes her husband's alibi, saying he removed the body earlier, she was scared, blah, blah, blah. You know all this already, all too well.'

'Sad, but true.'

'So we have to trash hers. Let's go back to square one.'

Oryński scratched his head. He couldn't keep playing the naïve trainee, the company mug, because now it was obvious. While Angelika could claim she'd kept quiet because Awit had intimidated her, Awit couldn't say the same. If he tried to blame her, he'd have nothing to back it up, and nothing to explain his silence.

'They're arguing,' Joanna went on. 'Awit gives her a shove, but Angelika isn't holding the child. Then what happens? Why would she want to kill her own daughter?'

'I can't think of any reason.'

'You're right, it's hopeless,' said Chyłka. 'Especially as Szlezyngier testified he saw the child after he'd set the alarm.'

'Angelika did too.'

'But now she's taking that back, saying she was intimidated into it.'

Kordian had to admit, albeit reluctantly, that Kosmowski had probably landed the innocent client. He didn't blame himself.

He'd never have been able to persuade Żelazny & McVay to represent her, no matter how skilfully he'd pleaded his case. She'd been hostile towards him ever since the accident, and there was no point deluding himself.

'Could they have killed her together?' he suggested.

Chyłka was silent for a moment, contemplating her beer bottle.

'It's the only logical option.'

'So that's the route we're going to go down?'

'In the absence of anything better, yes.'

'But how?'

'We'll prove the child was at home after seven p.m.'

'And how are we going to do that?'

'I haven't decided yet.'

'But it's just a matter of time?'

'Sure, yes, of course,' said Joanna, taking a sip. She grimaced as if she were lifting a giant barbell, not a small bottle of beer. She handed the bottle to Kordian, who quickly took the weight.

'What a weakling,' he said.

'My dear Zordon,' she said. 'If you'd been in that accident instead of me, I'd have been crying crocodile tears over your grave a long time ago.'

'Great. You always know how to fill my heart with joy.'

He smiled, trying not think how the accident was, indirectly, his fault. If only he hadn't called her that night, hadn't asked her to pick him up. As soon as she said she'd been drinking, he should have told her not to come. He could have found someone else to drive him. With a little forethought, he could have prevented it all.

He looked at the documents strewn over the bed, and wondered if they'd be poring over them now if the accident had never happened. Probably not. Angelika wouldn't have had that meltdown in court; and even if she had, Chyłka would have been quick to deal with it, refuting her testimony at once.

'You seem very pensive,' said Joanna.

'You know, somehow . . .'

'Are you blaming yourself?'

'Yes, to a certain extent.'

Joanna gazed up at him in silence, as if seeing something strange and unprecedented.

'Quite right too,' she said eventually. 'You've been an abject failure.'

'Thanks.'

'But you'll get a chance to make up for it. You just have to think of a way to prove Awit didn't kill his daughter.'

Kordian nodded, pulled one of the papers towards him and started to read it for the nth time. He felt as if he knew them all by heart.

8

The next day, at noon on the dot, Kosmowski called another press conference. Oryński had just settled Chyłka on the bed after a visit to the bathroom, when he appeared on the NSI news, sharp, well-groomed, and clearly no stranger to the tanning lounge.

'It looks like we'll be meeting every day until the trial starts,' he said to the journalists, as if he didn't know the cameras were already rolling. Then he flashed a smile to someone in the front row, took a breath, and looked into the lens.

'That miserable bastard could be a politician,' said Joanna.

Kordian sat on the bed and turned the volume up.

'Ladies and gentlemen,' Kosmowski began, 'I am well aware that legal battles can occur in many places, not just the court-room. Nor are they always within the bounds of the law. I can just about accept the first premise, but the second I find unacceptable. I cannot permit the integrity of the judicial process to be compromised by media shenanigans.'

Kordian and Chyłka exchanged glances.

'What the hell is he talking about?' she asked.

Kordian narrowed his eyes. This opponent might prove more dangerous than the one he was officially confronting in court.

'Chyłka . . .' he began feebly.

'Go on.'

'He's here, he's outside our hotel.'

'What the fuck?' she gasped, looking more closely at the background surrounding the slimy toerag. She didn't have time to examine it in detail, but Zordon could be right.

'Szlezyngier's defence team are staying here, in this guest house behind me,' Kosmowski went on. 'And, as it happens, so are two of my own assistants.' He paused for his words to sink in. 'They took a few photos on their phones, which I think you might find interesting.'

Kosmowski turned to one of his colleagues, who handed him a couple of digital printouts, at an angle the cameras couldn't immediately pick up. He sighed, and lifted the first photograph.

'As I'm sure some of you know, Szlezyngier's defence lawyer had an accident, allegedly suffering life-threatening injuries.'

Kordian looked at Chyłka, but she didn't take her eyes off the screen.

'Here you can see her being pushed in a wheelchair by her colleague. A heartwarming sight, isn't it? A lawyer, showing unstinting dedication to her work. She doesn't want to stay in hospital, she won't give her trainee authorisation to take the case over – no, she's going to defend her client herself, even if it literally kills her.'

Joanna looked out of the window, trying to spot the journalists. They must have gathered somewhere to the side of the building, although no doubt once this farce was over, they'd be at the window in seconds. Daniel Kosmowski had called the press conference for a reason. He'd clearly found something huge.

'At first, I thought: kudos, she's one tough cookie. But then I found myself feeling sorry for the prosecutor who would have to face her in court. Not because she seems indestructible, but because making her case from a wheelchair gives her an immediate advantage. I didn't realise then it was all a put-up job.'

A few journalists began firing questions at him, but Kosmowski silenced them with a gesture.

'Here's the next picture,' he said, holding it up. 'Here you see how her colleague is carrying her over the threshold into their room. Laughing and joking, which isn't surprising under the circumstances.'

Oryński got up and made to leave.

'Take it easy,' said Joanna.

Kordian grabbed the door handle, ignoring her.

'Zordon!' she hissed. 'That's exactly why he's holding this press conference here. He wants you to go out there all emotional and reckless.'

He glared at her, his anger palpable. But he turned round and walked back to the bed. Kosmowski was still holding the photograph of the two of them aloft, for all the world a blissful young couple.

'Why are they so carefree?' Daniel asked. It was, of course, rhetorical. 'Because it's all a masquerade. Joanna Chyłka does not need full-time care. She doesn't even need a wheelchair! My assistants were fascinated by what they had seen, and took more pictures.'

Kosmowski held them up one by one. In the first, she was sitting on the bed, bent over her files. The archetypal busy lawyer, no obvious sign of illness. Then the camera caught her trying to get to the bathroom by herself. She remembered what an ordeal it had been. She had only managed a few steps, but the photograph had been snapped just as she'd taken the first. Again, she didn't look ill. In the next she was sitting with a beer in her hand, and the last showed her laughing with Zordon.

'If this is someone who is seriously ill, we should wish all patients the same fortitude in dealing with their travails as Joanna Chyłka.'

Again the journalists tried to ask questions, and again Daniel showed no intention of answering. His script was prepared, and he wasn't going to deviate from it.

'I know this will make me unpopular,' he said, looking into the lens again. 'Questioning someone's suffering won't score highly in public opinion. But let truth prevail this time, and not a calculated marketing ploy.' He took a breath and lifted his chin slightly. 'Ladies and gentlemen, this is exactly why I left Żelazny & McVay – because I refused to be involved in this kind of manipulation. I know of a great many other breaches to which the firm turned a blind eye, but I am bound by a non-disclosure agreement and cannot discuss them. However, there is nothing to stop you launching your own investigation.'

After the statement he'd just made, the plural – *investigations* – would have been more apposite. Reporters from NSI or TVN wouldn't be so easily fooled, but the tabloids would descend on Żelazny & McVay like vultures onto a carcass. And that could make a considerable mess.

'And I will not allow them to appeal to the pity of the court to achieve their aims!' Kosmowski paused. Again there were questions, but he still hadn't finished his performance. 'Maybe this is the picture that interests you.' He held up the photograph showing Kordian carrying Joanna over the threshold. 'Because it does us. As soon as I saw it, I asked my assistants to look into it further. What they found was devastating.'

Oryński twitched, and Chyłka grabbed his hand. A gentle tug was enough to make him sit back down on the bed.

'We know that this is a supervisor with her trainee – a relationship governed by official statutes and regulations, not some rules concocted internally. If that wasn't the case, perhaps we could accept it.'

His colleague handed him the next picture, which showed Kordian leaning over Joanna as she lay on the bed. The next one showed him carrying her to the bathroom, but the angle from which it was taken made it seem like much more. He was holding her in his arms, her hands were clasped around his neck and they were gazing into one another's eyes.

Joanna remembered the actual moment. They had each drunk two beers, and in her state, the alcohol-free Lech seemed to be having a more intoxicating effect than a normal Bock. Oryński was taking her to the bathroom, and for a moment, their eyes had met. It had been a strange feeling – as if she was both totally vulnerable and in full control. She felt his breath on her lips, and knew it would only take a moment for it to turn into something more. She'd opened her eyes wide and urged him to get a move on. She couldn't let it happen. But the camera had caught only that second of hesitation.

'I instructed my colleagues to delete the remaining photographs,' said Kosmowski, then raised his hand in a gesture of thanks to the assembled crowd and set off back to his car. Journalists swarmed round him, as if he were a popular politician who, after winning an election, already knew the composition of the new government but couldn't yet share it with the public.

He got into the car, and he, together with his colleagues, drove away.

'Close the curtains, Zordon,' said Joanna in a thin voice.

'Weasel,' hissed Kordian, getting up.

He pulled the curtains to, then turned to face Joanna. 'No one will swallow this rubbish,' he said.

'You're joking.'

'Those journalists aren't idiots.'

'Of course they're not,' she answered, forcing a smile. 'Most of them will just ignore it. But the gossip magazines will have a field day.'

They sat in silence, listening for a moment, but soon heard sounds outside. The TV stations were setting up their cameras close by, while the first of the journalists were demanding information from the owners of the guest house.

'Fuck,' muttered Oryński.

'We've also got the Supreme Bar Council to think about.'

'Will we be in trouble?'

'What do you think?' she answered. 'I'd say an affair between a supervisor and her trainee doesn't exactly uphold their high moral standards.'

Kordian sat down on the bed and hung his head.

'We can easily refute this,' she said, 'and Kosmowski knows it.'

'So what was it all about?'

'Because by the time we explain it all to the Bar Council, the trial will be over.'

'So what do we do?'

'We leave well alone. It's a distraction. He just wanted to discredit us, so now we're a pair of immoral ambulance-chasers, exploiting my injuries to gain sympathy.'

'We can call a doctor who'll—'

'Call him where? There's no trial where he can testify. Unless I bring a civil suit against that slimeball.'

'Which you won't have time to do.'

'Precisely. Politicians can fast-track cases during an election campaign. Wouldn't it be great if we could do something similar before major trials?'

'We could call our own press conference. We could make him look a fool.'

Chyłka wasn't sure what effect that would have. Only the guilty went to great lengths to explain themselves, and besides, taking pains to prove she really was ill would give exactly the impression Kosmowski was talking about – that she was trying to win the sympathy vote. She explained it to Kordian, who admitted she was right.

'There's no point getting into a pissing contest,' she said, 'but saying nothing could work in our favour. If I turn up in court in my wheelchair with no further explanations, it'll say as much as ten press conferences.'

'OK then.'

'But I'll still need to advance some sort of argument.'

'Of course.'

'Did you find anything?'

Oryński turned to her, and from the look on his face she could see he'd spent the night in fruitless searching. As had she. There was simply nothing in the evidence that could help them.

'In that case we'll just have to wing it,' she said.

He didn't reply, and when she turned to him, she realised he was staring at the television. Chyłka looked too, and froze. The screen showed an NSI reporter standing outside the prosecutor's office in Suwałki, repeating everything Kosmowski had said at the press conference.

'They're in this together,' said Oryński, as the camera panned to Aronowicz leaving the building. There was a close-up where a woman – no doubt also from NSI – approached him, said a few words, then pointed to the lens. The prosecutor seemed to ponder for a moment, then came towards the camera.

'He's going to rip us to shreds,' said Kordian.

'Stop worrying.'

'Can't you see what's happening? It's all—'

'I can see very well, Zordon.'

Zbigniew Aronowicz stood beside the journalist, looking as if none of this was giving him the slightest satisfaction. The opposite in fact: his face was a picture of sadness and disappointment. The reporter introduced him, and at once the banner at the bottom of the screen identified him, giving his name and job title. The operator in the studio should have waited a bit, it would have looked more natural. This just proved they'd already known exactly who he was.

'Mr Aronowicz, did you see the press conference called by Angelika Szlezyngier's defence counsel?'

'I wouldn't call that a conference,' Aronowicz said, disgust apparent in his voice.

'What would you call it?'

'A speech. Or rather, a performance.'

Oryński was surprised. Chyłka less so.

'I don't approve of playing games when a court case is at stake,' he added.

'So you don't believe Joanna Chyłka is faking her condition?'

'It's not my place to judge. And neither is it the place of Angelika Szlezyngier's defence counsel.'

'Although neither of them is beyond reproach.'

'No, that's true,' said the prosecutor, sighing deeply, as though struggling with a tricky problem. 'My attention has recently been drawn to Mr Oryński's past, which is questionable to say the least. But again, as in the case of Ms Chyłka, it's not for me to judge.'

'Can you tell us more?' asked the reporter, moving her microphone closer.

'Alas, no. We're in the middle of a trial. Please respect that.'

The reporter nodded, and the prosecutor thanked her and walked off to his car. Joanna would have grabbed the remote and switched this garbage off, but it was too far for her to reach. She looked at Kordian, who seemed rooted to the spot.

They'd been hit from both sides, so hard they might never regain their footing.

'Zordon,' she said.

He still seemed to be in another world.

'Turn this shit off.'

'No,' he retorted, listening as the reporter summarised what they had just heard, and repeated the questions that had followed the prosecutor's short statement.

'Turn it off. Now.'

'They've made you out to be some sort of master manipulator, someone who'll even pretend she needs a wheelchair, for her own gain. And they say you're exploiting your trainee.'

'Anything else?'

'And that I'm someone who . . .' He stopped and shook his head. 'In a couple of hours, we'll be the most hated lawyers in Poland.'

'Probably.'

Chyłka knew very well what Aronowicz had been referring to when he'd talked about Kordian. She remembered him opening up to her during the Langer trial about how his mother had died. Now all the prosecution had to do was find Oryński senior, who would happily share his disdain for his son with the media.

But there was more, and worse. In the Langer case, Kordian had been forced to compromise his legal responsibilities, through no fault of his own. Żelazny & McVay hadn't sued him, and even Langer had no intention of pursuing him through the courts. The Supreme Bar Council knew about it, but as both partners had vouched for him, he wasn't even reprimanded.

But now it would all come out, before the trial even began, and they'd be seen in the courtroom as defendants rather than the defence team.

'So what now?' asked Kordian.

She didn't have an answer for him.

9

'I declare this trial before the regional court in Suwałki open,' announced the judge solemnly.

Kordian had arranged Chyłka's wheelchair alongside his own seat. They had considered whether it might be better for her to sit on the bench beside him, but decided that would bow to Kosmowski's pressure. As the presiding judge announced the case, Oryński sized up his opponent. As ever, Aronowicz was bent over his paperwork, occasionally raising his eyes and looking disparaging.

The judge then read out a list of those present, and when it came to Joanna's name, he graciously permitted her to stay seated. Unsurprisingly, he wasn't happy to be landed with this case: after Kosmowski's little performance, they were all in the spotlight. Usually, if a judge made a mistake in their sentencing, they were in no professional danger – the constitution guaranteed full judicial independence. But if it happened in a prominent case, like this one had become, it would be difficult to rebuild their reputation. On the other hand, neither was it a case in which a judge could become a national hero, sentencing some monster to the highest possible penalty. So the risks were considerable, but the benefits few.

For Oryński, risk no longer entered into it. He had been so badly battered by the media that it was hard to imagine anyone wanting to employ him if they lost the case. Even if they won, the outlook would be bleak.

Chyłka was in a marginally better position, but they still looked like two losers defending a third loser. Kordian had seen the looks the reporters were giving him as he came into the courtroom.

'Does either side wish to make any procedural requests which may affect the course of today's hearing?' droned the judge.

'No, Your Honour,' said Aronowicz, rising slightly. Chyłka had no such requests either.

They had hoped to find Sakrat Tatarnikov or Antoni Ekiel by now, but there was no trace. Wito had found a lead taking them much further inland, but even that had petered out. The fugitives could easily be at the other end of Poland by now.

Kordian glanced at their client. He too looked as if he had lost all hope. He'd seen the media frenzy, and if anyone understood the power of the fourth estate, it was Awit Szlezyngier, once a leading business mogul. Officially, the media had no influence on the verdict, but in this case, public opinion was clear, and the pressure great.

Oryński was worried a scuffle might break out before the trial even began. If he'd been Szlezyngier, he'd have given the two lawyers who'd led him into such deep trouble their marching orders. But Awit had given them a pleasant, if somewhat forced, smile, and walked silently into the courtroom.

The hearing began with Angelika's cross-examination. She walked to the rostrum, her legs shaking, and leaned on the lectern as if scared of falling.

'Angelika Szlezyngier, witness,' said the presiding judge. 'Thirty-nine years old, currently unemployed. Relationship to the accused: spouse.' He looked at the prosecutor, who nodded, and rose unhurriedly.

There seemed little that either side could ask Angelika. She had already given extensive explanations, which were now in the case file along with her previous statements, and that should have been perfectly sufficient. Nevertheless, Chyłka had called her as a witness.

'You've already outlined everything for us quite thoroughly,' began Aronowicz. 'I'm only missing one piece of information.'

Oryński looked over his shoulder and spotted Kosmowski in the public gallery. He had no doubt that the two men had prepared Angelika for this performance. As if to confirm it, Daniel winked at him.

'I'm wondering what you were doing between the time the defendant did what he did, and the time he hid the body.'

Angelika shuffled nervously and looked down at the lectern.

'I can't give you a detailed answer to that question,' she said.

The presiding judge sighed.

'Why not?' asked the prosecutor.

'I was in shock. I couldn't understand what was happening,' Angelika explained in a tremulous voice. 'One moment I was holding my little daughter, and the next ...' She stopped and shook her head. 'She wasn't there. I remember sitting down on the floor and crying. I didn't know what to do.'

'Didn't it occur to you to ring the police?'

'No,' she said without hesitation. 'I didn't understand what was going on. I didn't want to believe it. I hoped Awit would come back with Nikola in his arms and tell me none of it had happened.'

'Maybe you thought about calling an ambulance?'

'No, nothing like that.'

'Or ringing a friend, or a family member? Did you think about seeking any help at all?'

'I did.'

'And?' asked the prosecutor, not expecting anything much.

At least that was the impression he gave. By the time Oryński realised it was all a ploy, it was too late. He turned to Chyłka, who gave a barely audible moan.

'So you did call someone?'

Angelika lowered her head and sobbed. For a moment, the sound echoed through the courtroom, and Kordian thought that had there been a single person there who didn't yet hate them, they would have started doing so there and then.

'I . . .'

The prosecutor suddenly came to life.

'You rang someone?' he asked.

'Oh God, yes, I did.'

'Just after the murder?'

'Mr Aronowicz,' warned the second judge. 'Please remember that no one has yet been found guilty.'

Aronowicz raised his palms, but didn't even look at the judge. He looked instead at the witness, as if by simply gazing at her he'd drag her whole testimony from her.

'I rang Sakrat Tatarnikov.'

Joanna's eyes bulged. She turned to Kordian, but he just shrugged. He'd had no idea. Angelika hadn't said a word about it while she was still their client. Mind you, given everything they'd found out since then, that made perfect sense.

'I see,' said the prosecutor. 'After the argument with your husband and the alleged tragedy, you sought comfort from your lover.'

'Yes . . .' she stuttered.

'What did you talk about?'

'I . . .'

No one hurried her, and the court waited in suspense. The next words that came from her mouth could decide Szlezyngier's fate.

'I said Awit had pushed me and that I'd dropped the child.'

Oryński made a lightning assessment of how things might go from here. A statement from Tatarnikov would send their client straight to prison, but there was no chance of him appearing on the stand. If Wito hadn't found him, Aronowicz and Kosmowski certainly wouldn't have, and without him, there was no proof that Angelika was telling the truth.

He and Chyłka had been caught completely off guard, although they couldn't really blame themselves. They'd asked Kormak to check her phone for deleted text messages; calls were a bit more difficult. No mobile provider would give them access to their records just like that.

'And is that all you said?' asked the prosecutor.

'I don't know, I don't remember.'

'Luckily, I have a transcript of your conversation here,' said Aronowicz, holding up a piece of paper.

Chyłka rose from her wheelchair. She found it infuriating that the Polish court system didn't have a functional way of raising objections.

'Your Honour,' she said. 'The time for bringing a motion was at the start of the hearing.'

'I'm not bringing a motion,' said the prosecutor. 'I'm merely presenting evidence which may help Ms Szlezyngier remember.'

Joanna glared at him. 'Don't play games,' she hissed.

'Ms Chyłka,' said the presiding judge. 'Please remember where you are and respect the dignity of the court.'

Chyłka looked at him with loathing. Kordian was afraid that Joanna's poor health notwithstanding, they might be about to witness fisticuffs. The judge raised his eyebrows as if he was thinking something similar.

'Your Honour,' began Joanna, 'I rarely say this, but this time I will. This is unacceptable.'

'Unacceptable, but permissible.'

'I'm sorry?'

'The prosecution is simply going through the evidence given by the witness.' Oryński took Chyłka's arm and gently suggested he should take her back to her seat. He helped her to sit, fervently hoping no one could hear the curses she was muttering under her breath.

'Please continue, Mr Aronowicz.'

The second judge shook his head, almost imperceptibly.

'Thank you, Your Honour,' said Aronowicz, and turned to Angelika. 'Could you please look at this transcript? To refresh your memory?'

For a moment, Angelika seemed too confused to continue, but she pulled herself together and took the paper from the prosecutor.

'Could you read out—'

'Your Honour!' called Chyłka. 'This does not constitute evidence.'

Kordian swore to himself as the judge turned red with anger. The second judge, sitting by his side, came to the rescue.

'Mr Aronowicz,' he began in a conciliatory tone. 'Please respect the intelligence of the court and everyone in it. I understand you have your tactics, but please understand they may neither compromise the dignity of the court, nor show lack of respect towards your fellow men. Do I make myself clear?'

'Yes, Your Honour.'

'Then please continue.'

The prosecutor bowed gravely, put his hand to his chest and flashed Angelika a smile, as if to reassure her.

'Can you perhaps quote the words you said on the phone just after your husband had left?'

'Yes, I can . . . I remember them now.'

'In your own time.'

'I said, "My God, Sakrat, he killed her." Then Sakrat said, "What are you talking about?" So I said, "Awit knocked her out of my arms."'

Oryński listened with growing embarrassment. Chyłka too. Although it caused her pain, she wriggled restlessly in her wheelchair, as if she'd like nothing better than to jump up and silence Angelika once and for all.

Kordian was surprised to see the prosecutor using what amounted to scorched earth tactics, but he had to admit, the story sounded plausible. Szlezyngier really had been left holding a smoking gun.

He turned his head to look at their client. So far, Awit had managed to hold it together, but now he hung his head, wearily shaking it every now and then. It wasn't a good look, as if he didn't quite know what was going on – and that wouldn't give the panel a favourable impression.

'Awit,' whispered Kordian. 'Sit up straight.' He didn't respond. After a few minutes, however, when Angelika was in full flow, he lifted his gaze at last. In his eyes Oryński saw a fury he'd not seen there before. His upper lip was raised in a snarl – a predator ready to pounce on his prey.

'Awit,' Kordian hissed.

Chyłka heard the sound, turned towards it and also saw her client just a step away from catastrophe. Evidence notwith-standing, a court also bases its judgement on the behaviour of the alleged offender. If Szlezyngier erupted now, it would be game over.

Joanna got up again, with some difficulty.

'Your Honour,' she interjected while Angelika was speaking, 'I think we've heard all we need to hear.'

The presiding judge glowered at her, his open mouth forming the words to reprimand her for interrupting a witness, but the second judge leaned in to him and whispered something in his ear. The first man backed down, and Chyłka sat.

'We are indeed beginning to get into territory irrelevant to the case,' said the presiding judge. He wasn't wrong – Angelika was starting to describe in detail how Tatarnikov had tried to comfort her. 'We already have an accurate picture of what happened.'

Oryński thought how, just for saying such a thing, the presiding judge should be asked to hang up his chain of office for good. Because although the outcome of the case was already clear to everyone and reaching a verdict would take a matter of minutes, a presiding judge should never voice his opinion so categorically.

'I call a twenty-minute recess,' announced the judge.

Kordian looked at Chyłka. 'A stay of execution, more like,' he whispered.

She didn't reply. He wheeled her out, wondering why the judge had ordered a delay.

'They're giving us time to think about it,' said Joanna to Awit, who was walking behind them. 'They want you to change your statement.'

Without a word, he quickened his step and walked past them towards the toilets.

10

After the recess, the first witness to the stand was an expert, brought in to tell the court whether he thought a fall from a height of one to one-and-a-half metres could kill a three-year-old child. From all the jargon and medi-speak, Chyłka managed to deduce that theoretically, it could.

When Aronowicz had thanked the expert, Joanna rose slightly from her seat, but, unable to maintain her balance, sank back down. Before any of the panel had time to assure her yet again that there was no need to stand, she turned to the expert witness.

'I expect we all remember the case of little Madzia from Sosnowiec,' she said. It was no accident that she brought up that particular case now. 'The one where the mother killed her child, then covered it up. Perhaps some of us even recall what the experts said at the time. Most felt that a child falling from such a modest height wouldn't die, and that's what made everyone think Katarzyna W.'s testimony might be suspect. Do you recall the case?'

'Of course.'

'And would you say these were expert professional opinions?'

'Assuredly.'

'So could they also apply here?'

'Absolutely not,' replied the expert confidently. 'In the Madzia case, the child was just a few months old, an age at which the bones aren't yet fully fused.'

'I don't understand.'

'As I said before, a fall from this height can, in principle, only be fatal if the skull is fractured and the bone penetrates the brain. For the reasons I stated, it would be rare to see such an injury in a child just a few months old. Also, the younger the child, the more cerebrospinal fluid is present, acting as a kind of shield. So in this instance, that sort of fall could be fatal. But in the case you just mentioned, it would be very unlikely.'

'Thank you. No more questions,' said Joanna.

'The witness is free to go.'

Chyłka forced herself to stare straight ahead, ignoring the look of triumph on the prosecutor's face. This summed up the whole situation. She cursed herself for not checking the witness statements from little Madzia's case more thoroughly; she'd have been more prepared for the blow this expert witness had dealt her.

Next on the rostrum was a forensic technician, called by the defence, who was introduced as an employee of the forensics lab at police headquarters in Białystok and the person in charge of coordinating forensic examinations. He seemed perfectly competent. With a bit of prompting from Aronowicz, he repeated what everyone already knew – that there were no fingerprints other than those of the family, nothing to indicate someone had climbed through the rooflight and so on. When it came to her turn, Joanna decided she'd make no more abortive efforts to get up. She'd have felt more confident standing, but she had no choice.

'I have only two questions,' she said. 'They've been asked before, but now the situation is somewhat different. After my former client's most recent statement, we need to look at the forensics again, wouldn't you agree?'

'I don't understand.'

'If the child fell, there should be traces of blood, shouldn't there?' she asked. 'And if either Awit or Angelika cleaned them up, would there not be chemical traces from whatever it was they used?'

The expert nodded.

'We examined the floor thoroughly at the point where the child would potentially have fallen, and I stand by our findings at the time. There were no traces of fabric, secretions or excretions.'

'But the child must have been bleeding, mustn't she?'

'I don't feel qualified to—'

'What do you think, based on your experience?'

He wasn't happy that Chyłka was asking questions beyond the scope of his statement, but there was no hostility – like any other true professional, he simply didn't like to speculate.

'I would expect there to be traces of blood,' he said, 'at least if there was damage to the skull. But it's difficult to say if that's what happened. The body hasn't been found yet.'

'Let's assume the expert witness testifying before you was correct.'

The man nodded.

'If my former client's version of things were to be possible, there must have been blood. But you found no traces?'

'We found no trace of blood,' he confirmed. 'But we found traces of chemicals to show a cleaning agent was used.'

'Not altogether surprising. Even summer homes need to be cleaned from time to time.'

The expert said nothing.

'Tell me, was there anything at the crime scene to indicate murder rather than abduction?'

'No,' admitted the man, 'but there were no indications of abduction either.'

Chyłka was silent. The technician was making a fine impression, and she should use that to her advantage, but she couldn't think how to press him to say more than he should.

'Are you also responsible for mechanoscopic examinations?'

'I am. I coordinated the work of the whole team.'

Bullseye, thought Joanna. Noticing a few looks of confusion, she asked the expert to explain the concept.

'Mechanoscopics is a branch of forensics where we examine traces left by the interaction of one object on another. A skeleton key on a lock, a hammer on a door, etcetera. We look at changes in the surface geometry of solid objects.'

'Thank you,' said Chyłka. 'I am asking for a particular reason. Because if an abduction had taken place, shouldn't there be at least some of these traces at the scene?'

'Of course.'

'But there was nothing.'

'Correct.'

Joanna spread her hands, as if helpless. The next question risked clouding her own line of argument, but she had to ask it, to get to the core of the issue.

'Would that, in itself, be enough to conclude that a murder had taken place?'

'No, of course not.'

'And would it be enough to rule out abduction?'

'Also no.'

'In that case, what do you think took place?'

It was a crucial question, and one she'd been aiming to ask all along, but if she'd asked it at the start, the presiding judge would have quickly overruled it, and she would have had her wrists slapped. But he couldn't object now – it followed on logically from her previous questions.

'To be honest, I've never come across a case like this before,' said the expert.

Chyłka smiled to herself. It was music to her ears.

'Could you elaborate?'

He sighed, looking at the panel of judges, acutely aware that this was beyond the scope of the expertise for which he'd been called. Nobody seemed to care.

'Well, let me think,' he began uncertainly. 'This seems to be your classic British conundrum, "A case so puzzling it takes quite some effort to unravel." Have you read Conan Doyle?'

'I've read some.'

'Are you familiar with the final Sherlock Holmes novel, *The Valley of Fear*?'

'I'm afraid not,' she lied, inviting him to explain to the court what the plot entailed.

'In the story, a man is shot dead in a secluded castle. The killer uses a sawn-off shotgun, which causes so much damage it's hard to identify the victim. The conundrum lies in the fact that the house is locked up like a fortress, and can only be accessed through one entrance, which is sealed. It's a similar situation here, except instead of a moat, we have electronics. The alarm is the key to the puzzle. Without it, and the conclusions we reached on the basis of when it was activated, the case would have been obvious.'

'Meaning?'

'As a rule, lack of evidence of a break-in doesn't rule out abduction. On the other hand, lack of evidence of murder usually means no murder took place.'

It was a bit convoluted, so Chyłka gave the panel time to assimilate the idea.

'And I would suggest that that's exactly what happened here,' the expert went on, 'except that Mrs Szlezyngier's testimony gives us the only possible explanation. To paraphrase a classic, when we eliminate everything illogical, what we are left with is the truth.'

This wasn't going the way Chyłka had intended.

'Unfortunately, the only possibility is that the child was taken from the house before the alarm was set,' he concluded.

'It can hardly be called a theory, based only on circumstantial evidence.'

He shrugged.

'What else could have happened?' he asked. 'The little girl didn't just vanish into thin air.'

Joanna nodded her head, looking at the panel of judges one by one.

'But is that enough?' she asked, more of them than the expert witness. 'Aren't we reducing everything to mere speculation? And on this basis, we may be about to send a man to pr—'

'Ms Chyłka,' the presiding judge cut in. 'There will be time at the end for your closing speech. Do you have any further questions for our expert witness?'

'No further questions, Your Honour. Thank you.'

The man thanked the court and returned to his seat. And with him went her last hope of turning the trial around. All the witnesses had been heard, the expert reports presented and the evidence examined. The only thing that could save them now was the final speech; but one couldn't count on miracles. It had been a long time since Chyłka had faced such a hopeless case.

When it came to summing up, the prosecutor spoke first. He stressed that everything the court had heard pointed unequivocally to the defendant being guilty.

'The expert witness may be right,' said Aronowicz, 'when he says that lack of evidence is not evidence. But Ms Chyłka skilfully avoided the subject that interests us most. We have evidence. Substantial evidence. We've heard a witness tell us exactly how the crime happened.'

He paused to look at Szlezyngier, almost with sympathy. 'I cannot guess what is going on in the head of the defendant, but looking at him now, I can only assume he regrets it.' The prosecutor took a deep breath and puffed out his chest. 'So for this reason we are asking the court to return a verdict not of murder, but of manslaughter. We note the evidence does not suggest direct intent. This man did not want to kill his daughter, but kill her he did, and he must be punished for it. Thank you.'

Chyłka paused to consider her options. She had no real arguments left. She'd laid out everything she had while cross-examining the witnesses and interviewing the experts, and all her theories had been debunked. The judges and jury would remember that.

This time she gave it her all, and managed to stand up. She stood precariously, supported by Kordian's outstretched arm. He smiled and nodded to her, as if to say it was all right, but it hit her hard. It wasn't often she felt this vulnerable.

'Your Honour,' she began. 'I've spent a long time wondering how to start my speech, and I've decided to turn to the classics. We don't know who said the words I am about to quote, but I expect it was a representative of Roman jurisprudence, when the Roman Republic or Empire was in its heyday.'

The presiding judge glared at her, while the second judge placed his hands carefully on the table.

'*Qui accusare volunt, probationes habere debent,*' she said. 'He who wishes to accuse must have proof. We all know that officially, the prosecutor should also be the accuser. Yet in this case, he is not the defendant's opponent. That title belongs to Angelika Szlezyngier. It was she who started out as the co-accused, and it is she who has now placed the blame squarely on my client's shoulders. Ultimately, therefore, it is she who should provide evidence. Her testimony cannot simply be accepted as sufficient, credible explanation. She is doing everything she can to protect herself, and can thus scarcely be expected to act for the benefit of my client, whose conviction is tantamount to exoneration for her.'

The long speech had weakened Joanna. She swayed slightly, and Oryński flexed his arm to give her better support. The judge opened his mouth, but didn't speak.

'Those transcripts of the phone conversation?' said Joanna. 'They do not constitute evidence, as the prosecutor told us himself. They were simply there to . . . I can't quite remember how he put it . . . jog Mrs Szlezyngier's memory? If that's all they were, they should not be used as a basis for the verdict.'

She faltered again, and this time she had to sit down. Kordian helped her back into her wheelchair.

'This case is all about manipulation. Highly skilful manipulation. For instance the two press conferences, one after the other, called by Mrs Szlezyngier's d . . .' She lowered her head and took a breath.

'Do you need to take a break?' asked the presiding judge, although he didn't seem at all bothered.

'No, Your Honour, thank you,' she said, and looked back up. 'It's about pulling the wool over everyone's eyes, it's a con, like Mr Kosmowski and Mr Aronowicz's press conferences.'

It was never a good idea to use colloquial language in the courtroom, but Joanna was slowly beginning to lose control over what she was saying. She thought she'd better not say any more.

'That's all,' she said. 'And bearing that in mind, I ask that my client be acquitted. Thank you.'

The judges and jury did not deliberate for long. Although every minute seemed like an eternity, Chyłka had to admit that objectively speaking, they'd moved quickly. Which was hardly surprising.

As the presiding judge straightened his robe, his second-in-command looked at Joanna sympathetically. She knew that look. It said, *I know what you're getting at, but you have no proof.* She'd seen it before, though never directed at her.

But it crossed her mind she might have misread him, and she felt a glimmer of hope. She'd seen cases where the judge behaved like a complete snake in the courtroom, then ruled in her favour. Like everyone else, even judges had to keep up appearances. If her client were to be acquitted now, it would be hard to pinpoint any behaviour on the part of the judge that could be deemed controversial, but he had made it clear throughout the trial whose side he was on.

The next glimmer of hope was the look on the face of one of the jurors. He looked at her with both sympathy and satisfaction, making her think that perhaps not all was lost.

'Do you see that?' she asked Kordian, as the panel settled back into their seats and the presiding judge straightened the eagle on his chain of office.

'See what?'

'Look, that—'

'We will now proceed to the reading of the verdict,' announced the judge. 'Silence, please.'

Joanna realised that, behind her, people were quietly exchanging remarks, and that she was being an inveterate pessimist. Things might not be as black as they looked. She'd presented a fairly coherent argument in the end, showing that the only solid piece of evidence was a statement given by someone who could equally well be the perpetrator.

The transcript of the conversation could have destroyed Awit completely – but only if it had been introduced at the beginning of the case. By using it as a slur to confuse his defence, Aronowicz had made a grave miscalculation, which could come back to haunt him.

Chyłka looked at Zordon, who also felt a spark of optimism. He shuffled nervously in his seat as the judge lowered the microphone and cleared his throat.

'I declare in the name of the Republic of Poland that a verdict has been reached,' he began, and proceeded to recite the official stock wording.

Chyłka gripped the armrests of her wheelchair. A suspended sentence maybe. There was a host of possibilities, all it took was a little goodwill.

'The court finds the defendant Awit Szlezyngier guilty as charged, and, in accordance with Article 155 of the Criminal Code, imposes a sentence of three years in prison,' announced the judge without looking up from his paper.

Part 4

1

The Żelazny & McVay team quickly filed what was usually known as a Notice of Appeal, which consisted of a letter requesting a justification for the verdict. From that point they had two weeks to file for appeal, but had already done so within the first week. They indicated all the potential errors made by the district court, and expressed doubts about the factual findings.

Neither Joanna nor Kordian was happy with the outcome, but that was nothing compared to what Awit was going through. Three years in prison was like ten years on the outside, and given the way inmates treat child-killers, it would seem like an eternity.

After filing their writ, the pair sat in a little restaurant in the centre of town, on Chłodna Street. The appeal could be filed in the local court, so they hadn't had to go all the way to the Court of Appeal in Białystok, although it would have been on their way. They were packed and ready to go home, their belongings in a small Opel they'd rented from Gepard. They'd parked it outside the restaurant, determined to enjoy a meal before their journey. This past week, their moods had been low, and they hadn't even tried to raise each other's spirits.

'How long will it take?' Oryński asked when their food arrived. He'd ordered salmon, she'd asked for pork.

'It depends on the court,' she replied, stabbing the meat with her fork.

He looked uneasily at her plate. 'Are you pretending that's Aronowicz?'

'I don't need to pretend anything. They're both pigs,' she said, cutting off a juicy chunk of meat. She clearly had more strength than last week, although she still wasn't quite her old self and there was no way she could drive all the way back to Warsaw.

'More or less?'

'What?'

'How long will it take?'

'I already told you, I don't know. A few months at least, maybe six. It depends how busy the court is.'

'And how long the district court decides to take.'

She didn't answer; she was chewing on her pork. Even without her input, Oryński knew that the appeal would be carefully examined before it got any further. Only when they were absolutely sure all the conditions were satisfied would the district court send the file to the appeal court. Then it was a matter of keeping their fingers crossed that the hearing would be scheduled within the next couple of months.

'Awit will be pleased.'

'What about?' she muttered.

'That he's got a few months to go before the verdict becomes binding.'

'I expect he'll be ecstatic.'

Szlezyngier had not been remanded; he was still free. His behaviour in court had proved there was little danger of him trying to obstruct justice, although six months with a prison sentence hanging over his head was hardly a dream scenario.

Before Oryński began practising law, the whole system had seemed nonsensical. A murderer would go to court, be charged, sentenced and found guilty, but instead of being locked up there and then, they'd carry on with their normal lives until the verdict became binding. If neither party objected, this could be as little as twenty-one days, but if the case went to appeal, the verdict would not become final until the appeal court made its ruling.

'We've a long road ahead of us, Zordon.'

'I know.'

'And we have to find some evidence that'll explode in those judges' faces like a nuclear bomb.'

'Don't worry, we will. But at the moment, the only bomb they've got is that phone transcript.'

'Not really.'

'No?'

She shook her head, looking pityingly at his tiny portion of salmon.

'Aronowicz shot himself in the foot,' she said. 'He didn't present it as evidence, and he can't introduce new evidence in the appeal court if it's something he knew about earlier. He knew about this, so now he's been caught with his pants down.'

'Lovely image.'

'It would be infinitely more lovely if we could find something like that ourselves, something of that calibre.'

'Maybe we'll find Ekiel or Tatarnikov.'

'Possibly.'

'Or we might be able to show the child was at home at the time.'

'Uh-huh,' she mumbled, her mouth full.

'Or maybe we'll find her.'

Joanna didn't reply. They both knew the court's verdict was probably correct. The telephone transcript couldn't officially be included as evidence, but from an objective point of view, it was certainly enough to incriminate Awit.

The lawyers looked at one another as if they were both thinking the same thing.

'I once read an article in the Western press,' began Chyłka, 'about how psychopaths and bank directors – and businessmen in general – share a lot of similarities.'

Kordian cut off a corner of his salmon and put it on Chyłka's plate.

'Are you mad?'

'You really should try it,' he said, chewing. 'But carry on about those psychopaths.'

'They have a lot in common,' she said, putting the fish back on his plate. 'They're mentally resilient, they're sophisticated and they have charisma. And apparently when they compared their brain scans, even those were quite similar.'

'You learn something new every day.'

'They show courage, they're efficient, they're uncompromising . . . there's so much they share.'

'So what you're getting at is that Awit really could have killed her?'

Chyłka laughed, as if they were discussing a hypothetical case, rather than one they were working on. It was, Kordian had realised long ago, the only way to stay sane.

'To me, that's obvious, Zordon. And I can see it is to you too, which is the only thing that cheers me up about this whole sorry mess.'

'Glad to be of service.'

'And I'll tell you something else.'

'I'm not sure I want to hear it.'

She put down her knife and fork and looked straight at him. 'In Aronowicz's place, I wouldn't have gone for manslaughter.'

Kordian raised his eyebrows.

'With evidence like that, I'd have pressed for first-degree murder. I'd have proved that he hit his wife while she had a child in her arms, knowing it might cause the little one's death.'

'You're not serious.'

This time she raised her eyebrows.

'Why? It's as clear as day. I have no idea why Aronowicz didn't go for it.'

'Maybe he has more empathy than you.'

'That's quite a compliment, Zordon,' she said. 'You know just what to say to turn a woman's head.'

'I do my best,' he said with a forced smile. 'I already miss carrying you over the threshold.'

'Don't worry, you'll be doing a bit more carrying yet.'

'In Warsaw?'

She laughed. 'No, not in Warsaw. Did you think I'd be inviting you to live with me?'

'Kind of.'

'Well, you thought wrong. But you'll have a chance to carry me romantically to the car after we've eaten. Only without any accidental slobbering, OK?'

'I'll see what I can do.'

For the first time since losing the case, they smiled openly at one another, then finished their meal in peace, talking about Warsaw and deliberately avoiding the subject of Szlezyngier. But Kordian couldn't get Joanna's words about their client out of his head.

As they got into the Opel, he realised it wasn't that he objected to Awit being branded a murderer; he had long come to terms with the fact that they could be defending a child-killer. It was something Chyłka had said about the prosecution.

Kordian switched on the engine and looked at her.

'You're right,' he said. 'Aronowicz should have pushed for murder.'

'I know.'

'So why didn't he?'

Joanna pulled down the sun visor and examined her face in the mirror.

'He was scared,' she said.

'What of? Not us, surely, because we came off like a couple of—'

'I've got an excuse,' she said, leaning to the side and inspecting the fading bruises. 'I was barely alive. And you didn't do too badly. But let's leave it there, shall we?'

It was quite a friendly exchange by her standards, especially considering it was the perfect opportunity for a few choice insults.

'OK,' he agreed. 'But I'm still surprised that he didn't go for murder.'

'He didn't want to put Szlezyngier away for life, Zordon.'

'You think?' he asked, merging into the traffic.

'Three years is bad enough. When he comes out of prison, he'll be a different person.'

'He certainly will,' muttered Kordian. 'He'll be able to teach Warsaw's gay clubs a thing or two about bedroom technique.'

'That's for sure.'

Oryński indicated, and, to his passenger's consternation, pulled into the slow lane. She gave him the evil eye, but said nothing. Then she closed the sun visor and looked out of the window.

'So are you telling me Aronowicz was driven by his sense of decency?' he asked.

'Absolutely not. Ludicrous suggestion,' she answered. 'What he wanted was to be sure of a conviction, probably for his statistics. Accusing Awit straight out of murder would have been a bit risky, but with manslaughter, he'd be certain to win the case and get the verdict he asked for. Which would keep his superiors happy.'

'I don't buy it.'

'Because you like your conspiracy theories.'

He refused to let her shut him down.

'But supposing he knows something?' he asked. 'Something that casts doubt on the murder?'

'It doesn't change anything. As long as we don't know about it, he's got nothing to worry about, has he?'

'That's true, but if there is something—'

'If there is, it'll come out sooner or later,' Joanna interrupted. 'Now concentrate on your driving, because I have unpleasant memories of being a passenger in a car where the driver was incompetent.'

'You'll be back to driving yourself before you know it.'

Chyłka nodded happily. 'And I'll be behind the wheel of my X5.'

'Won't it go to scrap?'

'What a barbaric suggestion,' she declared. 'I might have to pay a bit, but I'll get it back. And I guarantee you, I'll get the money back from my insurance.'

'As long as you get back to your old legal self,' said Kordian. 'Because the way you are now, even I could crush you in court.'

'Rubbish. Didn't you hear my closing speech? It was masterful.'

'Until you started speaking so quietly no one could hear you.'

'Zordon, just shut up and drive.'

It took them a little over four hours to get to Warsaw, during which time Kordian endured a slew of wisecracks about how the X5, with Joanna behind the wheel, would have warped the space-time continuum and reached the capital in three.

At Chyłka's apartment block, she opened the gate with the remote control and ordered Oryński to take her bag upstairs along with his own. He stared at her.

'Something wrong?' she asked.

'You said not to even think about moving in with you.'

'You're not. You're my sofa-guest. Come on, let's go.'

'Makes me sound like some sort of pet.'

'You think that's a coincidence? Now lift me up, and let's face the fray. We could both use a drink.'

Kordian saluted and did as he was told, taking his supervisor upstairs, then coming back for their luggage. When he came in with the last of the bags, Joanna was sitting on the sofa, staring at the TV.

She looked as if she'd seen a ghost.

'What's wrong? Wojewódzki been knocked off his perch?' Kordian asked, surveying the flat. There was only one bedroom, so he'd be making do with the living room and its rock-hard sofa.

She made no reply, and he eyed her uneasily.

'What's wrong?' he asked again.

'Look.'

He stood beside her and looked at the screen. It showed a TVN24 news reporter standing on the shore of a smallish lake. The bank was overgrown, the police tape standing out clearly against the grass.

Kordian sat down beside Chyłka.

'We know that the victim did not live in the Drawsko Lake District,' said the reporter solemnly. He must have just got started. 'Unofficial sources tell us that the body was found in the water by an angler. Divers have found the victim's wallet, but no money in it. There was, however, an ID card, and according to our investigations, it seems the deceased was one of the witnesses in the high-profile criminal trial of Awit Szlezyngier, the businessman convicted last week of killing three-year-old Nikola Szlezyngier. The verdict is not yet binding.'

2

For this one evening, Joanna turned her flat into a centre of operations, a real live incident room. As soon as she'd got over the initial shock, she called Kormak to bring his laptop and any other equipment he felt might be useful. The young man had no idea what she was planning to do or what she might need, but she didn't elaborate. Then she realised Kormak didn't have a car. He was an obsessive user of public transport, which he rode while reading his Cormac McCarthy novels over and over. So she sent Kordian to fetch him, then opened a large Heineken in blissful solitude.

From her spot on the sofa, she watched the same information again and again, presented in various different ways. Under instructions from the police, TVN24 and the other stations were unable to release the victim's name, or even gender.

The reporter was clearly a rookie. He couldn't control his emotions and fidgeted in front of the cameras. He'd probably only got the story because he happened to be there first. Luckily for Chyłka, inexperience made him disclose a few details that, to her, were worth their weight in gold. He made it clear that the police were not treating this as a drowning, but as a death in suspicious circumstances, and also let slip that the case would be handled by the Drawsko Pomorskie district prosecutor's office.

Within half an hour, Oryński was back, Kormak in tow.

'So this is the famous Casa di Chyłka?' Kormak put the laptop bag down on the floor.

'Pretty impressive, isn't it?' said Kordian.

'I'm not sure,' Kormak replied. 'I was expecting to hear an Iron Maiden guitar riff from outside, then to be hit with the smell of meat and nicotine as I came in. But it's actually you who stinks of cigarettes.'

Joanna looked at Kordian crossly, but he just shrugged.

'Sit down and set up your stuff.'

Out of his bag, Kormak produced an old laptop, which didn't look anything like the latest model. Chyłka had expected her pet technology geek to have a spanking new MacBook, but this was more of an old-fashioned square box.

'What's that?' she asked.

'A ZBook.'

'Looks hideous.'

'It's tailored to its owner,' said Kormak, opening it. 'Ugly, but damned good at its job. Now tell me what it is you want. And what equipment did you want me to bring?'

The gleam in his eye suggested he'd been hoping for some illegal eavesdropping, or hacking, or another of the dubious activities he engaged in in his role as senior information specialist.

'I only mentioned needing equipment to entice you out of your burrow.'

'Right.'

'I know you, Kormak,' she said. 'It's not easy to force you out of your McCarthy cave. Now, shall we get down to business?'

Kordian went to fetch a beer from the fridge, while Chyłka looked at the television screen. There was a discussion going on in the studio now, with experts on anything and everything giving their opinions on the drowning.

'What's this rubbish?' asked Kormak.

'We need to know which of our witnesses is dead and why.'

'Your witnesses? In the Szlezyngier case?'

'Got it in one,' said Oryński, sitting down next to Chyłka again. He handed her a bottle, then took a gulp from his own. Neither bothered to offer Kormak a drink, because as far as they knew, he only drank carrot juice or water and never touched alcohol. Although he wasn't averse to a spot of Gandalf the White, as speed was generally known in the Skylight building.

Chyłka looked deep into his eyes, searching for signs of recent drug use. There was nothing, which was a little disappointing; with narcotic support, Kormak worked faster than Mark Zuckerberg devising new ways to make Facebook users part with their money.

'So one of your witnesses was killed?'

'Murdered,' Joanna corrected him. 'And we need to know everything there is to know.'

'Can't you ask the prosecutor's office? It sounds pretty important.'

'It is important,' said Kordian. 'But we don't know anyone in . . . where was the place again?'

'It doesn't matter,' said Joanna, waving towards the laptop. 'Google it, and find out everything you can.'

'But how am I supposed—'

'You know your way round the internet, you'll think of something.'

'So what, you want me to hack the police database?'

'I don't know, I'm not the one who said it.'

Kormak shook his head. 'We won't find anything there anyway,' he said. 'It'll take time for them to enter the data, and I can imagine some poor sap doing it tomorrow at the earliest.'

'That's why I'm telling you not to hack anything.'

'Right.'

For a moment, the trio sat in silence.

'So what do you want me to do?'

Joanna pointed to the screen. 'The police clearly didn't cordon off the crime scene in time. Look how many ghouls are there already,' she said. 'Like flies around a cow pat. And that means they'll be posting photographs online, along with their own opinions. You know where to look for that sort of thing.'

'I don't.'

'No?' she asked, surprised. 'But I thought I'd once caught you in your McCarthy cave looking at—'

'OK, OK, I'll do it,' he said, raising his hands in the air. Then he lowered them onto the keyboard and began hammering on the keys with gusto. He quickly found what he was looking for on the community discussion site Wykop. There were also links to other, less popular portals, whose moderators didn't seem to object to users posting photographs of a live crime scene. And although they were probably all taken on people's phones, the quality wasn't bad at all.

Kormak yelped when he saw a picture of the dead man, then skimmed through the available information before starting to dig deeper. It took him a moment or two to spot that his two colleagues were sitting rooted to the sofa, their beers still in their hands.

'What's wrong?' he asked, tearing himself away from the screen.

Then he realised – they must have recognised the victim.

'Fuck,' he said. 'You know who this is, don't you?'

Chyłka shook herself, took a gulp of beer and put the bottle down on the cabinet.

'With me, Zordon,' she said. 'And bring your cigarettes.'

They went to the kitchen, where Chyłka opened a cupboard

and pulled out an ashtray. Kordian followed a few seconds behind, while Kormak sat at his computer, trying to figure out who it was they had seen. The two lawyers stood at the window. Oryński had taken out his cigarettes, and Chyłka helped herself to one, lighting it before she had time to think. At first, the effect of the smoke was horrendous, and her whole body twitched. But along with that came a feeling of relief.

'I take it neither of us is in any doubt,' said Kordian, his voice flat.

'None at all,' Joanna confirmed. 'It's Antoni Ekiel.'

'But the reporter said a witness.'

'And he was right. We called him as a witness.'

Kordian inhaled deeply, then lifted his chin and blew the smoke out of the window.

'Why would anyone . . .' he began, then stopped, shaking his head.

'Ekiel must have known something.'

They fell silent, each puff helping them put the pieces together to build a cohesive picture. Then Chyłka flicked her cigarette-end out of the window, and Kordian did the same.

'Do you think Tatarnikov killed him?' he asked, turning to Joanna.

'I wouldn't like to speculate.'

'But it would make sense. Logically, I mean.'

'Logically?' she hissed. 'For something to be logical, it has to be based on some sort of premise. And what would that be, would you say?'

He looked at her and closed the window. 'We haven't got one,' he answered.

'Exactly. We have no idea what happened to Sakrat and Ekiel after they left the village. They could have gone their separate ways, they could have fled to Europe together, maybe they pissed someone off, or maybe the old man was simply in the wrong place at the wrong time. Whichever one you pick, it'll be a guess, not a logical conclusion.'

'I get it.'

They returned to the living room and looked hopefully at Kormak, who sat huddled over his laptop, his cheeks flushed, like an avid gamer showing his online opponents exactly why he was the number one player.

'Kormak,' said Joanna, 'have you found anything interesting?'

'I've found quite a lot of interesting stuff.'

'Yes, I can see by your face,' she said. 'But I meant interesting for us.'

'One of the rubberneckers tried to sell their pictures to NSI.'

'Sell them?' said Kordian. 'Don't they have a platform for citizen journalism?'

'They do. But this guy wanted money for his picture.'

'Why, what's in it?' asked Chyłka.

'A detailed close-up of the dead man's face,' said Kormak, turning his laptop towards the other two. 'Before the police arrived, two lads climbed into the water and turned the body over.'

Oryński looked at the gruesome image. Because the man's head was heavier than the rest of his body, there were visible signs of livor mortis. There was also evidence of washerwoman's skin all over the body, and in places the epidermis was swollen and almost completely white. The face bore little resemblance to a human being. The clothing was in tatters, revealing occasional fragments of flesh, and the presence of bluish petechiae bore witness to the victim's struggle for breath.

'Looks like he's been strangled,' said Joanna.

'What?'

'Look at his neck. Next to the patches of livor mortis.'

Kordian forced himself to look. The lower lip was swollen, as if it was about to fall off, and all around it was a white growth, resembling frothy saliva. Probably some type of fungus. Kordian shuddered, but managed to focus for long enough to see that there were unmistakable traces of strangulation.

'Well,' said Chyłka, leaning closer to the laptop, 'now at least we know why the police think this wasn't accidental. Someone murdered Ekiel and dumped his body in the water. And based on what he told me down by the lake that day, I'd say it was no more than a few days ago. That's quite ironic, that I can only estimate the time of his death thanks to him.'

'How did you work that out?'

'It's been hot, and the water's warm,' she said. 'If he'd been there for much more than a couple of days, the skin would begin to detach.'

'I'm sorry, what?' said Kormak.

'You'd be able to pull off the skin from the hand like a glove, fingernails and all.'

'I'm sorry I asked,' said Kordian, and hurriedly reached for his Heineken. 'We've got to get in touch with someone about this. Who the hell is running the case?' he asked Kormak.

'The district prosecutor's office in Drawsko Pomorskie.'

Kordian nodded, and sat down next to his friend, who turned the laptop screen so he could see it. For a moment they stared at the remains, until Kormak switched to another tab, and they both took a breath.

'You guys have a lousy job,' he said, 'but I guess you get paid for it.'

'When I last checked, you were being paid twice as much as I am.'

'Naturally,' said Kormak. 'I work like a dog all day, and then, in my time off, you ask me to do this sort of stuff for you. And who's going to have nightmares later? Me of course.'

'Says the one who's always reading Cormac McCarthy,' muttered Joanna, her attention on her phone. 'There were some pretty colourful descriptions in *Blood Meridian*. Graphic scenes of blood and guts on the sands between America and Mexico.'

'That's different.'

Chyłka dialled a number and settled back in her seat while her colleagues tried to listen in on her conversation. Oryński could only think of two people she'd call in this situation: Żelazny or McVay. And given that McVay's contacts were mostly abroad, she'd probably gone for Old Rusty.

'Is that Aronowicz?' she asked, and looked down.

3

'I'm watching TV,' barked a voice from the handset. Joanna's hackles rose instantly, but she had decided to ignore the recent past and keep her cool with him.

'Excellent. That means I don't need to explain anything.'

'I rather think you do.'

'I'm sorry?' she said, aiming for a neutral tone.

'I don't understand why you're calling me.'

Chyłka glanced at Oryński and Kormak, then leaned against the cabinet, placed her phone on the surface and switched to speakerphone.

'Hello?' said the prosecutor. 'Are you still there?'

'Yes.'

'So what do you want?'

Hearing his curt answers and abrasive tone, she felt tempted to commit an offence under Article 148 of the Criminal Code herself.

'Our witness has been murdered.'

'Is that right?'

Joanna looked at Kordian, who shook his head and took a sip of his beer, totally resigned. Kormak frowned and leaned back on the sofa, wondering who the dickhead was that Chyłka was talking to.

She, meanwhile, took a lungful of air and tried to keep her irritation in check.

'We've seen pictures of the crime scene,' she began. 'The deceased has ligature marks on his neck.'

'I haven't seen any photographs.'

'They'll be in your inbox any second.'

'Don't you dare,' he said firmly. 'I refuse to get my hands dirty with the kind of images you'd find in tabloids and gossip magazines. If that's what you want to do, it only shows how—'

'Listen to me, Aronowicz,' Joanna interrupted. 'We can snipe at each other until my phone battery dies, but it won't change anything.'

She fell silent, and for a moment the only sound was a faint buzzing on the line.

'What do you want from me?' said the prosecutor at last.

'I want you to do your job.'

'I am. To the best of my ability.'

'By charging an innocent man?'

Aronowicz burst out laughing. He forced himself to laugh long and hard, as if the laughing itself wasn't enough for him. Now the hearing was over, he'd dropped his mask, revealing the person he really was.

'Szlezyngier killed that child, whether he meant to or not. You must know that by now.'

'You think so? What about the body in the lake?'

'Firstly, you don't know if that was—'

'It was murder, there's no question. Open your eyes!'

'I did, as soon as Angelika stood on that rostrum and told us all what happened,' he said. 'Until that moment, I thought the child had been abducted by aliens.'

'And you can keep that kind of remark to yourself.'

'It's the only logical alternative. I'm surprised you didn't suggest it in court. Given all your other theories, it would fit in perfectly.'

Chyłka squeezed her lips together and held her hand out to Oryński. He threw her his cigarettes. She took one, placed it in her mouth and leaned over the candle.

'So you're just going to ignore the fact that a witness is dead?' she asked, blowing out smoke. It still made her lungs scratchy, and the taste made her think of old, spent chewing gum, but Joanna was in seventh heaven knowing she was actually smoking.

'No, not at all.'

She straightened up, and something clicked in her back. Maybe Aronowicz wasn't quite the hopeless case she had him down as. He could badger her all he liked, but in the end even he must be able to see that something about this case wasn't right.

'And I intend to take the appropriate action.'

'I'm very glad to hear it.'

'You shouldn't be.'

'I'm sorry?'

There was an ostentatious sigh from the receiver. 'The one person who saw the girl with Szlezyngier that night is dead.'

Again, Chyłka looked at Kordian, who got up and also lit up a cigarette. Kormak objected, but the lawyers ignored him. Oryński stood by his supervisor, and both stared at the phone.

'What are you talking about?' she asked.

'I'm sure you remember the old man's witness statement.'

'I remember it perfectly. And if he was here to repeat it, we'd have conclusive proof that your client – oh, I'm sorry, Kosmowski's client – is lying.'

The prosecutor burst out laughing again, but this time condescendingly, as if he couldn't believe how naïve she was.

'Antoni Ekiel's statement incriminated Szlezyngier, Chyłka,' he said. 'And he didn't say what condition the girl was in. If your client was carrying a body, Ekiel couldn't have known. Obviously, his testimony confirms everything we've established so far. Or it would, if I could ask him at the appeal hearing for more details. But meanwhile, here he is, dead. Which of us will benefit more from this, would you say?'

Chyłka picked up her phone and punched the red receiver icon. She didn't want to hear another word. She looked at Zordon, shook her head and took a deep drag on her cigarette.

'You know what? He's right,' said Kordian.

'Shut up.'

'Ekiel might well have seen Awit carrying the child.'

'Don't badmouth him now.'

'You know yourself it's the most likely scenario.'

Joanna stared absent-mindedly out of the window, then shifted in her seat and closed her eyes. Kordian was right, it could be exactly as the prosecutor had said. And if she saw that, so would the appeal judges. It would, of course, be difficult for Awit to be accused of Ekiel's death, but the implications were clear.

'I'm getting the impression everything's stacking up against you,' said Kormak. 'Don't get me wrong, it's good to watch you get knocked back from time to time, but this is starting to look suspicious.'

Kordian pointed his finger at Kormak.

'That's exactly it,' he said. 'And it's what I've been saying for a while.'

'Because you still hope it's all just one big conspiracy. The conspiracy theory of the century.'

'I'm not saying you're right, but I'm not saying you're wrong either.'

Joanna opened her eyes and looked at the two young men.

'Stop deluding yourself, Zordon,' she said. 'I understand that when things go wrong, we want to blame the whole world, not just ourselves. But in this case, you have to acknowledge your mistakes and face up to them.'

'Like you do?'

'More than you'll ever know,' she said. 'I'm fully aware of what could have been done and what I didn't do.'

Kormak closed his laptop and picked up the bag.

'I'd better be going,' he said, getting up. 'It's getting dangerous in here.'

He gave them both another smile, then looked at Kordian's Heineken. Clearly he'd have to get a taxi home.

And then the two lawyers were alone again. They didn't speak. Kordian picked up the remote and turned the TV back on. The drowned man was already old news, and the focus was now on farmers blockading one of the provincial roads. The court wouldn't forget so easily though, and Szlezyngier's defence team would have to scale the heights of sophistry to present their client in a favourable light.

'You know, I'm tempted to hire someone to follow him,' said Chyłka after a while.

'Who, Aronowicz?'

'No,' she said in surprise. 'Why would we want to follow him?'

'Because he might be mixed up in—'

'Oh yes, the Zordon conspiracy theory.'

He didn't answer, just scowled at her.

'And can you tell me what that theory would involve?' she asked, 'and exactly who would benefit?'

'Angelika.'

'You think so? How?'

'She'll be acquitted.'

When Chyłka had watched the hearing at which Angelika incriminated her husband, she'd thought so too, but on reflection, she wasn't so sure.

'Would she take such a huge risk?' she asked, more of herself than of him. 'They both stood a better chance of acquittal before she changed her story. If she's lying, as you seem to think, there's a good chance the truth will come out, and then she'll be behind bars for the rest of her life. As I see it, your version doesn't work for anybody. It would have been much safer for her to stick with her husband.'

'But...'

'So the only reason she'd change her story is to tell the truth. And that's where your conspiracy theory falls apart.'

Oryński lit another cigarette and contemplated the rising smoke. Chyłka knew it wouldn't take him too long to reach the same conclusion she had.

'So who is it you want to follow?' he asked.

'Awit, of course.'

'But why?'

'Because if he's got anything to do with Ekiel's death, I need to know.'

'And how will tailing him help?'

'Well, Szlezyngier would have hired someone to do the killing, wouldn't he? He wouldn't want to risk it himself if he didn't have to. So let's see who he contacts, who brings him packages, that sort of thing.'

'Packages?'

'He never leaves that summer house,' she said. 'I spoke to the guest house owner a while ago, and she said he buys everything he needs online. Oh, and that he went back to the lake house when Angelika went to Warsaw.'

'She's the one we should be following,' Oryński muttered.

Joanna turned back to the TV, although she doubted she'd learn anything new. Innocent people rarely provide their opponents with good arguments.

4

Two weeks later, Joanna was welcomed back to the Żelazny & McVay offices with much fanfare. Although Kordian had promised not to give away the exact date of her return, he decided it might be fun to spread the word then stand back and watch her reaction.

The twenty-first floor of the Skylight building was decked out with black balloons for the occasion, and an Iron Maiden album was playing in the reception area. Oryński waited for Chyłka downstairs, then got into the lift with her, keeping up a constant barrage of small talk.

When they arrived, the lift doors slid open to reveal a train of Żelazny & McVay staff waiting in the corridor. Usually at this time, the office was in the most infernal chaos, with people shouting over one another, passing unfinished documents back and forth and handing over letters to post. Now the only sound was Bruce Dickinson and the guitar riffs from 'The Wicker Man'.

Chyłka's eyes bulged, and she turned to Kordian. 'What the fuck is this supposed to be?' she whispered.

'Your welcome-back party.'

'You're going to regret this.'

'I don't doubt it,' he said. 'But it was worth it, just to see your face.'

Joanna gave him a sharp jab in the ribs with her elbow, then pasted on a smile and strode out of the lift. At the head of the line was Żelazny, and Kordian was reminded of his own welcome back to the firm a year ago. There hadn't been the same pomp and circumstance then, but Old Rusty had said a few words about him being a hero. This time though, he wasn't about to make a speech, aware of how painful the repercussions might be.

'Welcome back,' he said, shaking Chyłka's hand stiffly, as if they were heads of state at an official meeting. Someone took a photo on their phone, and Kordian positioned himself behind the two lawyers and snapped a selfie.

'Are you insane?' whispered Joanna through a forced smile.

'It's just a selfie with friends. A friendsie, if you like.'

'I'll give you friendsies. Watch out for them on your way home late at night – a couple of mates of mine.'

'I'll sprint.'

Chyłka shook hands with another dozen or so colleagues, then announced she had to return to work. With a feigned look of sadness, she went into her office, Kordian on her heels. He closed the door and looked at the strangely empty desk.

'I'm so sorry,' he said. 'I had to do it.'

'Actually, I should have expected it from you,' she said, sitting down in her chair. Oryński took a seat on the opposite side of the desk, on an uncomfortable chair designed to remind clients not to outstay their welcome.

'I could see you enjoyed it.'

'Oh yeah, sure,' she retorted. 'I've really missed the aura of hypocrisy those people give off.'

'They welcomed you like royalty.'

'Yes, Zordon, I noticed,' she said, switching on her computer. 'And I almost forgot they gossip about me behind my back like a bunch of old crones.'

'I've never heard a bad word about you.'

'No?' she said with a smile, scrolling through her inbox. 'What about: "That Chyłka, she always gets the best cases"? Or "She gets special privileges because she has a foot in both the Żelazny and McVay camps"?'

'Now you come to mention it . . .'

'Or you might have heard that I objectify people.'

'Ye-e-s,' he said with a smile, 'I have heard that. And I have to say, there's something in it.'

He waited for a biting response, but none came. Joanna was staring at her monitor. She tore her gaze away.

'We've got a date,' she said. 'The first hearing's in two months.'

'That was quick.'

'Because it's in the media. They want to prove that the Polish court system is like Usain Bolt.'

'Do you think we'll have mustered up anything new by then?'

'I don't know.'

Time marched inexorably on, and the chances of finding some way to turn Awit's fortunes around were waning.

Joanna and Kordian ate lunch in the Hard Rock Café next to the Skylight. Their food order remained unchanged, but their moods were gloomier than usual. And the next few days saw no improvement.

Kordian thought about the appeal less and less. He had a new client, a man charged with drunk driving. There wasn't a lot he could do, as the driver had thirty-five milligrams of alcohol in his breath. Oryński expected he'd be suspended and ordered to pay a fine of around five hundred zlotys.

It was a simple case, and a welcome distraction from the complications surrounding Awit and Angelika. They no longer featured in the media. The appeal might give the case a new lease of life – but then again, possibly not. It was usually only the initial hearing that attracted attention, until the non-binding verdict was delivered. What happened afterwards was of little interest to the public, especially in this case. Everyone was sure the appeal court would uphold the original ruling, and although Chyłka had been back at work for a month and a half, they still had nothing to show their client was innocent. And they still hadn't found any traces of the child.

Kordian didn't know what to believe. If Szlezyngier was guilty, at least Nikola was now at peace. If he wasn't, and she'd been abducted, she could be in some hellhole across the eastern border, being groomed for under-age prostitution. He shuddered at the thought.

The police had concluded that Antoni Ekiel's death was caused by a third party, but had ruled out strangulation – the marks on his neck turned out to have been made post-mortem. The forensic team had, however, found signs of a struggle on the lake shore. No one had yet been charged.

Szlezyngier was being followed as planned, but even that hadn't yielded anything. Chyłka and Oryński received daily reports from a private detective, whom they'd instructed to watch Awit from the minute he left his home. It wasn't easy, as he only ever left after dark, and then only to stroll around the lake, a distance of just over three kilometres. The tail didn't actually follow him, but stayed outside the house until Awit came back.

A few days before the trial, Joanna's phone rang. Kordian was sitting with her in the Hard Rock Café, hunched over his salmon and small beer; they tried to resist ordering large beers while working.

Joanna listened to what the caller had to say, then told them she'd ring them back.

'What was that?' asked Kordian, his mouth full.

'Our spook wants to follow Awit one night.'

'Around the lake?'

'Correct.'

'He's mad,' Kordian said. 'It's so quiet down there, even during the day. You could hear if someone stepped on a twig a hundred metres away.'

'He says he's been familiarising himself with the area for weeks, and claims he won't be noticed.'

'Do you believe him?'

'Not really. That's why I said I'd ring back. He'd like to do it tonight, because apparently the moon will be behind the clouds.'

'If Awit finds out he's being tailed, he'll cause a stink of epic proportions,' said Kordian.

'You don't say.' Joanna forked up a piece of beef whose spice levels were comparable to the fires of hell. Kordian had tried a small piece once. Never again.

'And before we could put a lid on it, there'd be an out-and-out scandal. And if the court found out, we'd—'

'I'm quite aware of what could happen, Zordon,' she said.

'And still you're wondering whether to let him go ahead.'

Joanna nodded.

'Why?' he asked.

'Because our man reckons it's odd that Szlezyngier walks around like that, night after night.'

Oryński put down his knife and frowned.

'Does he think he's meeting someone?'

'Apparently.'

'What makes him think that? Awit going out at night doesn't prove anything.'

'It might, if he goes out at specific times.'

Now Kordian put his fork down too.

'What?' he asked.

'You heard.'

'And we're only finding out about it now?'

'Because our detective has only just put two and two together.'

'I don't get it,' said Kordian. 'How can you spend nearly two months—'

'He goes out at different times,' Joanna cut in before Kordian had time to launch into a diatribe. 'And it's not necessarily the days of the week that matter, it's the days of the month. Our man says that on the first of the month he goes out at one o'clock, on the second at two and so on. Then on the fifth day, it all goes back to the beginning. He only identified the pattern yesterday, when he sat down with his diary and all his notes.'

'Is he sure?'

'He sounded sure.'

They didn't really have a choice; they had to risk it. The discussion went on for another fifteen minutes, and by the time their beer glasses were empty, they'd made their decision. Chyłka asked the detective to go ahead, and he assured her once again that Awit would never notice him.

'Maybe he has night-vision goggles, and will be watching from a distance,' Oryński suggested with a shrug.

It turned out the detective was very well-prepared. Not only did he have night-vision goggles, he had a tripod and a good camera, which, set to the right shutter speed, took very clear pictures. A dozen photographs landed in Chyłka's inbox the very next morning, and they opened them in her office.

He'd been right. Awit was meeting a man – someone they couldn't identify from the first few frames as he was wearing a hoodie and had his back to them. It was only when the two shook hands that Chyłka and Oryński recognised Kordian's smuggler friend Wito.

And he looked as if he'd struck gold.

5

Chyłka had no intention of confronting her client with this over the phone. As soon as they'd received the photographs, she put on her jacket and headed for the door. Oryński made no objections, and followed her. They didn't speak until they reached the X5. There were no more traces of the accident, other than the scars on Joanna's psyche.

'I take it we're going to Sajenko?' he said, as she started the engine.

'Have I ever told you your perspicacity known no bounds?'

'Yes, I think I've heard that somewhere before.'

'Key the address into Zygmunt.'

'What?'

'The sat-nav. That's what I call him, remember?'

'Sorry,' said Kordian, and leaned forwards to do as she asked. The system showed it would take them three hours and twenty-five minutes to reach their destination.

Under normal circumstances, Joanna would have been sure she could shave half an hour off that, but this time she figured the sat-nav was right. The journey from her home to the centre of Warsaw could be tricky these days. Not physically, as her body had healed now; the problem was her mind. She constantly felt that other cars were closer than they should be. She used to be able to almost brush up against them, dodging from lane to lane. Now she usually preferred to take a taxi.

Even so, old habits died hard – like when she pulled out onto Jan Paweł II Street and automatically put her foot to the floor.

Only now it triggered an irritating safety buffer in her brain, which made her slow down and pull into the right-hand lane.

'This will take me a while to get used to,' said Kordian.

'Don't panic, by the time you're used to it, I'll be up to my usual speed again.'

'Better you're up to speed in court than out here on the streets.'

She knew he didn't mean anything by it, but it was something that worried her more than her inner speed block. She'd never forget how Zbigniew Aronowicz had humiliated her before the entire court. The memory would come to her unbidden as she lay in bed. She felt that she had let him walk all over her, and that the appeal hearing would be a repeat of the same experience.

'Are you ringing Wito?' she asked, looking at Kordian's phone.

'I'm trying, but there's no answer.'

'He should accept your calls. I thought he was your best buddy.'

'Well, yes,' said Kordian. 'If you ignore the fact that he smashed my face in as a greeting.'

'That's how all the best friendships start.'

'Ours started with you telling me not to stink the place out, or something like that.'

'Ours isn't a friendship.'

He looked at her happily, but she left it at that. She looked in the wing mirror and moved into the left lane to overtake an ancient Micra.

'Well done,' said Oryński. 'Just a bit more on the accelerator and we'll be going as fast as that Polonez in front of us.'

Chyłka moved back into the slow lane.

'I thought you'd be the type to show me a bit of sympathy.'

'I need to enjoy the moment,' he said. 'Then I'll be able to tell our grandchildren there was a time their grandma drove as dictated by the rules of the Highway Code.'

'I have no intention of being a grandmother.'

'Never?'

She gave him a quick glance, then focused on the road again. She wasn't exactly crawling along, as Kordian had suggested; if anything, she was slightly above the speed limit, and they got to Sajenko at the time Zygmunt had predicted.

Joanna pulled up outside the Szlezyngiers' summer house, and the pair got out. It looked as if a bomb had gone off. No one had bothered to clean up after the journalists, many of whom had been camped out for some time, and there were piles of crisp bags and chocolate bar wrappers lying about, as well as the remnants of other snacks. And the number of cigarette butts was staggering.

'This looks weird,' said Kordian, as they headed for the house, both lighting up cigarettes. 'As deserted as Chernobyl.'

'They'll soon be back when they hear there's more to this case than anyone realised.'

Because that was how it seemed. Awit's meeting with Wito was not a one-off, and although Chyłka couldn't work out why Szlezyngier would want to see him on a regular basis, she had every intention of finding out.

They climbed the steps, and Oryński knocked. There didn't seem to be any sounds coming from inside. Then Joanna hammered on the door, but the result was the same.

'Maybe he's not in?' ventured Kordian.

'You mean today, for the first time in two months, he's decided to leave the house before dark?'

'Could be. Maybe he noticed yesterday. Maybe—'

'Shh,' she said, holding up a warning hand.

They heard footsteps, and moved back a little. The footsteps came to a halt on the other side of the front door. Szlezyngier was probably looking through the spy-hole. He gave a hoarse cough, then turned the key.

'This had better be important,' he said, opening the door a fraction.

'We wouldn't turn up here days before your trial if it wasn't,' said Chyłka. Awit had to step back to let her in. She looked around, taking a reluctant breath. The house stank of sweat, alcohol and cigarettes. She crossed to the living room and opened the window.

'What are you doing?' asked Szlezyngier.

She turned and looked him in the eyes. His were blank and unfocused, as if he'd just been drinking, but with the general surrounding stench it was hard to say if he had alcohol on his breath.

'The reporters will pounce on that,' he said, making for the open window.

'Which reporters, Awit?'

'The ones in the forest.'

Chyłka and Kordian glanced at one another. Szlezyngier slammed the window shut, clearly annoyed. Then he slumped on the sofa and stretched out his legs on the coffee table. Rubbing the several days' worth of stubble on his chin, he gestured for them to sit down opposite. Neither took him up on the offer: the armchairs looked as if takeaway pizza ended up on them more often than it did on the table.

'There aren't any reporters there,' said Oryński. 'Not anymore.'

'You're wrong.'

'But we checked.'

'Not thoroughly enough then,' said Szlezyngier firmly. 'They hide in the forest. I know they do. Sometimes they even walk with me.'

Chyłka tried to work out whether it was the alcohol addling his brain, or whether he'd actually gone mad. He didn't look very drunk.

'How much do you drink, Awit?' she asked.

'No idea.'

That didn't sound good.

'Let me put it another way,' she said. 'How often do you not drink?'

He shrugged.

'Have you lost your ability to communicate?'

'No. I just don't feel like it.'

Chyłka went into the kitchen. The state of it answered her question. She knew the recycling lorry came once a month to pick up the glass, so the number of empty vodka bottles spoke for itself. And the cupboard was stacked with full bottles, which made her think Szlezyngier must be walking around intoxicated twenty-four hours a day.

She returned to the living room. Awit was still not talking. Oryński had tried to start a couple of casual conversations, but it hadn't worked. The only way to handle this was to get straight to the point. She stood directly opposite Szlezyngier, arms folded.

'We know who you're meeting, Awit.'

He looked up, but said nothing.

'I mean on your late-night walks, in case you wondered.'

'I don't know what you're talking about.'

'You know very well.'

He puffed out his lips, picked his glass up from the table and drained the contents. Then he pushed the glass away and grimaced. He'd obviously had enough that day, although it didn't look like he had any intention of stopping.

'Can you tell me what you're doing meeting the man who helped Sakrat vanish?'

'Go fuck yourself,' said Awit, heaving himself off the sofa. Kordian made a move to follow him, but Joanna stopped him with a wave of her hand. They let Awit go to the kitchen and help himself to another drink, and watched as he returned to his previous position on the sofa.

'Well?' she asked.

'I don't understand the question, miss,' he answered rudely, taking a sip.

'What were you doing with that man?'

'Or what is it you do together, every evening?' Kordian added.

'None of your business,' Awit barked. 'And if that's how you're spending the time just before my trial, I don't see much of a rosy future.'

'You should have thought of that before you killed the child.'

Joanna regretted the words the minute they left her mouth, but it was too late to take them back. She half-expected Szlezyngier to get up off the sofa and launch himself at her, but all he did was raise his eyes. He took another sip, licked his lips and put the glass down.

'Get out of my house. Now.'

'Not unless you tell me what's going on.'

He got up and looked around the room, as if searching for something to use as a weapon. Oryński shuddered, remembering the two previous occasions he'd been in a fight. He'd come off lamentably in both.

'You don't understand, Awit,' said Joanna. 'If you don't want to be the chief whore in a certain block behind a certain high prison wall, you've got to start talk—'

'Get out.' He pointed to the door, but when the pair didn't stir, he made a move towards Kordian.

'Fuck off out of here!' he roared, pushing him. Oryński staggered slightly, but recovered himself quickly enough to push Szlezyngier's hands away. For a fraction of a second, Chyłka thought they'd hurl themselves at one another, but instead, each man took a step back and simply scowled. She scrambled over to Kordian, grabbed him by the arm and pulled him towards the door.

Verbal tussles were all well and good, but physically fighting with a client just before a trial would have been disastrous.

They dived outside, and the door slammed shut behind them. There was a stream of curses, then Awit seemed to go back to the living room, from where they heard the sound of breaking glass. They reached for their cigarettes as they walked down the steps.

Oryński turned to go to the car, but Joanna gestured towards the jetty. They walked to the end, sat down with their legs dangling over the water and lit up.

'It was worth coming, then,' she said.

'Like hell it was.'

'Since when have you been so keen to fight?'

'Since somebody told you to fuck yourself.'

She gave him a nudge, took a pull on her cigarette and smiled.

'You're quite the romantic, Zordon. You have your moments, anyway.'

He shrugged nonchalantly and tried to slip his arm around her. She sent him a warning glance, but it didn't have the desired effect.

'Get your limbs away from me,' she said.

He withdrew his hand, and for a moment they both stared at the headland opposite. There were no bad feelings, but that didn't change the fact that what they did have was one heck of a problem.

'We're all right, you know,' said Kordian.

His voice was serious, so she couldn't fool herself into thinking he was joking. She turned to face him, and realised he was gazing into her eyes.

'What do you mean?'

'This.' He gestured to her, then to himself. Then he took a pull of his cigarette and half-closed his eyes. 'We need only exchange a single sentence, and it starts to make the biggest pile of shit look insignificant.'

'OK, that's slightly less romantic.'

'I'm serious.'

'I can see that.'

He sighed, and stared straight ahead.

'Maybe one day we could talk without going around the houses.'

'Stop.'

'Stop? Just like that?'

'Any more of this and I'll get up and go, Zordon.'

'OK. It was just a thought.'

He gazed far into the distance, and for a moment sat totally still. There wasn't a hint of disappointment, anger or sadness in his face, but Chyłka knew him well enough to know that if he looked indifferent, his feelings were probably the exact opposite.

'Don't create drama where there is none,' she said.

'What?'

'Don't get melodramatic over our relationship.'

'I'm not, I just want to know if you—'

'*Hola, señor.* This is where I have to interrupt you.'

'Supposing I want to finish?'

'Then ring Kormak and confide in him.' She got up and flicked her cigarette butt into the water. It was reckless, she knew, but there wouldn't be any eco-warriors around to see her. They were completely alone.

Kordian got up too, and stood facing her.

'Whatever you say,' he said.

She rolled her eyes. 'You're a trainee, you idiot. And I'm your supervisor.'

'You don't say.'

'That'll change in two years' time.'

They stood for a while, looking at one another, and Joanna hoped that would be the end of it. And it was. Zordon wasn't stupid. What she hadn't said was as eloquent as what she had. He smiled and shook his head.

'Are we off?' he asked, gesturing to the X5.

Somehow, she knew he didn't mean back to Warsaw.

They made their way back to the car. Chyłka peered over to see if Awit was watching them through the window, but the curtains didn't move.

'Do you remember the way?' she asked as they got into the BMW.

'Not very well. I was a bit battered, a bit tipsy and a bit disorientated last time,' he replied. Then he picked up the sat-nav and entered an address in Lebiedzin.

6

Oryński tried to remember the name of the village where the smugglers had their hideout, but simply couldn't. It was where he'd met Jordi and the others and drunk Kenigers with them, but he'd arrived in the back of a delivery van. The only name he remembered was Lebiedzin.

They parked by the place they knew Sakrat and Ekiel had once hidden out, and got out of the car. The old hut looked completely abandoned, but they hammered on the door nonetheless. There was no answer, so they walked around the building, stopping at one of the windows at the back to look inside.

'Someone's been here recently,' said Chyłka.

'How can you tell?'

'Because they're lying over there.' She pointed to a leg sticking out from behind the door to one of the rooms. Kordian peered in the direction she'd indicated, and spotted the other leg, curled up.

'A body?' he asked.

'Can't rule it out,' she answered, 'but it's more likely to be a casualty in the eternal battle against alcohol.'

They walked along the other side of the building, looking for an open window. A couple of months ago, perhaps they'd have found one ajar, but now it was too cold.

'Break a window, Zordon.'

'I'm not falling for that again.'

'I mean it this time.'

'Like you did at Ekiel's house?'

Joanna sighed and looked around. There was a stone of just the right size lying a few metres away. She picked it up, took a swing and hurled it at the glass. Kordian was sure she was bluffing – until the moment the glass shattered.

He looked at her, and she shrugged.

'What?' she said. 'It's such an old hovel, no one will even notice. And besides, there might be a dead body in there. It's our moral duty to investigate.'

'Like hell it is.'

She wrapped the sleeve of her coat around her hand and picked off the remaining shards of glass. Then she put her hand through and opened the window. They both climbed in. Inside, it smelled like the aftermath of a good party: booze and puke, laced with a hint of smoke of indeterminate origin.

On the other side of the hallway lay the man they had seen. Joanna nudged him with her foot.

'Are you mad? Supposing he's dead?'

'Then he won't care,' she said, crouching down beside him.

Kordian did the same, and they began to examine him.

'He's breathing,' she said. 'Although given the fumes, I think I'd rather he wasn't,' she added, turning away. 'Do you recognise him?'

Oryński had been sure he'd recognise the faces of all the smugglers with whom he'd shared the cans of beer, but over time they'd all blurred into one, and he wasn't sure if he recognised this man. The tracksuit and T-shirt combo were familiar, but then the gang all looked disconcertingly similar: hench, a few millimetres of hair and a face you wouldn't want to mess with.

'I don't know.'

'You don't know? Surely you weren't that pissed.'

'You'd be surprised. We'd been drinking all day.'

Chyłka slapped the man's face. He mumbled something and grimaced, but didn't open his eyes. Then he tried to turn onto his side, but couldn't quite manage it, so he just drifted off again. Joanna plunged her hand into his pocket.

'What are you doing?'

'Rummaging in his trousers, isn't it obvious?'

'Yes, I can see that, but I'm wondering why.'

She pulled out a phone and held it up triumphantly. 'Now you can text your friend Wito and tell him to get himself down here while I move my X5 to the back of the building.'

Oryński raised his eyebrows, but took the phone.

'What should I say?'

'I wouldn't know,' she answered, heading for the exit. 'Try some street lingo. Yo, homie, get yo' ass down here, one of the bros is on the brink.'

'You think?'

'You'll come up with something,' she called as she walked away.

It didn't take Kordian long. He wrote that there was some guy in Lebiedzin asking for him, and added that he looked like that businessman accused of murdering his daughter.

Then he decided that if the gang was involved, that last part might look suspicious, so he deleted the whole message and simply said Szlezyngier was here. Everyone knew him from the media anyway, so even if these thugs weren't part of the plot, they'd know who Szlezyngier was. He's asking to see you straight away, Kordian added, then hit send.

In the meantime Chyłka had come back, and they waited anxiously for a reply. It came within minutes, and Wito's answer, despite its brevity, told them all they needed to know. I'm on my way.

Not a quarter of an hour later, they heard his car pull up outside, followed by the slamming of a door and hurried footsteps. Wito burst into the room like a tornado. Seeing the two lawyers standing with folded arms, he froze.

'What the fuck—'

'Surprise!' sang Joanna. 'Let's have a little chat.'

Wito looked ready to turn on his heel and leave, so Chyłka added, 'Think of it as an opportunity that we're giving you out of sheer curiosity, before we go to the police and tell them a few things that might interest them.'

He stood at the door, watching them.

'Do you understand what I'm saying?'

'What I understand is that you're determined to die.'

Joanna unfolded her arms and invited him in, as if she were the host. Which in a way, she was. Wito closed the door, but didn't move from the hallway.

'If I see police anywhere near the house . . .'

'You'll fill your pants,' she finished for him. 'Now cut the bullshit, because I'm tired, annoyed and hungry, and there's nothing in this dump that isn't completely rotten.'

He opened his mouth, but she didn't give him time to speak.

'If we want to drop you in it, we can and we will,' she went on. 'Oryński has seen enough, and a few hundred zlotys will soon persuade some of those morons you work with to tell us what we need to know. As far as you can call it work.' She looked at him, waiting. Kordian wanted to back her up, but she'd said it all. Now Wito just needed to admit she was right. And finally he did.

'What do you want from me?'

She smiled and pulled out a pack of Marlboros.

'We know you and Szlezyngier meet every night,' said Oryński while she lit up.

'What?'

'Awit makes it look as if he goes out for walks at random times, but we know those times are fixed, depending on the day of the month.'

'Have you been following us?'

'Absolutely not,' said Joanna, puffing out smoke, 'which doesn't alter the fact that you've just confirmed it.'

'But . . .' He stopped, glancing round as if he thought he might be being watched here too. 'Just a minute, I . . .'

'Take it easy, Wito,' she said. 'There are no cameras or listening devices here. You can talk freely.'

It took a moment for everyone to check that their phones weren't recording, then they went to the kitchen and sat down. It was relatively tidy – there were no beer cans, at least. It seemed everyone drank in their rooms.

'Now talk,' said Kordian. 'Why are you meeting? And who killed Ekiel?'

Wito looked at them, fear etched on his face.

'Just a minute. Surely you don't think I—'

'No we don't,' Chyłka cut in. 'That's not the type of crime you get involved in. But you could have been an intermediary.'

'A fucking middleman? What in?'

Joanna clasped her hands behind her chair and looked down at Wito.

'This is what I think happened. Awit was paying you to look for Tatarnikov. You couldn't find him, but you did track down Ekiel, and you told Awit that during one of your nightly escapades. He then gave you a pile of cash to find someone to kill him. Getting Ekiel out of the picture was crucial for Awit, because if Ekiel had decided to testify again, he may have mentioned he'd seen him down at the lake, carrying the child. And even if the old man hadn't wondered whether the child was alive or dead, the court certainly would. Szlezyngier knew he had to get rid of him.'

Wito, who'd been sitting motionless, suddenly burst out laughing. Shaking his head, he pulled out a packet of cheap Belarusian cigarettes and lit one.

'Jesus Christ,' he said, 'you know nothing.'

It was his turn to puff out smoke, while the lawyers looked on in silence.

'Correct me if I've gone wrong anywhere,' said Chyłka.

'I wouldn't even know where to start.'

'At the beginning.'

Wito sighed. 'If you hoped I could give you something concrete, you're wrong,' he began, looking around for an ashtray before he realised Joanna was flicking her ash onto the floor. Not that it would make much difference.

'What were you doing for him?' Kordian asked, leaning over the table.

'He contacted me some time after the trial. He didn't know who else to turn to, seeing as even his defence team believed he had killed the child. He knew I had friends in . . . let's say various places, so he came to me.'

'More like he knew you'd do anything for money,' said Joanna.

'There's that too,' Wito admitted. 'Anyway, we met. And he offered me a tidy sum to keep looking for the girl and Tatarnikov, and to give him daily progress reports.'

After losing the trial, Kordian was counting on Wito to carry on looking for Sakrat, but Wito had been quick to say that all traces of him had vanished, and that he didn't want to go chasing all over Poland after ghosts. Which wasn't really surprising.

'So I kept looking. Or rather I coordinated the search.' He shrugged. 'I wasn't expecting to find Tatarnikov, because if he'd gone to ground, he'd have done it pretty well. The body gave us a bit of hope, but it came to nothing.'

'And?' asked Chyłka.

Wito shrugged again. 'And nothing. That's it. So much for the great mystery you thought you'd uncovered.'

Joanna smiled in a way that told him plainly she had not a shred of sympathy for him.

'Bullshit,' she said. 'If what you're saying is true, Szlezyngier would have told us the minute we stepped into his house.'

'Have you talked to him then?' asked Wito.

'We've tried,' replied Oryński, 'and Chyłka's right. If it was about looking for the girl and Sakrat, he'd have told us.'

'You've got no idea what's going on in that old dipso's head. Now you'll have to excuse me, I'm getting the fuck out of here.' With that, he got up, threw his cigarette butt in the sink and made for the door.

'Not so fast,' Joanna warned. 'You walk out of here, you make enemies of us both.'

'I couldn't give a fuck,' he said. 'I've told you everything I know. If you want to concoct more theories, be my guest. But I won't be here. If you want to know more about what I've been doing for Szlezyngier, you can ask him. We'll get back to you when we find the body.'

He went out without bothering to shut the door. Kordian looked at Chyłka, but she dismissed him with a wave.

'We'll get nothing more out of him,' she said.

'Do you think there's something more to get?'

'Definitely, Zordon. I think there's more to this case than we realised.'

'What makes you say that?'

Chyłka watched as the car pulled away.

'Because that bastard was lying like a cheap rug.'

On the morning of the hearing, Chyłka stood at the mirror in her hotel room, examining her reflection. The room in Białystok's Hotel Gołębiewski wasn't cheap, but Chyłka had given the bill only a cursory glance before putting it away in the file she'd later hand to the admin team at Żelazny & McVay. The location was good. It was only fifteen minutes to the appeal court building, and the walk, she decided, would clear her mind. It was chilly, but not so cold it would bother her. She looked in the mirror again. Her hair was appropriate for a court hearing but not overly conservative, and her make-up was light, with just a hint of aggression. The rest didn't matter, as her robes would hide it anyway.

She looked her reflection in the eye, nodded, and left the room. Kordian was waiting in the corridor, nervously shuffling from foot to foot.

'Ready to rumble?' he said.

'Keep saying things like that and I'll feel like an adolescent schoolgirl facing an exam rather than a ruthless lawyer out for blood.'

'Then maybe I can get you a juicy steak?'

'Meat doesn't cause aggression in humans, Zordon.'

'Strange,' he replied. 'Because I thought people accused vegans of not being predatory enough because they don't eat other living creatures.'

'Rubbish. When you eat meat, some primordial instinct kicks in, and your body gets the message that everything's OK, that you've been hunting, and now you've eaten your fill. If you don't have meat, you remain in a state of constant alertness, because your body thinks you haven't been out hunting yet.'

'Is that your personal theory?'

'No, not at all. I read about it in *National Geographic* or something.'

'Right.'

They took the lift down, and Kordian was shocked to discover they wouldn't be driving.

'Surely not,' he said. 'Are we walking?'

'Yes.'

'On our own two feet?'

'Looks like it.'

He looked at his watch, and pondered for a moment.

'Are you worried you'll drive like a wuss again, and lose your confidence even more?'

'How perspicacious you are, Zordon. Or should I call you Sigmund Freud?'

'Call me what you like, it doesn't alter the fact that I know you well.'

She didn't answer, as she realised he might be right. When she'd looked in the mirror, she wasn't altogether sure she was seeing the same Chyłka who, just a few months before, would have strutted into the building and burst into the courtroom full of vigour. She hoped she was still the same person, but there was no time for a dress rehearsal. Never mind – it would all come out in the wash.

The walk, as predicted, took quarter of an hour, and as they had another half-hour before the trial started, they bought coffees from a nearby Tchibo, and sat down in the park to drink them. Normally Joanna would have waited in the corridor outside the courtroom, but today, that would have put her under too much stress. She'd do better to arrive at the last minute.

They finished their coffees, then Chyłka took a deep breath and threw her cup in the bin.

'Right, it's time,' she said.

'Aronowicz has probably already filled his pants.'

'I bet he has. I bet he's trembling like a leaf, and is already planning what he'll do when they throw him out as a prosecutor.'

'He could retrain as a barrister, but after this debacle I doubt anyone would hire him.'

'Not likely. He's blown his chances in the legal profession.'

'He could be a parking attendant.'

'Not outside the court though. They wouldn't have him.'

'At the station then.'

'Maybe,' said Chyłka.

Standing outside the court building, Chyłka had no regrets about leaving the car behind. She'd have had trouble finding a space in the tiny car park anyway. She looked up at the newly renovated façade, then they went inside.

They checked that nothing had changed on the cause list, and they made their way up the stairs to the first floor. There were still a few minutes to go. Szlezyngier was standing outside the courtroom. He wouldn't look at them, but Aronowicz greeted them enthusiastically.

'Welcome, Chyłka.'

'You can only welcome someone to your own home,' she retorted.

'What?'

'And it expresses the superiority of the one welcoming to the one being welcomed,' she added, 'which in this case is completely inappropriate, because by the end of the day I'll be scraping you off my shoe, not the other way round. Now bugger off.'

The prosecutor opened his mouth, but Joanna wouldn't let him get a word in.

'Quickly now,' she urged. 'You might just have time to use the toilet before the hearing starts.'

In fact, it was her stomach churning, but she had no intention of letting it show. The prosecutor gave her a feeble smile, shook his head in disapproval and moved away.

'Good opening speech,' remarked Oryński.

'Thanks.'

'Not particularly subtle, but I know you like to get straight to the point.'

'You can bugger off too,' she said under her breath, and they both fell silent, waiting for the case to be called.

Which it then was, sooner than Chyłka would have liked. A neatly dressed woman opened the door and announced the hearing, the cue for the throng of people to stream into the room. The presiding judge welcomed the crowd warmly, urged them to respect the dignity of the court, then read out a list of attendees. Witnesses were ushered into the corridor and told they would be called by name.

On the defence bench, Chyłka felt Kordian's hand on her thigh. She turned to him to give him an earful, then realised it was because she was tapping her foot. He took his hand away and gave her a sly smile.

'You're like a school kid,' she whispered.

'I'll take every chance I can get.'

'Shush now.'

Chyłka straightened her light woollen robe and appraised their client. Szlezyngier looked as if he really didn't care, and kept staring at the ceiling; he was just waiting to have the verdict confirmed.

Then she looked at the panel of judges. There was no doubt they were excellent lawyers. Two women and a man, which more or less reflected gender distribution in the Polish justice system, where the average judge was female, around thirty-five to forty years old.

Appellate court judges had to spend at least ten years working in the district court system and emerge with an unblemished record. They'd spend the same again on the regional circuit, and only then could they be appointed to the appeal court. These were no amateurs.

The presiding judge eyed the thick bundles of files arranged on the judges' bench as if at an exhibition. Then she looked at both sides, and proceeded to open the hearing.

The presiding judge started by summarising Joanna's grounds of appeal. Joanna tried to tell from the tone of his voice whether he was secretly for or against, but he spoke so dispassionately, it was impossible.

Slowly, she began to calm down. She was on familiar territory, and felt confident. The judge continued in the same monotone. He gave an outline of proceedings from the regional court, then introduced the charges raised in the appeal.

Chyłka and Kordian had challenged the lower court's ruling in its entirety, arguing that the conviction was effectively based on a misrepresentation of the facts.

No one was surprised. It had been their only option, as all previous proceedings had been conducted within the letter of the law, and it would have been difficult to contest the verdict on any other basis. Their only saving grace had been that the prosecution had overstepped the mark in trying to prove Awit guilty.

As soon as the judge-rapporteur had finished, the presiding judge took over, announcing it was time to move to the evidentiary proceedings.

As a rule, this wouldn't be part of an appeal hearing. The appellate court's role was more to do with scrutiny than evaluating content, and it was not there to repeat what had already been presented in the lower court. Evidentiary proceedings were an exception, permissible only if they were expected to streamline the procedure and speed up delivery of a verdict. In this case, these conditions were deemed to have been fulfilled.

Witold T., otherwise known as Wito, was invited to take his place on the rostrum.

He did so, clearly agitated. He was used to appearing before district and regional courts, but this was a very different experience. In the appeal court, one could somehow feel the solemnity of the court and the seriousness of the case.

'The witness will now take the oath,' the judge said, peering at him. 'Please repeat after me. In full awareness of the significance of my words and—'

'Your Honour,' Wito chimed in.

The judge looked at him. Chyłka didn't know her, but as soon as she heard who would be on the panel, she'd got in touch with her contacts in Białystok to learn more. Apparently Judge Wilnowska valued precision, judged well, and while on the regional circuit had prided herself on the fact that none of her rulings had ever been overturned on appeal.

Looking at her now, Joanna saw an intelligent, down-to-earth judge, who was also trying to contain her annoyance.

'Perhaps the witness could explain why he feels it necessary to interrupt the court?' she asked.

'Do I have to swear the oath?'

'Yes.'

'I didn't before.'

'The judge in the previous trial waived the oath. This court does not. So please repeat after me. In full awareness of the significance of my words and my responsibilities before the law, I solemnly swear that I shall tell the whole truth, concealing nothing that is known to me.'

The court, judges included, rose. Wito reluctantly repeated the words, pausing in the middle to check he'd remembered them correctly. The oath wasn't hugely significant, and taking it didn't change much. The witness could be held criminally responsible for not telling the truth and concealing facts whether they had sworn the oath or not.

Formalities completed, everyone took their seats, and Judge Wilnowska gave the floor to Aronowicz.

He rose slowly, as if stung that a witness was being asked to testify at all.

'Do you have anything to add to what you already told the previous court?' asked the prosecutor.

'No.'

'Absolutely nothing?'

Wito hesitated, and Aronowicz picked up on it straight away.

'I mean anything at all that might be related to the case.'

'No. If you mean about the girl, I've told you everything I know.'

Aronowicz shrugged, thanked the judge and sat down. Now it was Chyłka's turn. She wasn't at all surprised that Aronowicz had little to say. He wasn't expecting any threats, and had no need to launch a pre-emptive attack.

Chyłka rose briskly. 'Thank you, Your Honour,' she said. She looked at Wito uncertainly, not sure how far he'd go to protect his own interests. The oath had rattled him, although he probably had no idea whether it meant anything much. She straightened up and lifted her chin slightly.

'Has the witness ever made contact with the defendant?'

Wito looked at Szlezyngier, who seemed completely uninterested in what was happening around him.

'Please answer the question,' Wilnowska said.

'Well, yes, I have.'

Aronowicz fidgeted nervously.

'Regarding what, exactly?' asked Chyłka.

'He wanted me to do something for him.'

'What sort of something?'

'He wanted me to find Sakrat Tatarnikov and Antoni Ekiel.'

'For what purpose?'

Wito looked at her as if she'd lost her marbles, and needed the most obvious things explained to her.

'To find the child, of course.'

'And when did he ask you to do this?'

Wito took a deep breath and proceeded to describe to the court everything Joanna and Kordian had established over the past couple of days. He didn't leave out a single detail, which astounded Joanna. She'd expected it to be like pulling teeth, with Wito hiding behind his right to refuse to answer. But here he was, spilling for all he was worth. She didn't even have to encourage him to add details. Faintly disconcerted, she looked at Kordian, but he just shrugged.

He must have got advice from someone before the trial, she concluded. As long as he stuck to what he was doing for Awit, there was no way he could incriminate himself. On the contrary, in fact, because this made him look like a man who had no problem talking openly about his activities.

'And did you find them? Ekiel and Tatarnikov?'

'No, I'm afraid I didn't manage to track them down,' he said, looking at Szlezyngier. 'Although we did come across some clues here and there. And in the end, we did find Ekiel, but we all know what happened to him.'

The panel eyed the witness, as if trying to establish whether perhaps he had killed Antoni Ekiel, but his candour seemed to contradict their suspicions.

'And unfortunately, we found no sign of the girl or her kidnapper at the scene.'

Chyłka bowed her head as if in contemplation.

'What makes you so sure Nikola was kidnapped?'

Wito shrugged.

'Why would Awit pay me a fortune to find her otherwise?'

8

The cross-examination wasn't going badly, but the judges weren't as impressed as Kordian had hoped. But then again, he shouldn't expect miracles. Chyłka had told him over and over that evidence presented on appeal rarely had the power to shake up the whole case, unless it revealed something fundamentally different that shed a whole new light on it.

That was not happening here, and she maintained the outcome would depend almost wholly on their closing speeches. That was where they could expect results.

Szlezyngier also had the right to make a statement, but had chosen not to exercise it. He didn't speak, either during Wito's, testimony, or the subsequent ones, which came from members of Wito's gang involved in the search for Tatarnikov.

Wito had been Chyłka and Oryński's last card, and now all they had left was Chyłka's closing speech. The principle of *favor defensionis* dictated that the defence had the right to speak last, giving them the opportunity to counter any arguments advanced by the prosecution. It also meant the judges would remember them better.

So Aronowicz began.

'Your Honour, I move to uphold the verdict of the previous court. Throughout the course of this appeal, the defence has failed to demonstrate any error in its findings of fact, and has therefore not established sufficient reason to question the legitimacy of what has already been ascertained. We have heard the same speculations raised from the very first days of the trial, and seen not a single piece of evidence to prove that the lower court's findings were incorrect. And, if I may speak frankly, it is hard to imagine how such a thing would be possible in a case as clear-cut as this one. We have no body, it's true, so no material evidence of the defendant committing the crime, but that doesn't mean he did not commit it. In the regional court trial, the defendant's wife explained the events in such a way that Mr Szlezyngier's guilt could not be in doubt. The facts of this have not changed.'

Aronowicz continued in the same vein for some time, until Kordian was almost comatose. He assumed the judges were feeling the same way, which was why the prosecutor had chosen this particular tactic: he was going to bore them until they were in no fit state to listen to another speech.

At last he finished, having once again requested that the initial ruling be upheld. Then he thanked the court and took his seat.

Oryński looked at Chyłka. At first glance, she looked as she always did, and it was only on closer inspection that he caught a flicker of uncertainty in her eyes, which was never normally there.

If at any time during this case the weight of responsibility had come close to crushing her, it was now. Awit's fate hung on what she was about to say.

He tried to send her a secret smile, but she didn't even glance his way, just got up and straightened her robe. Then she looked at Aronowicz and sighed.

'Your Honour,' she began. 'I request that the case be referred back to the regional court for reconsideration.'

It was a good start. Oryński would probably have moved to quash the original conviction entirely, but that might have been a step too far for the rather flimsy arguments they had. Joanna tried to point out errors in establishing facts, but none were so serious that they would turn the case on its head. Ultimately, the child had vanished, and there was little doubt that it made sense to see Awit as the guilty party. Even with the most compelling arguments in the world, it would be hard for the judges to see it otherwise, so a retrial seemed the logical choice.

'During the proceedings, it was assumed *a priori* that my client was guilty of this crime,' she said, her voice none too assertive. 'Then every effort was made to fit the evidence to the hypothesis.' She swallowed, and had to pause for a moment. Kordian wanted to give her a nudge, or hum the chorus of 'Afraid to Shoot Strangers', but he couldn't even give her the briefest glance of support; she seemed to be completely ignoring him. She needed to deal with this on her own.

'Until Angelika Szlezyngier changed her statement, everything was shaped to fit the prosecution's theory. The person on the lake shore that night was assumed to be my client, although we still don't know who it actually was. The bloodstained rod was assumed to be the murder weapon, although we now know that it was taken from the workshop, and that the blood had been on it for some time, as per the sticking plaster.'

She paused again, but this time it was deliberate. She was, Kordian saw, becoming increasingly confident.

'Who planted that rod, Your Honour? The trial did not answer that question. I'm not saying there was no adequate answer, I'm saying there was no answer at all.'

Up to that point, Aronowicz had been focused on the papers spread out on the bench in front of him. Now he looked up at Joanna with hostility.

'Did this rod find its own way into the forest?' she continued. 'I find it uncomfortable even to articulate this question, as I feel it offends the dignity of this court. I felt the same way in the previous trial, but the panel seemed to ignore what I was saying. Why would that be? Because, as I said at the start, it had already been assumed my client was guilty.'

Oryński felt like applauding.

'I find this an unacceptable omission. If we had discovered who planted the item where it was found, our picture of the crime may have been very different to the one the prosecution has been painting for us.'

She stopped to take a breath. Kordian watched Wilnowska and the other judges, but they betrayed no emotion.

'There was no investigation into Aleksander Soboń, the young man living on the outskirts of the village, who was badly beaten; it was he who suggested we talk to Antoni Ekiel when we were searching for Nikola, and he was attacked that same night. And the fact that the person to whom Soboń tried to lead us was killed just a short while later proves there is more to this case than meets the eye. It is particularly interesting that Aleksander Soboń was reluctant to speak to us, and it took a lot of effort to persuade him to give us any information about Ekiel.'

Kordian was pleased to see the presiding judge frown. A reaction at last, he thought.

'Finally we come to Sakrat Tatarnikov,' said Chyłka. 'The man no one can find, who went to ground when the whole affair started. Am I the only one who finds it suspicious that he vanished at the exact same time as little Nikola? I'm not saying there's necessarily a connection, because we have no evidence of one. All I'm saying is that it's worth looking at with an open

417

mind, and I feel that referring the case back to the regional court for retrial would help us do just that.'

At this point, Joanna's speech was due to reach its conclusion. Kordian had skimmed it through a few times, and she must have read it at least a hundred times, because she had stuck pretty much word for word to what was printed on the page. But Chyłka didn't look or sound as if she was about to finish.

She gazed at the eagle icon on the wall, the Polish coat of arms, and paused.

'Ms Chyłka?' prompted the judge.

'Just another moment, if I may, Your Honour.'

The judge nodded. Chyłka could have kept up her monologue for a while yet, but worried it would alienate the adjudicating panel.

'There's one more thing I find strange,' she continued. 'And that's Angelika Szlezyngier's behaviour. She called me in the middle of the night, quite rightly, but didn't seem unduly distraught. More like someone who'd misplaced a cherished item than someone whose child had gone missing. That, of course, is my subjective opinion, but during the trial I had the impression that her husband was more distressed than she was. She seemed . . . well, neutral.'

Aronowicz looked pleadingly at the judges. Personal opinions were of little use in a court of law, and the prosecutor wasn't interested in them anyway. Kordian was also concerned that speculation wouldn't help. But he saw the glint in Chyłka's eye, and recognised she had stumbled onto something which she had no intention of letting go.

'None of this mattered much to me – until Angelika turned against her husband. Your Honour, as I'm sure you remember,

I was defending both Mrs Szlezyngier and her husband at the time. My first thought was that Angelika was trying to avoid liability, but I reasoned that even if that were so, she would have done better to stand by her husband. That way, she could have turned him against her, and it would have been his word against hers.'

The judge-rapporteur stifled a yawn.

'So why did she do it?' Joanna asked, looking at Aronowicz. 'Because she wanted Awit out of the picture. And there, Your Honour, lies the nub of the problem. I think we have all missed a very significant point.'

The second judge took off her glasses, folded them up and placed them in front of her. The third judge also looked as if Chyłka had his full attention. Only the presiding judge seemed unmoved.

'As Angelika Szlezyngier testified, her husband wasn't the father of her child. Subsequent DNA tests proved that to be true. And up to that point, I believe she had been telling the truth. But from then on, nothing added up.'

Oryński knew now where she was going. It could end in one of two ways: either the judges would be outraged at all these speculations, or they'd admit that her version of events was plausible enough to have the case heard again.

'As I see it, there was indeed an argument when Angelika told my client about her affair, but he did not push her: there were no marks on her body to indicate a violent altercation. And not only did the child not fall, she wasn't even in the room.'

The judge-rapporteur narrowed his eyes.

'While her parents fought, Nikola was upstairs in her bedroom. Angelika Szlezyngier told her husband about her affair, and announced she was leaving him.'

Aronowicz looked helplessly at the judges again. They didn't notice; they were all fully focused on Chyłka.

'Because what she's been telling us all this time isn't true,' Joanna continued. 'Nikola's mother had no intention of leaving her lover. Quite the contrary. She wanted to spend the rest of her life with him. Him and his daughter.'

The prosecutor tutted his disapproval so loudly that the judges heard, and the presiding judge sent him a scathing look.

'My client, meanwhile, did not want his wife to leave him. He loved her very much, obsessively, even. When she threatened to go, he set the alarm in their home so she couldn't go out. Then there was another exchange of words, lasting until the early hours. Eventually they acknowledged they weren't going to settle it that night. Except that my former client had a plan.'

Joanna paused to give her next words more weight.

'May I remind the court that Angelika Szlezyngier had deleted all the text messages between Sakrat Tatarnikov and herself from her phone. Why would she do that? After all, her husband already knew about the affair. The answer she gave us was not altogether convincing. She claimed that she was concerned for Tatarnikov, and that the police would accuse him of abducting the girl.'

Chyłka was back on her game, thought Kordian. Giving it her best. Even the presiding judge was hooked. Her reasoning was sound, and she'd certainly convinced her trainee. He turned to their client, but Awit was staring blankly ahead.

'Was it altruism?' asked Joanna, 'or was Angelika driven by her love for Sakrat Tatarnikov, the father of her child? Whichever it was, her behaviour was suspicious, to say the least. And now we know why.'

Chyłka looked at the prosecutor, who was struggling to keep his composure. Bringing all this out in the closing speech had been a good tactic, Oryński thought. If she'd mentioned it earlier Aronowicz would have shot her down, but now all he could do was sit quiet as a church mouse, waiting for the grand finale.

'I think we all know Sakrat Tatarnikov kidnapped the child,' Joanna said. 'He and Angelika made it look like murder, and put the blame on my client in order to get rid of him. Then as a knock-on effect, Mrs Szlezyngier would gain a say in the running of her husband's logistics company, and despite their separation of assets arrangement, she'd at last have power over his accumulated capital. She knows the members of the board of directors and the trustees, and has shown herself to be a skilled manipulator. So, Your Honour, Angelika Szlezyngier could hope for two positive outcomes: she and Tatarnikov could bring their child up together, and she would have access to my client's assets. A dream scenario.'

Chyłka broke off, and raised her head.

'So with this in mind, I request the case be referred for retrial.'

9

The two lawyers stood outside the court building, smoking nervously. Joanna was overjoyed to find her confidence had returned. She took a pull on her cigarette and blew the smoke out.

'Once you started, I thought you'd never stop,' said Oryński.

'I know,' she said. 'My mouth's completely dry.'

She spotted a shopping centre at the next junction, and she and Kordian hurried towards it. They stopped at the first newsagent they found, and Chyłka bought herself a cola, taking a swig at once with obvious relish. It tasted incredible – as if she'd spent half the day in the desert – and the several teaspoons of sugar it contained gave her a burst of energy.

'I think you convinced them,' said Kordian as they left the centre.

'Maybe the two either side. The presiding judge looked a bit sceptical.'

'We don't need her.'

'You're right, we don't,' said Chyłka. 'We only need two votes.'

'And if the case goes back to the regional court?'

'No judge will be happy to take it on. For them, it would be spitting into the wind, because if it does get referred back, it means there were problems, and we'll make sure every fool can see what they were.'

Kordian nodded. 'Well, you've convinced me,' he said.

'That means I can convince the other idiots too.'

He scowled at her, then took the cola bottle and drank from it himself. 'Even Aronowicz looked uncomfortable by the time you'd finished.'

'I can't quite believe that,' said Joanna. 'He must have been through it in his head, every scenario and every possibility. But he couldn't give a monkey's. His job is to focus only on evidence that supports the charges.'

Oryński shrugged and gave her back her drink.

'Only Awit looked sceptical,' he said on the walk back to the court building.

'Awit lives in a different world now,' she said. 'He knows he's minutes away from being put away, and is only too aware of what will happen to him in prison. Even at its best, the prison service can only do so much. The other prisoners will find out who he is, then he'll be battered and raped with whatever they can get their hands on.'

'True.'

'You'd be spooked too if it were you.'

They smoked another cigarette each and returned to the corridor, to find Aronowicz nervously pacing from one end of it to the other. He saw them and turned his back.

'Now there's a new potential secret admirer.'

'Are you feeling threatened? He might topple you from your position as chief admirer of my humble personage.'

They sat down on a bench along the wall, impatiently eyeing the courtroom door. The judges' meeting was still in progress. Joanna would have done anything to sneak a quick look through the keyhole, and the longer the door stayed closed, the greater the temptation grew.

Half an hour later there was still no news. Awit sat a little way further down, gazing outside longingly, possibly thinking this was the last time he'd see the world through an unbarred window.

'How much longer is this going to take?' asked an exasperated Kordian.

'There must be some sort of uncertainty.'

'Is that good or bad?'

'How am I supposed to know?'

'You're an experienced lawyer. You should understand these things.'

'I do. I understand that if it takes this long, there's some sort of doubt.'

Oryński propped his elbows on his knees and lowered his head. He pulled out his phone, scrolled through his notifications, then swore to himself and put the phone away. He looked up at the door again.

'What happens if they uphold the verdict?'

'Szlezyngier will learn some new bedroom tricks.'

'Be serious.'

'I am,' she said, folding her arms. 'Awit will be able to give the Moulin Rouge girls a run for their money.'

'Moulin Rouge is a cabaret. If you want something a bit wilder, try De Wallen in Amsterdam, or Soi Cowboy in Bangkok.'

Chyłka looked at her trainee with fresh admiration. 'I didn't realise you were so knowledgeable, Zordon.'

'That's because whenever I've stayed at your place, you've made me sleep on the sofa.'

She shook her head with a smile, then they both fell silent again, waiting anxiously for the judges' decision. Another fifteen minutes passed, and Joanna began to think this might be a bad sign.

'If this fails, can we go on to final appeal?' asked Oryński.

'On what basis?'

'I don't know. We can think of something.'

'My little story may stand up as part of a closing speech, but it wouldn't cut it in an appeal statement. It wouldn't stand a chance.'

'Not even the slightest?'

'Not even the slightest. It all gets decided now. Besides, even if another appeal were accepted, Awit will have been slaughtered in prison long before the first hearing.'

'You're right,' said Kordian.

Chyłka was preparing to explain how difficult it would be to find absolute grounds for appeal or prove a serious legal error in this case, when the door to the courtroom opened. Szlezyngier looked up. Aronowicz stopped pacing, and within moments, everyone stood in their appointed places, waiting for the judges to enter.

When they did, Joanna tried to catch a glimpse of their faces. The presiding judge caught her eye, and didn't look pleased. What could that mean? She'd seemed ill-disposed towards them earlier. Maybe she'd lost to the other two judges? And that would mean . . .

'Please sit,' said Wilnowska. 'I don't have much to say, and I'll do it as quickly as possible. You've waited long enough.'

She adjusted her chain of office and looked at the open book on the bench in front of her.

'In accordance with Article 411 of the Criminal Code, this court hereby defers pronouncement of a verdict.'

The prosecution and defence teams glanced at one another. Neither had expected this.

10

Chyłka and Oryński had to extend their stay at the Gołębiewski. It cost over three hundred zlotys per room per night, but no one was about to take issue with that. As evening fell, they sat on comfortable, pale-brown armchairs by the window of the Patio Café. The deep-red carpet, lavish chandeliers and voluminous plants left them in no doubt that the prices on the menu were unlikely to be competitive.

Kordian scanned his menu and grimaced.

'What's wrong?' asked Chyłka. 'No fillet of soya?'

'What on earth is one of those?'

'I don't know,' she admitted. 'You're the one who eats pseudo-foods, not me, so you should know. I'm sure they make steaks and things from soya.'

'This is only cakes.'

'That's normal for a café. Are you having anything?'

He ordered tea sweetened with rose-petal jam. Chyłka rolled her eyes, and asked for chocolate cake and coffee.

'How do you burn all those calories? I always wonder.'

'Give me a break, Zordon.'

'It's not fair, that's all I'm saying.'

'Stop moaning and get yourself an ice-cream cake.'

He'd have loved to, but he hadn't brought his running shoes, and would have no way of losing those excess calories for over a week. Then he remembered. The Gołębiewski had a swimming pool, Olympic size, or so he'd been told.

He ordered the cake.

'You're like an old woman,' said Joanna.

'And you're like a peasant farmer, so somehow we complement each other.'

'Complement? I don't even know where to start with your weird eating habits.'

'You love it really.'

'Yeah, right,' she said, taking a bite of cake.

Oryński busied himself with his own dessert, and silence fell. After a while he put down his spoon and looked at Joanna.

'So how does it look?' he asked. She pretended to size him up.

'Not great,' she admitted. 'I mean, overall it's OK, but if you look more closely at your—'

'I meant the case.'

'Oh, I see.'

'Well?' he persisted. 'Do we stand a chance?'

'I'm not the Oracle of Delphi.'

'But you can make an educated guess.'

'My educated guess is that it's all one big unknown,' she answered, her mouth full. 'If I had to speculate though, going by their expressions I'd say Wilnowska is against us, the others in favour.'

Kordian thought for a while.

'And how long can they defer?'

'Officially? Three days.'

'Can they extend that?'

'Yes, up to a week. Anything beyond that and the case gets heard again, right from the beginning.'

'That's ridiculous.'

'Possibly, but in our position, it would be a good thing. Maybe even better than if they referred it back to the regional court. We've sown seeds of doubt in the minds of the panel; we could water it with a few litres of legal prestidigitation and see what comes up.'

Oryński drank his tea, staring into the white mug. You didn't have to be here long to sense the breath of bygone times. The shabby carpet in particular was a reminder that the décor probably dated back to . . . earlier times.

'Any chance of a retrial?' asked Kordian.

'No. They'll reach a decision in the time allowed.'

'Are you sure?'

'Yes, Zordon. That's one thing I am sure of.'

'I guess you're right,' he said. 'No one wants to risk listening to you going on again like that.'

She kicked him under the table, but smiled. They finished their cakes, chatted about topics unrelated to the case, then took a stroll around the hotel. The corridors were a little oppressive, and here and there guests had stepped out of their rooms to try and connect to the Wi-Fi. They wandered around aimlessly until nine o'clock, when the night club opened.

Then they went in, settled themselves comfortably on a sofa and ordered a beer each to warm up. An innocent enough start to the evening, although Oryński guessed their first beer wouldn't be their last. As the court had announced it was deferring its decision for three days, they were free the next morning, so there was no reason why they shouldn't get wasted.

'I can't stand this,' said Chyłka after two gulps.

'This what?'

'This techno, the lights, the bass, everything. It's awful.'

'This isn't techno, it's dubstep.'

'You're not seriously telling me there's a difference.'

Oryński pondered for a moment, trying to remember all he'd recently had to learn about Iron Maiden.

'If there's no difference between techno and dubstep, then there's no difference between power metal and heavy metal.'

She narrowed her eyes.

'Don't,' she said. 'That's sacrilege. The mere mention of proper music in this . . . in this den of insipid clamour is blasphemy to my ears.'

With each passing minute, the music grew louder, while the lights grew dimmer. And when a wave of young party animals poured in through the door, it was the last straw.

'What is all this?' she said.

'Shall we dance?'

The lasers were changing colour, the floor was shaking, and Kordian knew the throbbing bass line would be echoing in his head long after he'd gone to bed.

'What kind of dancing are you talking about?' barked Chyłka. 'Because that,' she said, pointing to two teenagers on the dance floor, 'looks more like some bumbling form of foreplay. I don't see any dancing going on here.'

Oryński looked at the teenage couple. They were certainly getting to know one another – he was moving his hands rhythmically from her back to her buttocks, and she was fondling his muscular shoulders.

'Watch,' Chyłka went on. 'The tonsil tennis will start soon.'

'Nobody calls it tonsil tennis anymore. Not for years.'

'Well, making out then.'

'Or that. So last-season.'

'OK, Mr Know-It-All, what's it called these days then?'

'How would I know?' he answered, taking a gulp of beer. 'Sucking face?'

'Hopeless.'

'You're interested, though.'

'I see my presence here as an opportunity to further my anthropological studies through participant observation,' she said, lifting her beer mug. 'But another two of these miserable excuses for tunes and I'm off. I can't take much more, although I hope you can see I'm trying.'

He could, and he appreciated it. If anyone had asked him an hour ago if Joanna would ever contemplate drinking in a club where they played electronic music, he'd have laughed in their face. Yet here she was, sitting quietly, watching the lip-locked young pleasure seekers.

Eventually though, she finished her beer.

'Enough is enough, Zordon.'

She got up, and without another word, headed for the exit. It took Oryński a moment or two to realise that on her way to the door, Chyłka had forcibly shoved one of the drunk teenagers aside.

He followed her, finishing his beer as he went, then put the bottle down on the table next to the bewildered youth on the receiving end of her anger.

'Is she some sort of freak?' he complained as Oryński was passing. 'All I said was she's a bit of a babe.'

Kordian smiled. 'Did you hear?' he shouted to Joanna, trying to make himself heard over the thumping techno. 'This bloke says you're—'

'I heard, thank you,' she yelled back from the doorway. 'And I suggest we leave straight away, or I'll be tempted to go back and rearrange his septum.'

Oryński sent the boy a sympathetic glance, then stepped into the corridor with Chyłka. It was a relief to be outside the door.

'Sodom and Gomorrah,' remarked Joanna.

'Are Iron Maiden fans any better?'

She shook her head in disbelief. 'Listen,' she said. 'I'm giving you a new assignment for this term.'

'Surely it's not for you to . . .'

'Go to Woodstock this summer and see what it means to have a good time. You can get drunk in style, and then get a proper shagging, not some adolescent fumbling on the dance floor.'

'Squelching around in mud isn't exactly my idea of—'

'Let's go,' Chyłka cut in, moving off down the corridor.

'Where are you going?'

'I don't know yet. Somewhere we can get lots of alcohol.'

It wasn't a bad idea, Kordian admitted. The hotel restaurant closed at eleven, so they wondered whether to find somewhere in town, but eventually decided they were too tired to wander around in search of a night-time binge. If the worst came to the worst they could always buy drinks from the shop across the road.

'One thing intrigues me,' said Oryński.

'Just one?'

'Do you really think Awit did it?'

She wiped the condensation from her glass and didn't speak for a moment. Kordian had rarely seen Joanna look so serious, and it made him uncomfortable. He coughed and began to fidget. After a moment she looked up, but didn't say anything, just kept staring.

'In court, it sounded like you thought Angelika and Tatarnikov had abducted the child themselves,' he ventured.

Still no answer.

'Are you pretending to be Langer?' he asked.

Chyłka smiled and took a sip of beer. 'I don't know what to think, Zordon,' she said in the end. 'When I took the case on, I was sure we were defending a guilty man.'

'And now you're not convinced?'

'No.'

He nodded, and took a sip too. The beer was disappearing at an alarming rate, but it was just what they'd needed that evening.

'Someone must have planted that rod, mustn't they?' she said, narrowing her eyes. 'And basically, that's the only mistake they made.'

'So without that, the police wouldn't have locked Awit up?'

She shook her head.

'It would have happened sooner or later. Whoever planned it should have been a bit more patient.'

'But they were in a hurry.'

'Quite possibly,' she said.

'Sakrat wanted Angelika out of temporary custody as soon as possible,' Kordian added, feeling he might have hit the nail on the head. 'They wanted to be together.'

The lawyers' eyes met, and they were silent for a moment.

'It's possible, I suppose,' said Joanna. 'But there's one thing that doesn't sit right with me. And the court will likely think the same.'

'And what's that?'

'There's a hole in the logic that brings the whole hypothesis tumbling down.'

He raised his eyebrows, waiting for her to continue.

'If Tatarnikov kidnapped the girl – how in God's name did he do it?'

'What do you mean?'

'The alarm was set, the doors and windows were closed, and Szlezyngier was probably in too much emotional turmoil to sleep much anyway.'

Oryński scratched his head. Before Awit had got the blame for everything, they'd considered every possible scenario, but had found nothing which could explain the kidnapping. Maybe that's why the police were happy to believe the child had been murdered, and her body removed, before the alarm was set.

'It's a conundrum,' he said.

Chyłka smiled and pulled out her cigarettes, turning the pack over and over in her hand.

'Let's hope the court sees it as a conundrum too,' she said, 'because if they don't, there'll be no retrial.'

They went outside to smoke. Kordian turned to go back in, but Chyłka grabbed his wrist to stop him. He was puzzled, as she rarely allowed physical contact.

'They're closing,' she said, turning her phone screen to show him. 'Let's get beer from the shop and take it to our rooms.'

'That doesn't sound very safe.'

'Tonight isn't about being safe, Zordon.'

'How am I supposed to take that?'

She turned around without giving him even a fleeting glance. They bought their drinks and went back to the hotel.

11

Just two months ago, a hefty dose of hops and alcohol would have put Joanna in a tailspin. Now she was back on form, both in court and in terms of alcohol consumption. She felt relaxed and happy, but nothing worse.

'I don't know if we're allowed to bring this in,' Kordian said as they walked across reception.

'Of course we are.'

'Is that your opinion as a legal professional?'

'No,' she shrugged, 'as somebody needing a drink.'

They got to the corridor, and Oryński stopped short. 'I've got a better idea,' he said.

'Have you?'

'They've got a pool here.'

'I'm not going to drink and swim.'

'Who said anything about swimming? There's a jacuzzi next door.'

'Don't even think about it.'

He looked surprised. Was she sending him mixed messages? Maybe. She clearly had no intention of explaining herself. Kordian wasn't stupid.

'A game of pool then?' he suggested.

'I've never played.'

'You'll pick it up in no time,' he said smugly, gesturing for her to follow him. Chyłka looked at her beer, then at her trainee, then she nodded. It wasn't a bad option. In the pool or jacuzzi they'd have been close together, wearing very little. It could have ended badly.

In the pool room, Oryński pulled out his wallet. Joanna looked around, but couldn't see any staff.

'So what now?' she said.

'You really haven't done this before, have you?'

'I can't think of a single reason why I'd have wanted to,' she said, standing by the table. 'I'm not particularly keen on golf either, so it shouldn't surprise you.'

'What's golf got to do with pool?'

'Here you hit a round object with a cue, with golf you hit it with a club. Same difference.'

'I guess you're right,' he smiled, placing a coin in the slot and pushing the button to release the balls. They fell with a clatter, and Kordian reached for the triangular rack to set them up.

'Do you really know the rules, or are you pretending?' Chyłka asked.

'No, my father taught me before he decided that ... well, you know.'

She nodded. In uncomfortable silence, they remembered a conversation they'd had during the Langer case. Kordian had opened up to her, and quite frankly, she didn't want that ever to happen again. At least not while they were still trainee and supervisor.

'I always thought you'd be a dab hand at pool.'

'Why?'

'Because I can imagine a young Chyłka, still a student maybe, sitting in a smoky old pub where the beer flowed freely, listening to Black Sabbath and Iron Maiden against the constant click of pool balls.'

'Chyłka the student always had her nose buried in a textbook.'

'That doesn't sound very rebellious.'

'How else would I notch up the grades I needed to get into Żelazny & McVay?' she asked, taking a cue from him. 'And don't worry, I've made up for it now.'

He nodded, and pointed to the triangle, putting on his best teaching face. Before he even had a chance to say anything, Joanna levelled the cue at him. 'You're enjoying this, aren't you, you little . . .'

'Definitely. My one and only opportunity to teach you something.'

'Right, let's get on with it. And make the most of it, because as you say, you won't get this chance again.'

'OK,' he said, turning the cue in his hand. 'Let's play a game of eight-ball. So first, choose your colour.'

'They're all different colours.'

'I mean stripes or solids.'

'Solids. You're more suited to stripes – less decisive, more dithery.'

'Thanks.' He turned his focus back to the table.

'You have to pocket all the balls in your colour, and then the eight-ball. That's basically it.'

'And if I pocket one of yours?'

'Doesn't matter.'

'What about if I pocket the eight-ball before the others are in?'

'Then you lose.'

'And if I whack my opponent across the head with the cue?'

'Then you win,' he said, and beckoned her over to the table. 'I'll explain the rest as we go along, but first let's see if you can hit the white ball at all.'

'I'm not that drunk,' she said. 'And if either of us has gross motor issues, it's you, Zordon.'

She rested her cue on the cushion and leaned over the table.

'To start with, just hit any ball into any pocket.'

She lined up her cue and extended it in front of her; it glanced off the cue ball, giving it a slight spin. Not exactly a great shot. She heard Kordian behind her, giving a polite cough.

'You need to lean over a bit more,' he said, 'and your feet should be wider apart.'

'Is that right?'

He stood behind her and gently corrected her stance.

'Back knee straight, front knee slightly bent. The cue under your chin, but not touching it.'

'OK.'

He came up closer, and she could feel his body touching hers.

'Put one arm out in front of you,' he went on, guiding her hand forwards, 'and with the back arm . . .'

He stopped. Their bodies were now so close together they couldn't pretend any longer. Chyłka slowly put her cue down and began to turn around. Kordian didn't move.

'What are you doing?' she whispered, uncertain if he could hear.

'I don't know.'

'I can see that.'

They were only inches apart, yet a gulf separated them. Chyłka tried hard to remember that, but it was a struggle, especially as she could feel his arms sneaking around her waist. He picked her up gently. She sat on the table and parted her legs, while he came even closer, his eyes on hers.

'This would be unbelievably stupid,' she said.

'I know.'

She felt his breath on her lips, and trembled. If they didn't end it now, they'd be waking up in the same bed tomorrow morning. She swallowed, looked down, and very gently, pushed Kordian away. He didn't protest. He took a step back and drew a breath.

'If someone saw us,' she said, 'it would be the end of our careers, not to mention the Szlezyngier case. Do you understand?'

'Totally.'

They were silent for a moment.

'Besides, we've got a game of pool to play.'

Oryński smiled and walked to the other end of the table, re-racked the balls and made space for Joanna. She wasn't particularly bothered about the game, but felt she needed to do something with herself. For about ten minutes, they played as if their lives depended on it. Kordian explained the rules as they went, and she tried to focus. It didn't go too badly. After a beer each, it was even better.

'We need some sort of forfeit,' said Joanna.

'A competition without a potential trophy is no fun for you, is it?'

'Got it in one, my dear trainee.'

Kordian hit the ten-ball into a pocket and straightened up with a grin.

'In that case, here's my suggestion. If you win, I renounce my position as your trainee. If I win, you renounce yours as my supervisor.'

'Good idea.'

'We can draw up an agreement after the game. Our word can be our bond.'

'If you say so.'

'Then all we have to decide is your room or mine.'

He hit the eleven-ball, and Chyłka could scarcely contain her smile.

'Pool clearly brings out your inner confidence,' she remarked.

'Do you think so?'

'Absolutely, and it makes me uncomfortable. Especially as when I see you like this, it makes me want to . . .' She paused, and looked at him with a sparkle in her eye.

Oryński missed his shot, and she winked.

'Well done, Zordon,' she said, getting ready for her turn. 'But for the sake of your future clients, I hope you're not so easily distracted in the courtroom.'

They resumed their game, and for the rest of the evening, they skirted the subject at the top of their minds, talking about anything and everything else.

And so the time passed, in painful neutrality, until the day of the verdict.

12

On the fifteen-minute walk from the hotel to the court building, Oryński almost felt sad it was all over. With a bit of luck, he'd be able to look back on his time in Białystok as groundbreaking. He constantly reminded himself he only had two years left as a trainee, then the road ahead would be clear. The company had no policy regarding personal relationships between professional equals.

He and Chyłka smoked a cigarette each, then went in. There was a quarter of an hour to go before the decision would be announced. The prosecutor was perching on a bench by the door, and Szlezyngier stood a little way away, his back to everyone.

This time they were to meet on the ground floor, in a room significantly smaller than the last one. Kordian spotted a few reporters in the distance, but they didn't seem as interested in the outcome of the trial as they had been in the clashes during it. The media weren't the only ones for whom attendance was optional: the prosecutor and the defendant had no obligation to be there. As long as the court reporter was present, the hearing would be considered valid. No one else was needed, the aim being to keep to the time limit, as exceeding it would mean starting all over again.

Kordian and Joanna stopped beside Aronowicz. Kordian looked down on him, and thought how symbolic it was.

'I hope they don't fire you, Zbigniew,' Chyłka greeted him.

'And I hope they don't transfer you to another department,' he said, not bothering to look up. 'Insolvency law would probably suit you, as everywhere you go, morals seem to fall to an all-time low.'

'What a pleasant comment to start the day.'

'A day I hope you'll come to see as the start of your own personal downfall.'

'We'll see,' she said, and turned to look at Szlezyngier.

Awit didn't share his defence team's good humour. On the contrary – he looked as if he'd like nothing better than to resolve everything early by jumping out of the window.

Joanna nudged Kordian and gestured towards Awit. Kordian obeyed her unspoken instruction and went to him. He stopped at the end of the corridor, by the window overlooking the buildings behind the courthouse.

'Awit.'

The businessman turned around. 'What do you want?' he asked.

'To tell you to try and stay hopeful.'

'I thought you couldn't guarantee success.'

'We don't,' said Kordian, looking out of the window. It was a cool, bright day. 'But positive thinking never hurt anyone.'

'My positivity ended when my wife incriminated me.'

Kordian tried to think of something cheerful to say, but couldn't. He decided to keep his client company, in silence, until the verdict was pronounced.

Szlezyngier's breathing was loud and ragged. His eyes constantly flitted around, from the figures in the distance to the cars stopping in the car park on the left. He didn't smell of alcohol, although, Kordian thought, a drop or two might help calm his nerves.

Suddenly Awit turned to Kordian. 'Do you believe it?' he asked.

The young lawyer frowned.

'Believe what?'

'What Chyłka said in her closing speech. Do you believe Sakrat and Angelika kidnapped my daughter?'

Szlezyngier was whispering, as if saying the words out loud caused him physical pain. In his eyes, Oryński saw suffering that had nothing to do with the prospect of spending time behind bars. This was the grief of losing a child.

Awit swallowed with difficulty, while Kordian simply stood, unsure what to answer.

'Chyłka sounded as if she believed it,' Szlezyngier said.

'Maybe she did,' replied Kordian. 'It seems likely. To me, anyway.'

Awit nodded, and didn't speak again. Kordian watched him a moment longer. Szlezyngier hadn't asked because he didn't believe her – if he wasn't guilty, he'd have probably put it all together long ago. He simply wanted to know if there was anyone left who thought he was innocent.

When the court reporter stepped into the corridor to call them in, Kordian clapped his client on the back. It was a paltry gesture, but it was all he had to offer.

'I don't believe you did it, Awit,' he said as they moved off towards the open door.

'I hope you're not the only one.'

As they entered the room, Oryński thought he probably wouldn't be. At least one person on the adjudication panel must have seen it the way the lawyers had done, and it only took one more, then Szlezyngier would be free.

What were the chances? He felt the scales were beginning to tip in their favour. You could even see it on Aronowicz's face. Although he tried hard to keep up appearances, his unease was starting to show.

They entered the appointed room and took their places. The presiding judge went through a few formalities, but as Kordian noted, nothing could be inferred from her demeanour. The same went for the other two judges, who also remained stony-faced.

'We will proceed straight to the verdict,' said the judge. 'All rise, please.'

Everyone rose, and Kordian thought how if Szlezyngier was pronounced not guilty, the search for the child would start again, and this time the police would redouble their efforts, trying to make up for the mistakes they'd made the first time round. Which meant they might also find Sakrat Tatarnikov.

Oryński forced his mind back to the presiding judge. Unlike the rest of the court, she and her two colleagues were seated. She was staring straight at her monitor, seemingly undaunted that Awit's fate rested in her hands.

'In the name of the Republic of Poland,' she began, 'on this twenty-fourth day of November 2015, the Białystok Court of Appeal, Second Criminal Division, comprising Appeal Court Judge Anna Wilnowska and Judges Piotr Dobrowolski and Katarzyna Tkacz, with Zbigniew Aronowicz of the Suwałki Regional Prosecutor's Office, after hearing on the twenty-first day of November 2015 the case against Awit Szlezyngier, charged under Article 155 of the Criminal Code as a result of an appeal filed by the defendant's legal representative against the verdict of the Suwałki Regional Court . . .'

Kordian swallowed.

'. . . hereby upholds the verdict as pronounced, deeming the appeal to be unfounded.'

He lowered his head, while Chyłka swore under her breath. Neither noted that Awit had also been ordered to pay costs.

Two policemen appeared in the room and stood by the public gallery. Szlezyngier turned to look at them, and Kordian had to support him as he slumped backwards.

Meanwhile, Wilnowska was giving the reason for the verdict, as if she hadn't a care in the world.

'The evidence submitted by the defence is not really evidence,' she said. 'It is conjecture, which, in some places, has not been thought through. One of their key arguments concerned the bloodstained rod, which, they claimed, had been planted by the lake shore. However, the only fingerprints found on it belonged to the defendant. There was no forensic evidence to show anyone else had come in contact with it. This casts doubt on the supposition that the defendant is the victim of an alleged conspiracy. Conspiracies are the stuff of media – they do not belong in a court of law, at least as long as there is no concrete evidence to support them, only vague conjecture.'

Joanna swore again, more loudly this time. And again, this time, none of the judges heard her.

'Then there were two pieces of evidence the defence failed to refute. Firstly, the witness who saw the defendant that night with the child. It's difficult to argue he would have changed his testimony if he were still alive. If we went down that road, we would be in a position to call into question every verdict, in every case.' Wilnowska paused for a moment, but didn't look away from her screen. 'The second piece of evidence was the statement made by the defendant's wife, the credibility of which the defence team also failed to destroy. Even the most fanciful speculation does not bear the weight of fact, so we cannot conclude that the witness was not telling the truth.'

At last Wilnowska looked up, and straight at Chyłka.

'The remaining arguments were simply not sufficient to even contemplate a retrial. The fact that a resident of the same village was assaulted cannot be seen as supporting any kind of theory, and it's difficult to see how it is relevant to the case on the cause list. The same applies to Sakrat Tatarnikov's disappearance, in the absence of any real evidence to show he had anything to do with the disappearance of the child.'

Joanna pressed her lips together and scowled at the presiding judge, who was now no longer reading from her screen.

'Because that's what a trial is based on,' she was saying. 'On evidence. However compelling the rhetoric on either side, we must not be swayed by it if it does not give us facts. And there is nothing to prove that there were errors in finding of fact when the case was heard in the lower court.'

Wilnowska carried on a while longer, but Kordian was no longer listening. This whole time, he'd been supporting Awit, who didn't seem to realise what was going on. Two things were clear in Oryński's mind: firstly, that Awit wouldn't make it through his first week in prison, and secondly, that he was innocent.

13

Chyłka stood at the reception desk waiting for her invoice to print. Although they'd had an unexpectedly good evening, now they wanted to leave Białystok as soon as possible. Their luggage was in the car, they just had to settle the bill.

On their return to Warsaw, they had a meeting arranged with Szlezyngier – he was to be held at the Białołęka facility for first-time offenders, as the local prison in Białystok was for repeat offenders only.

Not that it mattered. The other inmates would catch up with him sooner or later wherever he was. And although the wardens took care to keep high-risk individuals safe from attack, the prisoners always managed to find a way. And 'culling child molesters, grasses and other worthless characters' was a point of honour.

Kordian waited for Chyłka in the car. She took her seat behind the wheel and they set off from the hotel with a squeal of tyres.

'I'm glad to see you're ready to race again.'

'I'm the female Kubica.'

'You said it,' Oryński commented as she drove out of the side road, cutting across two lanes. 'Shall I do the sat-nav, or do you know the way?'

Joanna nodded her head at a huge sign indicating the exit they needed for Warsaw. She shifted down and squeezed into the other lane, between a green and white bus and a small Opel.

'At this rate we'll be at Białołęka in two and a half hours,' Kordian remarked.

'Two hours, more like.'

Chyłka's estimate proved more accurate, although the unusually light traffic helped. It was still a little early for their scheduled prison visit, so they stopped at a roadside restaurant in Michałów-Grabina, where they sat in silence, eyeing each other nervously. Neither wanted to address the elephant in the room, although sooner or later it had to be done. Awit had spent the night in prison, and they were preparing to see him in a pit of despair.

'He'll be begging us to get him out,' said Joanna, flicking through the menu.

'I'll bet.'

'You've never had to see it with your own eyes though.'

'No, not so far.'

'Then get ready for something quite grotesque.'

She knew Kordian was ready to face whatever the afternoon would throw at him. She'd taught him the theory during the Langer case, and although he hadn't witnessed it in practice, he'd seen enough in his year at Żelazny & McVay to know what he was in for. They ate unhurriedly, then set off for Białołęka.

Arriving at the appointed time, they went straight to the visiting room, bought a can of cola and a bar of Milka from the vending machine and sat down at a table. They'd only been there a few minutes when a procession of inmates appeared in the aisle – a dozen or so men, all greedily looking around as if each new face would inject some colour into their grey existences.

Chyłka rarely did prison visits, mainly because her clients usually ended up on remand rather than in a real prison. But none of these prisoners were here temporarily, and they stared at her, as if committing her face to memory. She tried to push the thought away, but it was probably justified. In closed prisons, visits were allowed only twice a month, so how many opportunities would they get to see a woman?

Awit shuffled in at the end of the line. His eyes were fixed on the floor, and he wouldn't even have noticed the two lawyers if the warden hadn't pointed them out. He came to the table and slumped heavily onto the metal chair, then took the cola, opened it and drank, as if he were enjoying the finest wine. Then he opened the chocolate.

'We've got an hour,' said Chyłka.

Szlezyngier muttered something, his mouth full, and Kordian leaned over to him.

'If there's anything you n . . .'

Chewing on a large piece of chocolate, Awit stared at him, not taking his eyes off the young man until his mouthful was finished.

Chyłka had expected to see a broken man, hardly able to hold back his tears. Instead, he just looked crazy. He took a long gulp of cola and slammed the can down on the table. The drink spilled onto the table, and at once a guard made a move towards them. Szlezyngier turned to him and apologised.

'Thank you,' he said to the lawyers, 'for the cola and chocolate.'

'If you need anything else . . .' Kordian paused, meaningfully.

Awit was wealthy, but money meant nothing here, unless you found a way to get it in. Before they arrived, Chyłka and Kordian had agreed they'd help Awit in any way they could, which meant that if he needed support inside, they'd find out which of the inmates would be happy to take his money.

'No,' Szlezyngier said now, 'I don't need help with anything.' He pushed away the rest of his chocolate.

'Not inside, anyway. I'll be OK in here. It's not easy, but I'll manage.'

Joanna didn't want to imagine how her client had spent his first night.

Awit sniffed and looked around.

'They call me a child-killer, did you know?'

They didn't answer, and he twisted the empty cola can round and round on the table. Eventually he took a deep breath and sat up straight. Now Joanna could see how swollen and bloodshot his eyes were. He gave the two lawyers a fleeting glance, then looked away into the distance.

'When I went to my cell, I thought I'd be with men who'd been sent down for crimes similar to mine. How wrong I was. There are five of them, paedophiles mostly, but they've never taken any-one's life. And for some sick reason, they think . . . they want to . . .' He broke off and shook his head. 'Let's just say if prisoners have the chance to make another prisoner's life hell, they take it.'

The lawyers lowered their heads. Joanna didn't want to hear the rest, but Awit wasn't about to let her off.

'They have to vent somehow,' he went on. 'To their minds, killing a child is infinitely worse than raping one. I thought it might just be coincidence that the others in the cell . . . that they . . . at first, I thought everything would be OK. Then they came for me in the night.'

He rubbed his forehead and looked around again.

'They got the brush from the toilet and poured the water over me, then three of them held me down and . . .' He stopped again, but this time he didn't carry on. 'But I'll be OK,' he said. 'No one's going to kill me.'

Chyłka nodded. If Awit was going to lose his life in here, it would be by his own hand.

'I've got three years,' he said. 'When can I start applying for parole?'

In cases such as Awit's, prisoners were eligible for conditional early release after serving half of their sentences, but Joanna didn't want to start getting his hopes up. It was hard to imagine the court agreeing to parole, even if Szlezyngier proved to be an exemplary prisoner.

'Eighteen months,' she said.

'But I can tell from your voice you don't think I have much chance.'

'It all depends on your behaviour,' Oryński chimed in. Chyłka looked at him, about to protest, but she changed her mind and said nothing. Even so, Szlezyngier understood there was little reason for optimism.

'Right,' he said. 'Three years. That's not so much.'

It wasn't, if you were free. Inside it was different. Just twenty-four hours here would drive the average person to despair. Being alone in a bedsit was hard enough, but in a cell with several others? And with the toilet just a few steps away from your bed?

'But I'd still like you to keep representing me.'

'Of course,' said Chyłka. 'We'll keep representing you if—'

'I keep paying the bills,' he cut in. 'And I will.'

'I meant that we'll do everything we can to get you out. It's not murder anyway, but manslaughter. Maybe at some point we'll be able to persuade a judge to release you with some kind of electronic surveillance. We'll see.'

'Thank you,' said Awit, with genuine gratitude. 'Hope dies last, and when you've got good lawyers, it doesn't die at all.'

Joanna didn't know what to say to that.

'And since you're still representing me, I take it you're still bound by client confidentiality?'

'Of course.'

'And you can't, under any circumstances, tell anyone what we talk about?'

Chyłka and Kordian looked at one another. This sounded ominous.

'No, not under any circumstances,' Chyłka confirmed. 'We have to keep what you tell us to ourselves. And nothing can release us from that.'

'What about, say, in fifteen years' time?'

'Lawyer/client privilege lasts indefinitely. There's no time limit.'

'And there's no way anyone can force you to talk?'

Joanna shook her head, feeling, rather than seeing, Kordian's anxious stare.

'There are two exceptions,' she said, 'but both apply to counter-terrorism.'

Szlezyngier let out a breath and broke off a small piece of chocolate. He offered the rest to the lawyers, but they declined.

'What's this about, Awit?' asked Oryński.

'I didn't kill my daughter,' he said quietly.

'We'd worked that much out ourselves,' said Chyłka.

He nodded, lost in thought. 'But your theory's not right either,' he said. 'My wife didn't run away with her lover, taking Nikola with her.'

This time, they knew he wasn't going to leave them hanging on, and that at last they'd find out what had happened to the child. They waited.

'Now that the case is closed, there are a few things I need to tell you.'

'Go ahead,' Joanna urged.

'And then I'll need you to do something for me. In fact, if my sentence can't be reduced, I'll need you to keep doing it for the next three years.'

'Go on.'

Awit leaned over the table, but not enough to arouse the suspicion of the guards. He looked at them closely, first at Chyłka, then at Oryński, then he took a deep breath.

'Allow me to start from the beginning,' he said. 'That night, Angelika and I did have a fight. We screamed at each other, we brought up old grudges from long ago ... it was no-holds-barred. I pushed her, she gave me a shove and, suffice to say, it wouldn't have taken much to do something stupid. But then I heard Nikola crying in her room, and I came to my senses. Angelika too.'

Chyłka checked her watch, worried they'd run out of time. But there was plenty.

'We went to Nikola's room to help her settle, and in the process we managed to calm ourselves down as well. Angelika stayed in there while I went to set the alarm. I thought she'd probably want to go to him that night – seek solace in his arms – and I wasn't about to let that happen. In the end I slept on the sofa in the living room, and she had our room. I'd drunk more than I should have done, and she probably had too.'

Chyłka frowned. 'So how did Nikola vanish?'

'I didn't understand it myself at first, and it was only when ... well, when things became clearer that I put two and two together. You'll do the same, I'm sure.'

'So what happened next?' asked Kordian.

'Angelika woke me in the morning, screaming and waving her arms about. She grabbed me and dragged me out of bed, still yelling, and swearing like a trooper. She was in tears. She pulled me to the door and ordered me to turn off the alarm, shrieking into my ear that Nikola was gone. She said the rooflight was open and the child had disappeared.'

Chyłka reached for the chocolate.

'I turned the alarm off, and she sprinted out of the house calling her name,' Szlezyngier went on. 'It took me a while to grasp what was happening. I raced to Nikola's room, and when she wasn't there, I bolted upstairs. And that's when Angelika must have come back and taken Nikola.'

'What?' Oryński snapped.

'I don't know where Angelika had hidden her, but there were a few possibilities. The kitchen, the other room ... anywhere but the living room, her room and the attic.'

Awit stopped for a moment and looked at the two lawyers, trying to assess if they believed him. He spoke with such calm and conviction that Chyłka had no doubts.

'Sakrat Tatarnikov was waiting nearby,' Awit continued. 'He took the child, and Angelika came home. She called me to help her search, so I did. I had no reason to disbelieve her, certainly not as regards Nikola. At that time her intention was to do exactly what you suggested, Chyłka,' he said, looking at her. 'She wanted to get her hands on my money, then live out her days in the sun with Sakrat and our ... I mean his daughter.'

'She's your daughter, Awit,' said Kordian, 'and no one will ever take that away from you.'

Awit nodded.

'Tatarnikov was supposed to take her away for a few days, hiding first in that hunting lodge, then somewhere outside the town. Angelika told Nikola it was an exciting holiday away with her uncle. Angelika had made sure our daughter was well prepared for her "abduction".'

He hung his head and his voice broke.

'Angelika was sure Sakrat loved her unconditionally, as she did him. But she was wrong.'

'What do you mean?' asked Kordian.

'I mean Tatarnikov exploited the situation. He had the child; he'd left no forensics and he could be sure that no one would suspect him for at least the next two weeks. Even Angelika wasn't expecting to hear from him right away.'

'So . . .'

'So he demanded a ransom,' said Szlezyngier. 'Angelika conned me, and Sakrat conned her.'

'Then what happened?' asked Oryński.

'At first, Sakrat kept quiet. It had gone just as he'd planned. Although I guess I should say "they", because there was more than one person behind it.'

'Ekiel?'

'He only helped,' said Awit. 'Sakrat was like a son to him, and when he asked for help, Ekiel didn't hesitate. Tatarnikov told him she was his daughter, and that he had to take her away from the man who was raising her. Ekiel agreed to lie for him, saying he'd seen us at the lake that night. Then he helped Sakrat disappear. But I expect he realised at some point it had all gone too far. When he started to ask too many questions, Tatarnikov got rid of him. He'd killed before.'

'Who was working with him?' asked Chyłka.

'His old employer, Wito.'

Kordian froze.

'They'd put the plan together, the two of them, thinking it would make them rich. No more smuggling, no more risk, no more work. With my money, they'd become millionaires. And they did.'

'But . . .'

'I couldn't pay the whole lot at once,' continued Szlezyngier, 'because the banks have to report any transactions over fifteen thousand euros. That's about sixty-two thousand zlotys. Then they don't even have to disclose it to the tax authorities, who step in only when some sort of financial crime is suspected.'

'So you had to pay in instalments.'

'Yes, and that's what I've been doing for the last few months. I set up new accounts and transferred funds from various other banks, muddying the waters as much as I could. And I did it all online. So if someone tried to trace the history of the payments, they'd have trouble working out where they came from and how. I deposited cash abroad, used the money to buy shares, transferred assets . . .'

'And that's what those night-time meetings with Wito were for,' Joanna remarked.

'Yes. Every time we met, I gave him access to the accounts he needed.'

'How much have you paid them?'

'Over these last two months? More than I've earned honestly in my lifetime.'

Neither Joanna nor Kordian commented. Given that they had also given Wito money for his supposed searches, he'd made the deal of a lifetime.

'In return, they guaranteed that not a hair on my daughter's head would be harmed, and that she'd have a great holiday with her "uncle".'

Joanna shook her head.

'That's insane,' she said.

'Not really, it was the only way to keep the child safe.'

'What about Angelika?' Oryński cut in before Chyłka had a chance. 'When did she realise Sakrat had set her up?'

'Too late. They got to me first. We made a deal, but the condition was that Angelika had to go free.'

Joanna was surprised. Why would Tatarnikov or Wito care if Angelika was found guilty? And then she realised.

'It wasn't their condition, it was yours. You imposed it.'

'Of course. I had to be sure Nikola would be safe. How better to do that than make sure she was with her mother?' he asked. 'There's a lot of things I could say about Angelika, but in her own slightly twisted way, she really loves my daughter. And for me, that guarantees her safety.'

'Where's Nikola now?' asked Kordian.

'I don't even know.'

Joanna ran her fingers through her hair, pushing her fringe aside. 'Are they going to hold onto her for three years?' she said. 'Is that how you imagine things will go?'

'No, they'll let her go early.'

'How can you be so sure?'

'Otherwise Angelika won't give them the rest of the money.'

'So she's got access to your accounts too?'

Szlezyngier smiled bitterly. 'I had no choice,' he said. 'It was the only way I could guarantee my daughter's safety.'

'And your own freedom.'

'Yes. Because when all this comes to light, I want you to file another appeal. The sentence will be overturned, and I'll leave prison.'

'Plenty of time for you to rot in here before that happens,' Chyłka said quietly. 'Besides, you'll be charged with financial malpractice.'

'Will I?'

'Yes,' she answered. 'Remember the exceptions to client confidentiality I mentioned? One of them is money laundering.'

Szlezyngier leaped from his chair.

'What do you mean?'

'We're not obliged to keep any information relating to money laundering confidential.'

And at that point, Awit went berserk, leaping up, shouting the odds and cursing. But before he managed to articulate his threats, the prison warders swarmed to their table and, to the delight of the onlookers, cuffed him and led him away, still screaming and threatening.

One of the other inmates looked Chyłka up and down.

'What the fuck did he expect?' he said. 'That his lawyers wouldn't screw him over?'

14

Kordian followed Joanna into her office and closed the door. She stood by the window, tilted it open, pulled out a packet of Marlboros and lit one. Then she tossed the pack to Oryński.

'It's hopeless,' he concluded, lighting up.

'It would be hopeless if our hands were tied. But they're not.'

He sat at the desk and pulled the ashtray over.

'I'm not so sure,' he answered. 'From a legal point of view, it's questionable to say the least. From a moral standpoint . . .'

He stopped when he saw Joanna glaring at him. 'You can shove your moral standpoint,' she said. 'These bastards need to be brought to justice.'

'Last time I checked, bringing people to justice wasn't part of our remit. Our job is to defend clients. At least that's what my own supervisor keeps telling me.'

Chyłka took a seat on the opposite side of the desk and opened her laptop.

'So what do you propose?' he asked.

'Just the usual. I'll submit the information to the prosecutor's office, and Tatarnikov and Wito will be put away. The girl will be returned to her father, and the mother will lose her parental rights.'

It was difficult to argue with that, Kordian thought. Legally speaking, it would probably go exactly as Joanna described. The problem was that even though they had that route open to them, they'd be acting directly against their client's wishes, and that could cause all sorts of problems.

'Isn't there a danger they might hurt the child?' he asked as she prepared to print out her document.

'Not if they don't know what's coming.'

'How can we be sure of that?'

She peered up from her screen, her expression suggesting he was getting too involved. She was probably right.

'If the police get there in time, Nikola shouldn't be in any danger.'

'What about Awit?' Oryński asked as the printer sprang to life.

'What about him?' Chyłka answered. 'They'll reshape his backside a few times in prison, then he'll be released. We'll lodge a cassation appeal and get the case over with quickly, and that first presiding judge, the one from the district, will be saying goodbye to a stellar career.'

She got up and walked over to the printer. Oryński got up too, and moved towards her, stopping just a step away. She turned, and they looked at each other, both seeking support.

'This goes against everything you've taught me,' he said.

'Up yours, Zordon.'

'It's not just that it's a rather dubious reason for waiving client confidentiality,' he added, 'it's because it goes against our client's express wishes.'

'So what do you suggest?' she said, taking a step back. 'Should we ignore the case and leave the child with some lowlife scum who's already killed two people? Or maybe you think her mother will take care of her?'

'I think—'

'Our duty to our client is to find the best solution for him, legally speaking,' she went on. 'And if that means acting against his wishes, then so be it.'

'But—'

'We are under a statutory obligation to act in the best interests of our client,' she cut in. 'His legal best interests, not any other. And it's up to us to define what that means.'

They were standing so close together that Kordian was becoming intoxicated with her scent. He swallowed, cursing himself, then stepped away and sat back down at the desk.

'We can't do it,' he said.

'Can't we? Just watch me.'

'You can't make decisions for your client, Chyłka.'

'I can, if there's terrorism or money laundering involved.'

If the circumstances had been different, Kordian knew, she'd be vigorously defending the principle of client confidentiality. She'd said more than once that Article 180, Paragraph 2 of the Criminal Code, which allows the principle to be waived, was shameful, and should be withdrawn. But in this case, her emotions had got the better of her. And she just wanted to get the child away from Sakrat. Which was hardly surprising. The only problem was, it could mean kissing her own career goodbye, and Kordian couldn't let that happen.

'But Awit hasn't been laundering money,' he said, and hung his head.

'What are you talking about?'

'He hasn't done anything illegal.'

'Bullshit.'

Kordian turned around to see Chyłka leaning over the filing cabinet, signing her report.

'The only thing he did wrong was to fail to register a donation.'

She looked at him and straightened up.

'There's nothing to stop him giving money to Sakrat and Wito if he wants to,' Oryński went on, more confident now. 'He can pay them as much as he likes, and there's nothing we can do about it. The only thing the state's interested in is tax. There are three rates, if memory serves, up to twenty per cent. And if Szlezyngier hasn't paid, there's nothing we can do about it. We don't have the right to disclose that information.'

Chyłka moved closer and looked down at him.

'You're wrong,' she said. 'They're not donations, and this goes against the concept of normal social coexistence.'

'It doesn't matter what you call it, you still can't disclose it.'

They scowled at each other as if potential adversaries rather than allies.

'He's protected by legal privilege, Chyłka.'

'I don't think so.'

'He hasn't laundered money, and he's not engaging in terrorist activity.'

'But someone else is laundering that money.'

'We don't know that.' He stood his ground. 'You don't have access to the accounts, and you have no way of knowing what's happened to the money. Your only evidence is what your client told you – and that client is in a risk situation and may not be thinking clearly.'

He thought that might get through to her, but she didn't seem to see any version of events other than the one she had talked herself into.

'Get out of my office,' she barked.

Kordian hesitated, taken aback by a tone he'd never heard before. Her abrasiveness usually had an undercurrent of humour, but not this time. He got up and left without a word. As he closed the door behind him, he hoped he'd made her see sense, but didn't know if he should be proud of himself, or ashamed. He had done what was expected of him legally speaking, but how much did that have to do with how he should act as a person? He had no idea what Chyłka would decide to do.

It all became clear a few days later. She didn't report Awit to the prosecutor, and she gave Kordian a wide berth whenever she saw him in the office. He let her be, assuming she'd speak to him again when she was ready. Joanna wasn't easily influenced – apart from this one time, when he'd managed to convince her not to break client confidentiality.

So when she unexpectedly came to his office one day, he was surprised.

She thrust a sheet of paper under his nose. He glanced at it, then leaped to his feet.

'No,' he said. 'We agreed.'

'We agreed nothing.'

'Chyłka, you have no right.'

She turned on her heel and strode towards the door. He followed.

'If you submit this, I'm handing in my resignation,' he said.

She turned her head and looked at him.

'I can't work with someone who doesn't give a damn about professional regulations.'

'Excellent,' she answered. 'Then you'd better give them your notice before you change your mind.'

'I won't change my mind.'

'Really? You won't let the promise of a six-figure salary sway you?' she said, turning to face him. 'Are you that much of an idealist, Zordon?'

'I'm not an idealist, but . . .'

'We'll see,' she said, and marched out.

15

It had taken Chyłka a few days to reach her decision. She'd thought everything through again and again, although she already knew she had no other option. Sakrat Tatarnikov would never let the girl go, even if Awit paid the whole ransom. He had no reason to, and doing so would incriminate his lover; Joanna assumed they still had feelings for one another. Maybe they were in this together. Maybe he hadn't betrayed her. That might have been a story concocted for Szlezyngier's benefit, to make him more willing to agree to their terms.

Kordian was right. There had been no money laundering, at least not by Awit. Chyłka contacted a friend in the tax office and asked officials to look at the paperwork from Awit's logistics company. They soon discovered that the funds transferred by Szlezyngier were being put into circulation in a variety of ways, which bore all the hallmarks of a financial crime. And that gave Joanna the right to waive client confidentiality.

She arranged a meeting with Aronowicz and told him the whole story, and the case was referred to the regional prosecutor's office in Warsaw. They did not have to wait long to see results.

Witold T. was put under surveillance until he led police to the house in Ustka where Sakrat Tatarnikov was in hiding. Armed officers broke down the door and burst inside, finding not only Tatarnikov, but the child as well.

The two men were charged with child abduction, while Awit was cleared of all charges. Angelika shared the same fate as her lover, and ended up in the women's prison in Łódź.

Chyłka had to admit she'd made the right decision. And Oryński hadn't resigned. She was afraid he might have done, given how stubborn he was, but common sense had clearly prevailed. He could hardly have been expected to risk his career to defend the rules and regulations of the Polish Bar Association, which were bent so often it would be a lost cause anyway. He was still avoiding her, even turning away if he saw her in the corridor.

The day after the kidnappers were sentenced, Joanna passed the closed door of his office, and remembered with a pang those few days in Białystok. It would be difficult for them to ever return to that level of intimacy.

So she carried on walking, to the office at the end of the corridor, where she knocked on the door.

'Come in,' called Artur Żelazny.

She pushed the door open. She knew exactly why she'd been summoned.

'Don't even sit down,' he said.

She walked up to the desk and glanced at the sheaf of papers he'd pushed over to her.

'By mutual consent,' said Old Rusty.

'I see.'

'Are you going to be awkward?'

'No.'

'I hope you understand,' he said, but there was no regret in his voice. 'No client wants a lawyer who gives away their secrets.'

Chyłka knew that. She had known it when she did what she did. If this had been a much smaller firm, it wouldn't have crossed anyone's mind to kick her out, but Żelazny & McVay's clients were rich, and as such, usually had something to hide. No one would trust her with their secrets now.

Joanna signed the papers, took the copies and headed for the door.

'Good luck,' Żelazny called after her.

She ignored him. The corridor, as always, was teeming. Pushing her way through the hustle and bustle, she thought how she'd miss this. She needed it like she needed oxygen; it was her natural habitat.

As she passed Oryński's office, she toyed with the idea of going in to say goodbye. He had no idea they were going to fire her, or he'd have said something. He probably thought Harry McVay would stand up for her – and possibly he would have, if he'd known. But since her termination of employment was 'by mutual consent', he didn't need to be informed.

She slowed down at Kordian's door and hesitated, but then picked up her pace again. It didn't take her long to pack her things. She took the lift down and walked to the car park.

Chyłka placed her box of belongings on the passenger seat and turned on Iron Maiden. And to the strains of 'Afraid to Shoot Strangers', she drove her X5 out into the street.